T RETIRING BOOMER'S FINANCIAL HANDBOOK

The Twenty
Financial Decisions
You Must Make
at Retirement

Ray E. LeVitre, CFP®

The Retiring Boomer's Financial Handbook
Cover design, layout, and illustrations by Beckie Rock
Edited by Jerry Kerns, Morningstar
Printed in the USA by Alexander's Digital Printing

To order this title, or for further information about this book and related
subject matter, please call (801) 566-6639.

Library of Congress Cataloging-in Publication Data

LeVitre, Ray E.
  The Retiring Boomer's Financial Handbook
  by Ray E. LeVitre
  ISBN: 0-9727882-1-2
  Library of Congress Control Number: 2005908016

To the awesome women in my life –
My wife, Jana, and my daughters, Brianna and Alexis

Special Acknowledgements

Jana LeVitre – Thanks for your never failing support and unwavering confidence in me. Without your constant willingness to endure my often overzealous, entrepreneurial spirit, this book would never have come to fruition. Thanks for believing with me that even the loftiest goals can be achieved and for making me want to be better than I am. Also, thanks for your tireless hours of editing and feedback.

Ray and Judy LeVitre – You are truly great parents. Thanks for your encouragement and support. A special thanks for helping me over the hurdles that life has thrown my way. Life's challenges are much easier to face when your parents and family are always there for you. I love you for always believing in my dreams.

Chuck L. Cutler – You are a rock-solid mentor and role model. Thanks for giving me a solid financial planning foundation. Without your help I would have missed out on many opportunities and would surely not be where I am today. I owe you a great deal.

Eugene Banks – Because you hired me and gave me the opportunity to work for the largest brokerage company in the world, I owe much of what I have learned in the financial services industry to you.

My Clients – A special thanks to each of you for placing so much trust in me as your financial advisor and for giving me the opportunity to help you develop a strategy to reach your financial goals. The strategies outlined in *The Retiring Boomers' Financial Handbook* are a culmination of my experience in working to develop fundamentally sound solutions to your unique financial situations.

And finally, I would like to thank the many companies that have invited me onto their corporate campuses and into their work sites to teach their employees how to manage a retirement plan distribution and develop a solid investment strategy.

About the Author

Ray E. LeVitre is a fee-only CERTIFIED FINANCIAL PLANNER™ who specializes in helping people develop and manage their financial plans at and through retirement. Ray has seen all sides of the financial services industry. Early in his career he spent time at Fidelity Investments, Citicorp, and Mutual of New York and later went on to build a career at Merrill Lynch working as a financial consultant and branch manager. Ray now runs an independent fee-only financial planning practice. He has been retained by many Fortune 500 companies to teach financial management seminars to their employees and has been quoted by *Newsweek, Business Week*, and several financial industry magazines.

Ray can be contacted to answer questions or arrange speaking engagements.

Mail:	Net Worth Advisory Group
	6975 Union Park Center, Suite 465
	Midvale, Utah 84047
Phone:	801-56MONEY (801-566-6639)
Email:	ray@networthadvice.com
Web:	www.networthadvice.com

CONTENTS

Section Three: Developing a Successful Investment Strategy

Warning and Advice from the Author

If you are reading this book you are likely retiring right now. So, congratulations are in order. CONGRATULATIONS! From now on every day is Saturday.

I have spent the past fifteen years helping people successfully make the financial transition from the workforce into retirement. This book is a culmination of my experience with my clients.

During my time in the financial services industry I have worked for some of the biggest and most well known financial institutions in the United States. While I am grateful to each of these firms for the employment opportunities they provided, I think that their business models are severely flawed. They seem to be much more concerned with making money for themselves rather than making money for their clients. You should be aware of the conflicts of interest that exist in the financial services industry as you seek financial advice and buy financial products at retirement. Making a mistake now could negatively impact the way you live for the next 30 to 40 years. Here are some words of warning and some advice to follow as you make the financial transition from the workforce into retirement.

Warning #1 Hidden Agenda

Most people have the need for a financial advisor to help them make money decisions at retirement. The problem with this is that most financial advisors work on commissions and have a hidden agenda to sell something. While most are well-meaning, keeping their jobs ultimately means they've got to make a commission. In their intense efforts to meet sales quotas and pay their mortgages, they wind up pitching loaded financial products (mutual funds, annuities, and life insurance) to make a quick buck. If this occurs you will wind up with investments and insurance that are best for your advisor and his/her firm and not necessarily what is best for you. Read Chapter 3, *Fire Your Broker!*, to see how to find an objective advisor who is more interested in your goals than in theirs.

Warning #2 Expensive Products

The investment and insurance products sold by commissioned

advisors are expensive. When you buy loaded (i.e. commissioned) financial products, the product sponsors simply build in additional up-front, back-end, and annual expenses so they can compensate your advisor. Since these fees are often hidden most investors never really know what they are paying. You can read Chapter 15, *"No-Load" Means Lower Costs*, to learn how to avoid excessive fees.

Warning #3 Poor Service

Because commissioned advisors are under such extreme pressure to make money for their firms, they have to keep finding new clients and selling more expensive products. This is a problem. When an advisor is focused on acquiring new clients, little time remains for existing clients. The bottom line is that most people receive poor to no service from their advisors. Unfortunately, this is accepted as the norm, thus advisors are not held to higher standards. As an investor you should know what you are paying in fees (both those seen and those hidden) and make sure your advisor is providing service equal to the fees you are paying.

Advice

Due to the complexity of the financial world I believe most people should hire a financial professional to help them develop a plan and make all the financial decisions outlined in this book. I also believe that investors need to be educated so they can monitor the advice they receive and hold their advisors to much higher standards. If you read this book you'll have a good idea of the issues your advisor should be addressing, the way he/she is compensated, and the types of products and services they can offer. Armed with this information you can make sure your advisors are working for you and not just pushing products to meet the pressures of corporate sales objectives.

To avoid the major problems in the financial services industry I believe all investors should follow these four basic principles as they pursue financial success:

- Work with a fee-only Certified Financial Planner™ (CFP®) who has at least 10 years of experience.

- Develop a written comprehensive financial plan and review it with your advisor often.

- Create an investment policy statement to act as a framework for making investment decisions.

- Purchase only low-expense, no-load financial products (mutual funds, annuities, and life insurance).

The fact that you are reading this book says that you are serious about your retirement and making the right decisions with your money. Making the right decisions now will provide peace of mind and ensure financial success throughout retirement.

"If we take a late retirement and an early death, we'll just squeak by."

Are you retiring now? If so, this book is for you. There are thousands of retirement planning books which focus on helping baby boomers manage their money in the years leading up to retirement. *The Retiring Boomers' Financial Handbook* is the only book of its kind, written specifically for people who are retiring now.

If you are ready to leave the workforce and begin retirement then the pressure is on to make the right choices with your retirement money. The decisions you make at this critical juncture, many of which are irrevocable, will profoundly affect your financial security and your lifestyle for the next 30 to 40 years. There is much more to retiring than simply deciding what to do with the money in your 401(k). *The Retiring Boomers' Financial Handbook* addresses the 20 major financial decisions people must make as they transition from the workforce into retirement. Making all of these decisions is a big task, but one that is well worth it since the next 30-40 years are riding on the decisions you make right now.

The Twenty Decisions You Must Make at Retirement

Every chapter deals with a decision you must make at retirement. My recommendation is to begin by reading Chapters 1, 2 and 3 on financial planning and choosing a financial advisor, then proceed through the rest of the chapters, reading about the topics that are the most pressing to you right now. Each chapter was written independent of the others so it is not necessary to read the book in its chapter order. The *Twenty Decisions Checklist* on page 20 will help you track your progress as you check off each decision you make and help ensure that nothing falls through the cracks.

Do-it-yourselfers and Delegators

If you are a do-it-yourselfer you'll find all the resources necessary to develop and manage your financial plan on your own. However, I think you should seek a second opinion periodically from a financial professional who works on an hourly basis. If you are a delegator then my advice is to use the book as you meet with your advisor to discuss each retirement decision. Being educated before you meet with your advisor will help you ask the right questions, address all the issues, and hold your advisor to higher standards.

You Only Retire Once. Do It Right!

Each of the six sections of the book addresses various components of retirement planning. For instance, **Section One: Retirement Planning**, will help you assess what your current retirement situation looks like and determine whether you are on track to meet your retirement goals. This section also outlines the importance of having a written comprehensive financial plan, how to find objective financial advice, how to determine a safe portfolio withdrawal rate, and what to do if you plan to retire early.

In **Section Two: Sources of Retirement Income**, we'll explore the issues surrounding Social Security; teach you how to maximize your company pension benefits; and teach you how to avoid the most common investor mistakes so that you can be sure not to sabotage your most important retirement income source–your investment portfolio.

Section Three: Developing a Successful Investment Strategy covers important investment planning techniques. After all, reaching your retirement goals will depend largely on how successful you are as an investor. This section deals primarily with how to develop successful investment strategies, including asset allocation, proper portfolio diversification, choosing investments, ongoing portfolio management, how to protect principal while investing in the stock market, and how to handle company stock positions.

In **Section Four: Insurance and Retirement**, we'll discuss how to obtain health care coverage during retirement, and whether or not you need long-term care insurance. Without these safeguards in place, you could prematurely deplete all of your hard-earned assets. In addition, we'll figure out what to do with the life insurance policies on which you've been paying for so long. This section will teach you how to evaluate how much insurance you will need and when and how to purchase it.

Section Five: Other Retirement Considerations will help you determine what to do with your mortgage and also which estate planning documents you need to obtain.

Section Six: Retirement Plan Distributions is intended to be a retirement plan distribution guide. This section deals primarily with the issues and choices facing people who, at retirement, take a distribution from an employer-sponsored retirement plan. Before making any decisions about your money, be sure to reference this section for a very detailed analysis of your retirement options.

The Retiring Boomers' Financial Handbook explains, in basic terms, the highly complex financial concepts that you need to understand in order to make twenty critical retirement decisions. Use it as a comprehensive information source on retirement planning and successful money management techniques. *The Retiring Boomers' Financial Handbook* is an important resource that will help you build a financial strategy to guide you toward the retirement lifestyle you deserve. *You only get to retire once. Do it right!*

✓ THE TWENTY DECISIONS CHECKLIST

☐ Decision #1: Do I have enough money to retire now?

☐ Decision #2: Should I get a comprehensive financial plan?

☐ Decision #3: Should I fire my broker and hire an advisor who can be objective and isn't pitching products?

☐ Decision #4: How much can I safely withdraw from my portfolio?

☐ Decision #5: If I retire early how can I get the money out of my IRA without penalty?

☐ Decision #6: When should I begin taking Social Security?

☐ Decision #7: Which pension payout option should I choose?

☐ Decision #8: How should I manage my personal savings?

☐ Decision #9: How much should I invest in stocks, bonds, and cash?

☐ Decision #10: How should I diversify my investment portfolio?

☐ Decision #11: What should I do with my company stock?

☐ Decision #12: What criteria should I use to identify the best investments?

☐ Decision #13: Should I buy load or no-load mutual funds, annuities, and life insurance?

☐ Decision #14: How will I manage my portfolio on an ongoing basis?

☐ Decision #15: How will I cover my medical expenses during retirement?

☐ Decision #16: Should I buy long-term care insurance?

☐ Decision #17: Should I cancel my life insurance policy since I no longer need the coverage?

☐ Decision #18: Should I pay off my mortgage at retirement?

☐ Decision #19: What strategies should I use to ensure that my estate passes to my heirs and not to Uncle Sam?

☐ Decision #20: Which retirement plan distribution option should I choose?

■ SECTION ONE ■

RETIREMENT
PLANNING

ONE

Retiring Now!

✓ RETIREMENT DECISION #1: *Do I have enough money to retire now?*

Are you ready for the time when every day is a Saturday? When it comes to retirement planning, too many people face a reality gap. Seventy percent of American workers and retirees are confident that they will have enough money to live comfortably during retirement. That same survey revealed that only 39 percent would actually have enough money saved to enjoy the kind of retirement lifestyle they envision.[1] Other studies indicate that middle-income baby boomers will need much more than $1 million in their investment accounts the day they retire.

Where do you stand? Are you overconfident that you will reach your retirement goals?

 America fails the Retirement IQ Test with an average score of 33%.[2]

When you add up all your financial assets on the first day of retirement, what will your portfolio need to total in order for you to reach your retirement goals? How far are you from that goal? You need to take a good hard look at your overall retirement situation to answer these questions and to ensure that your savings nest egg will generate enough retirement income to last for decades.

Figure 1

+ **Brokerage Accounts**
+ **IRA Accounts**
+ **401(k)'s**
+ **Insurance Cash Value**
+ **Annuities**
+ **Savings Bonds**
+ **Bank Accounts**
+ **Other Investments**
_____

(**???**)

Of course, the amount needed at retirement differs for everyone and ultimately hinges on your answers to the following questions:

- When will you retire?
- What is your current income?
- What percentage of your current income will you need each year during retirement?
- How long do you estimate you will be in retirement?
- What will your income sources be during retirement?
- What will be the rate of return on your investment assets during retirement?
- What impact will inflation have on your retirement goals?

The best way to see if you're on track is to submit yourself to a retirement analysis. Don't worry. It's not that painful. I'll walk you through each step. To develop a retirement analysis, you will need to take the following nine-question quiz. Once you've completed the questions, I'll refer you to some retirement calculators online. We'll simply plug in some numbers and you'll see where you stand. Friends of mine, Ron and Linda Hansen, have already taken the quiz. To help spark your thinking as you evaluate your own situation, I've included the Hansens' answers as a case study. I'll also discuss each question to ensure you consider the right factors in your answer. Let's get started.

1. When do you plan on retiring?

If you are reading this book you are probably planning to retire soon. The average American retires at age 62.[3]

---

1 Question #1: When do you plan on retiring?

Your Answer: _____

Case Study: Ron and Linda Hansen, age 59, plan on retiring at age 60.

---

2. How much annual income will you need during retirement?

Financial planners suggest you'll need to have about 70 to 80

Only four in 10 workers have tried to calculate how much money they need to accumulate for retirement. Only one in 10 has done the calculation in the past year.[2]

percent of your pre-retirement gross income to maintain your current standard of living. This, of course, can vary widely depending on your lifestyle.

During retirement you will pay less taxes, save less, spend less on your children, and have less of a mortgage burden than you did while working. While many expenses will decrease during retirement, others will increase. Figure 2 outlines some of the most common changes in spending during retirement.

Figure 2

Expenses likely to decrease	Expenses likely to increase
• Home Mortgage • Savings • Income Taxes • Work-related Clothing • Life Insurance • Commuting • Education Expenses	• Healthcare • Travel • Second Home • Further Education • Hobbies/ Recreation

The way you decide to spend your retirement years will have an impact on how much income you will need. Have you thought about what you want to do during retirement? The following poll reflects the most common desires of retirees.

Moving to another city will also greatly affect your income needs. According to the American Association of Retired Persons, only one in 10 Americans age 55 and over is interested in relocating when he or she retires. However, if you do plan to move to another city, you must adjust your estimated retirement spending depending on the cost-of-living differences from region to region. A cost-of-living calculator, like the one at www.homefair.com,[4] is an easy way to see how your new home will affect your living expenses.

Figure 3

Poll Results

How do you want to spend your retirement years?

Travel the world	19.6%
Pursue creative passions	16.7%
Give back by volunteering	11.3%
Start a second career	11.2%
Sit home with my feet up	10.1%
Keep working (I need the money)	9.1%
Spoil the Grandkids	4.2%
Launch my own business	3.6%
Keep working (I love my job)	3.4%
Go back to school	2.1%
Other	8.7%

Source: www.mygeneration.org

Use the worksheet in Figure 4 to help you get down to the nitty gritty of your annual retirement costs. The more you detail your spending habits, the more accurate your retirement picture will be. Figure 4 shows a list of annual expenditures for the average American couple older than 65. How your expenses match up to these average figures depends on your lifestyle.

In the column titled *Your Budget Now*, estimate your current annual expenses. To make it easier, take your monthly expenses and multiply by 12. Then in the last column, *Your Budget At Retirement*, estimate what these costs would be if you were to retire today. This figure is your yearly retirement income need.

How much annual income will you need during retirement?

Your Answer: _____

2

Case Study: The Hansens' housing expenses will drop dramatically as they pay off their mortgage. They plan to travel during retirement and have set their retirement income goal at $75,000 per year (in today's dollars).

Figure 4

Annual Retirement Expense

	Average Budget for a Married Couple 65+	Your Budget Now	Your Budget at Retirement
Housing	$10,922		
Transportation	$6,592		
Food	$5,541		
Health Care	$4,502		
Utilities	$2,825		
Taxes	$2,035		
Household	$1.983		
Insurance	$1,957		
Contributions	$1,891		
Entertainment	$1,578		
Miscellaneous	$1,336		
Clothing	$1,245		
Personal Care	$561		
Total Spending	$42,968		

Source: Consumer Expenditure Survey, 2001-2002

3. How many years will you spend in retirement?

Most financial planners assume people will live until about age 85. This assumption is based on average life expectancies (see Figure 5). For example, a man who is currently 65 can expect to live to 81, while a 65-year-old woman can expect to reach 84.

In one aspect it is good news that we are living longer. Because of advances in science, medicine, and nutrition, we're aging slower. There are twice as many people—70,000—older than 100 today than there were just a decade ago. By 2050, it's estimated that more than 1.1 million people in the United States will be older than 100.

Figure 5

Life Expectancy

Male		Female	
Age	**Life Expectancy**	**Age**	**Life Expectancy**
50	27.7	50	31.7
55	23.5	55	27.3
60	19.6	60	23.1
65	16.1	65	19.1
70	12.8	70	15.4
75	10.0	75	12.1
80	7.5	80	9.1
85	5.5	85	6.6
90	4.1	90	4.8
95	3.0	95	3.5
100	2.4	100	2.7

Source: National Vital Statistics Report, 2002

On the other hand, longer life expectancies present a dilemma in developing your retirement plan. Let's assume you and your spouse are planning to retire at age 65. If you presume that you will live for 35 years, until 100, you may have to settle on a dramatically reduced level of income to make your nest egg stretch for so many years. However, if you assume you will live to age 85, as mortality tables suggest, and you or your spouse live to age 100, you run the risk of outliving your money. In fact, some people will spend more years in retirement than they did in the labor force. Consider the example of Anne Scheiber. Anne retired from her $3,150-per-year IRS auditor job in 1943 at age 47 and passed away in 1995 at the age of 101. She spent more than 52 years in retirement.[5]

So how do you plan to optimize your chances of making your money last? Much like the investment decisions you have made, you must decide if you want to be a little more aggressive or a little more conservative in your planning. It is better to err on the conservative side. This can best be accomplished by adding at least five years to the life expectancy figures in Figure 5. For example, a married couple retiring this year, both age 65, should plan to be in retirement for 24 years (19.1 years in the table, plus five) or until they reach age 89.

Question #3: How many years will you spend in retirement?

Your Answer: _____

3

Case Study: Ron and Linda have decided to be even more conservative. They're both in good shape and members in both of their families tend to live long. They are adding 10 years to their life expectancy figures and are planning for 33 years in retirement.

---

4. How much income will you earn annually during retirement?

Half of American employees think they will be forced to work during retirement.

Now, we need to take an inventory of your retirement income sources. List your income in Figure 6. Will any of your sources of

Figure 6

Sources of Income Worksheet

Annual Income Sources	$	Annual Increase %
Your Social Security		
Your spouse's Social Security		
Your pension		
Your spouse's pension		
Rental income		
Income from continued work		
Other income		
Other income		
Total income (excluding investments)		

income be adjusted each year for inflation? For example, Social Security has a cost-of-living adjustment. Your company pension may or may not adjust annually for inflation. If you own rental property, most likely you will increase the rent periodically to keep pace with inflation. This is an important element to factor into your retirement planning. For this exercise, exclude any income you'll earn from your investment portfolio (non-real estate investments).

What sources of income will you have during retirement?

Your Answer: _____

4

(Complete the worksheet in Figure 6 to total your anticipated retirement income sources. Also, estimate how much the income source will increase each year during retirement.)

Case Study: The Hansens are anticipating retirement income of $30,000 from the income sources outlined in Figure 6.

5. What inflation rate are you going to use in your planning?

Inflation is a measure of the annual increase in the costs of goods and services you buy. It's an unavoidable fact that the price of things you need in life will increase over time. During the past 70 years, inflation has averaged about 3 percent per year, as it has since 1989 (Figure 7). However, during the past 30 years, inflation has averaged 5 percent. The U.S. economy experienced double-digit inflation during the period from 1977 to 1981, when inflation averaged a whopping 10 percent.[6]

If you fail to factor inflation into your retirement planning, you'll find prices rising while your income remains level, and eventually you'll

Figure 7

Inflation Since 1989	
1989	4.65%
1990	6.11%
1991	3.06%
1992	2.90%
1993	2.75%
1994	2.68%
1995	2.54%
1996	3.32%
1997	1.70%
1998	1.61%
1999	2.68%
2000	3.39%
2001	1.55%
2002	2.60%
2003	1.99%
2004	3.64%

Source: CPI

be forced to lower your standard of living or deplete your assets. A fixed income in a rising-cost world is slow financial suicide. In Figure 8, you can see how the average costs of various products and services have increased over time and what they could cost in the future if they continue on the same inflationary course.

Figure 8

Cost of Living Comparison (1900-2003)

Year	House	Car	Milk	Gas	Bread	Postage	Income
1900	$4,000	$500	$.30	$.05	$.03	$.02	$637
1910	$4,800	$500	$.33	$.07	$.05	$.02	$963
1920	$6,396	$500	$.58	$.10	$.11	$.02	$1,179
1930	$7,146	$525	$.56	$.10	$.08	$.02	$1,428
1940	$6,558	$810	$.51	$.15	$.08	$.03	$1,231
1950	$14,500	$1,750	$.82	$.20	$.14	$.03	$3,216
1960	$30,000	$2,275	$1.04	$.25	$.20	$.04	$5,199
1970	$40,000	$2,500	$1.32	$.40	$.24	$.06	$8,933
1980	$86,159	$5,412	$1.60	$1.03	$.48	$.15	$11,321
1990	$128,732	$9,437	$2.15	$1.08	$1.29	$.25	$14,777
2000	$205,000	$17,700	$3.35	$1.56	$1.72	$.34	$21,950
2003	$261,100	$26,077	$2.32	$1.72	$1.95	$.37	$22,250
Average inflation	**House 4.14%**	**Car 3.41%**	**Milk 2.52%**	**Gas 3.50%**	**Bread 4.14%**	**Postage 2.90%**	**Income 3.50%**

Source: www/seniorliving.about.com

Where prices are headed if past inflation repeats itself

Year	House	Car	Milk	Gas	Bread	Postage	Income
2010	$346,840	$34,108	$3.98	$2.18	$2.59	$0.45	$28,327
2020	$520,362	$50,053	$5.03	$3.08	$3.89	$0.60	$39,997
2030	$780,694	$73,452	$6.36	$4.35	$5.83	$0.80	$56,474

Of course, you don't know what the inflation rate will be during your retirement, so you must make assumptions. Here again, you have a choice between aggressive planning, in which you optimistically assume a lower inflation rate than the average, or more conservative planning, using a higher inflation rate assumption. Most financial planners assume a 3- to 4-percent rate in their planning.

If inflation remains at 3 percent during your retirement, you will need to increase your income by 3 percent each year to buy the same amount of goods and services you purchased the previous year and maintain your standard of living. Essentially, you should give yourself a 3 percent raise each year by withdrawing more money from your investments. For example, if you need $75,000 in the first year of retirement, you will need $77,250 the second year, $79,567 the third year, and so forth to maintain your purchasing power. At this rate, in the 20th year of retirement, you will need $131,512 to purchase the same items that can be bought with $75,000 today. Figure 9 shows the impact of inflation during retirement.

Figure 9

Year	Amount Needed	Year	Amount Needed
1	$75,000	11	$100,793
2	$77,250	12	$103,817
3	$79,567	13	$106,932
4	$81,954	14	$110,140
5	$84,413	15	$113,444
6	$86,945	16	$116,847
7	$89,553	17	$120,352
8	$92,240	18	$123,963
9	$95,007	19	$127,682
10	$97,857	20	$131,512

Equivalent of $75,000 today assuming 3% annual inflation

Because of inflation, your investment portfolio must be structured to provide you with a rising income stream during retirement. This is especially critical if your pension or other sources of retirement income don't have built-in cost-of-living adjustments.

5

Question #5: What inflation rate are you going to use in your planning?

Your Answer: _____

Case Study: Ron and Linda are using a 3 percent rate.

---

6. How much money have you accumulated?

Do you currently have enough money set aside to be on track to reach your retirement goals? The chart in Figure 10 will tell you if you are in the ballpark. Simply multiply your current annual income by the factor that best represents your situation.

For example, if you are a moderate investor making $100,000 per year and planning to retire in five years, you should have $773,000 already accumulated in your various investment accounts (7.73 multiplied by $100,000) to maintain your pre-retirement standard of living during retirement. This assumes you will spend 25 years in retirement, save 8 percent of your income each year prior to retirement, reduce your exposure to equities at retirement, experience 4 percent inflation, and exhaust all of your savings during retirement. (Figure 10 does not take Social Security or pensions into account.)

Alternatively, if you're an aggressive investor planning to retire in 10 years and currently have a $50,000 per year income, you would need to have accumulated $231,500 by now to be on track, using the same assumptions as above.

Figure 10

Are You On Track?

Years to Retirement	Aggressive Investor	Moderate Investor	Conservative Investor
0	9.57	10.46	11.48
5	6.75	7.73	8.90
10	4.63	5.58	6.76
15	3.07	3.93	5.05
20	1.93	2.68	3.69
25	1.09	1.72	2.61
30	.48	.98	1.74
35	.03	.42	1.05

Source: Wall Street Journal

In Figure 10, the thing that determines whether you are an aggressive, moderate, or conservative investor is the amount of your portfolio invested in stocks and bonds. A portfolio consisting of 80% stocks and 20% bonds before retirement and 65% stocks and 35% bonds after retirement is considered aggressive. Moderate investors are those with 65% of their portfolio's invested in stocks and 35% in bonds before retirement and 50% stocks and 50% bonds after retirement. Those investors who maintain a portfolio of 50% stocks and 50% bonds before retirement and only 35% stocks and 65% bonds after retirement are labeled conservative.

Take an inventory of all your investments and complete the worksheet in Figure 11. (You'll also need this information for Question 7.) This will help you determine what type of investor you are.

Figure 11

Portfolio Allocation

Retirement Accounts (IRA's, 401(k)'s, Profit Sharing Plans, etc.)

Stocks or stock mutual funds	$_____
Bonds or bond mutual funds	$_____
Cash equivalents	$_____

Non-Retirement Accounts

Stocks or stock mutual funds	$_____
Bonds or bond mutual funds	$_____
Cash equivalents	$_____

Total Investment Assets (retirement and Non-Retirement Assets)

Stocks or stock mutual funds	$_____	_____ %
Bonds or bond mutual funds	$_____	_____ %
Cash equivalents	$_____	_____ %
Total	$_____	100 %

How much money have you accumulated?

6

Your Answer: _____
(Use the chart in Figure 10 to see if you are on track to reach
your retirement goals?)

Case Study: The Hansens earn $100,000 per year and are
moderate investors. They are in the ball park, having
accumulated $1,200,000 in assets ($100,000 multiplied by
10.46 equals $1,046,000.)

7. At what rate do you expect your investment portfolio to grow?

You now know how much your portfolio is worth and you've
broken it down in asset classes. But how do you know if it's enough
money to last you? To determine if you are on track to reach your retirement goal, we can forecast a reasonable rate of return you can expect to
achieve between now and retirement, and your return once you are in
retirement. In Chapter 11 we will examine, in more detail, the expected
growth rates of various investment portfolios.

For our purposes here, let's keep it simple: Since 1925, stocks
have averaged a 10.7 percent rate of return; bonds, 5.3 percent; and
Treasury bills (cash), 3.8 percent.

Figure 12 illustrates how
different mixes of stocks, bonds,
and cash performed, on average,
from 1926 through 2002. Find
the portfolio most resembling
your own now. What is its expected rate of return?

What will your invest-
ment returns be during retirement? Most investors reposition assets from stocks into
bonds and cash during retirement
to reduce their risk. This also
reduces returns. I recommend

Figure 12

Asset Allocation
(Annual Returns 1926-2002)

Stocks/Bonds/Cash %	Average Return
90/0/10	11.36%
80/10/10	10.70%
70/20/10	10.04%
60/30/10	9.38%
50/40/10	8.72%
40/50/10	8.06%
30/60/10	7.40%
20/70/10	6.74%
10/80/10	6.09%
0/90/10	5.13%

Source: Ibbotson and Associates

that you remain conservative in your planning and assume a rate of return no higher than 7 percent per year during retirement.

At what rate do you expect your investment portfolio to grow?

7

Your Answer:
Before retirement: _____
After retirement: _____

Case Study: Ron and Linda expect their portfolio to grow at a rate of 9 percent before retirement and 7 percent during retirement.

---

8. What is your annual savings rate?

The personal savings rate in 1997 was 2.7% (as a percentage of after-tax income). In 1998, the savings rate turned negative for the first time since the 1930s.[8] Today, the rate hovers around 1%.

If you are still a year or two from retirement you should be saving no less than 10 percent of your gross income; if married, you and your spouse should save 10 percent of your combined income. In most cases, you should work toward saving 15 percent. To accomplish this goal, control your expenses and strive to live within your means. The recent best-selling book *The Millionaire Next Door* outlines characteristics of America's millionaires. The book's authors, Thomas Stanley and William Danko, conclude that the reason most millionaires accumulated so much wealth was due to their high savings rate and ability to live within their means.

Only 58% of American workers are saving money for their retirement.

To be a good saver, you need discipline and consistency. The best way to do this is to set up a systematic savings plan and have money drawn directly out of your bank account or paycheck and deposited into an investment account at least monthly.

Here's a simple rule: If you can't get your hands on it, you won't spend it. That's why company-sponsored retirement plans work so well. The money is invested even before you receive your paycheck.

8

What is your annual savings rate?

Your Answer: _____

Case Study: The Hansens save 10 percent of their income, or $10,000 per year.

---

9. How much do you want to leave to family or charity?

It's natural to want to leave an estate to your heirs or to an organization or cause about which you care deeply. Be sure to incorporate this into your retirement planning. Determine how much you wish to leave; this is the amount of your financial portfolio you will not spend during retirement.

9

How much money would you like to leave to family or charity?

Your Answer: _____

Case Study: Ron and Linda are not planning to leave an estate to their heirs.

Case Study Results

Are Ron and Linda Hansen on track to reach their retirement goals?

To answer this question, the Hansens visited www.Fidelity.com, one of many places to find an online retirement calculator (see below) and plugged in the following assumptions:

- Ron and Linda, both 50, are planning to retire in 10 years.
- They need $75,000 per year of retirement income (in today's dollars).

- They will need this income for 30 years of retirement.
- They are expecting income from various sources to provide them with $30,000 per year.
- They have accumulated a $500,000 investment portfolio made up of 65 percent stocks, 35 percent bonds.
- They save $10,000 per year (10% of their income).
- They've assumed an inflation rate of 3 percent per year and are anticipating their investments will grow at 9 percent annually between now and retirement, with a 7 percent growth rate assumed during retirement.

Based on these figures and assumptions, Ron and Linda are on track to reach their goal. Their analysis indicates that when they hit retirement they will have a $1,027,231 nest egg (this represents a $115,535 surplus). In fact, if they choose, they can retire one year earlier than planned. The Hansens passed the retirement quiz with flying colors.

Your Results: Are you on track to reach your retirement goals?

Now you have all the information you need to determine if you're on track to reach your retirement goals. There are a couple of ways to crunch the numbers.

The first involves simple linear equations in which you assume a constant rate of return on your investments during retirement (this was used in the Hansen case study). This approach is easy and works well, as long as you assume a conservative rate of return and you still have 10 or more years until retirement. If you are investing for the long term, chances are you will enjoy a rate of return that is close to the long-term averages. Most Web calculators use this approach.

The second is a little more complex. It involves probability calculations to determine the chances of reaching your goals, given the fact that rates of return will fluctuate from year to year during retirement. This approach is referred to as Monte Carlo analysis (see Chapter 3). It is more appropriate for those on the verge of retirement and those already retired. If you fall into this category, you do not have as many years to invest and your retirement savings would be devastated by an unexpected and extended market downturn. Monte Carlo analysis can account for the unexpected and will provide a more accurate view of whether or not you are on track to meet your retirement goals[9] Monte Carlo analysis will also help you determine how much you can withdraw from your investments during retirement without running the risk of depleting your assets. T. Rowe Price's retirement calculator will perform the Monte Carlo analysis for you (see Web references on next page).

Financial advisors have access to planning tools and software that can take into account the many variables that will change during retirement. These factors can include a spouse who plans to work several years after you retire, changes in tax rates, the impact of inflation on some income sources, and different interest- rate assumptions for each of your investment assets.

If you have a large asset base or if your financial situation is more complex, it is highly recommended that you seek the counsel of a professional financial advisor to develop a retirement analysis. Otherwise, you can simply use one of the many retirement calculators on the Internet. Whether you decide to work with a financial advisor or develop a retirement plan on your own, you will need the answers to the questions asked in this chapter to complete your retirement analysis. Surprisingly, just a little over half of American workers have ever tried to figure out how much they need to save and accumulate for retirement.[10] Put yourself ahead of the crowd by visiting one of the Web sites listed below and determine if you are on track to reach your goal of never-ending Saturday's.

Now back to the burning question: Are you on track to reach your retirement goals? Hopefully, the answer is "Yes!" If not, don't panic. You just may need to save more money each year or adjust your investment portfolio to obtain better returns. If you have a lot of catching up to do, you might have to work longer before you can retire, or retire with less than you had originally planned. But at least you now know where you stand and you can plan accordingly.

If you are ahead of the game and don't need to seek a high rate of return, you may want to reposition your investments more conservatively. Why take additional and unnecessary risk if you are able to reach and exceed your goals without that risk?

Remember that retirement planning is not a one-time event. You should update and review your retirement analysis yearly at the least.

Find It On The Web:

Retirement Planning Calculators

- Fidelity Investments: www.Fidelity.com
- Wall Street Journal: www.wsj.com
- KJE Computer Solutions: www.javacalc.com
- Quicken: www.quicken.com/retirement/planner/
- CNNmoney: www.money.cnn.com
- Smart Money: www.smartmoney.com
- The American Savings Education Council: www.asec.org (Click Savings Tools)
- T. Rowe Price: www.troweprice.com
- AARP: www.aarp.org
- American Funds: www.americanfunds.com
- Vanguard Funds, www.vanguard.com

Moving at Retirement: Cost of Living Calculator

- www.homefair.com

TWO

Double Your Money

✓ RETIREMENT DECISION #2: *Should I get a comprehensive financial plan?*

Want to double your money? Would you like a $1 million retirement portfolio instead of one with $500,000? What if I told you it's easy? Studies indicate that people with financial plans have twice as much money in savings and investments as those without plans. Imagine that, the mere act of developing a plan and updating it regularly could put twice as much money in your pocket. Of course, developing a financial plan won't magically double your money overnight. A plan is nothing more than a road map that provides a guide for making all of your financial decisions, motivates you to push a little harder to achieve your goals, and acts as a yardstick to measure your progress. Without a map, it can be very easy to start down the wrong path and never arrive at your desired destination.

 Only one out of five preretirees or retirees has a written financial plan. LIMRA International

Goal Setting

Financial planning is nothing more than goal setting. You determine where you are now, and where you want to be in the future. You then spell out a specific course of action to get you from point A to point B. It's no secret that setting goals will increase your chances of accomplishing them. Committing your goals to writing will further increase your chances. Setting up a plan to reach your goals and reviewing your progress regularly will again boost the odds of success. By going a step further and regularly reviewing your goals with someone else (a coach, a trainer, a teacher, an advisor), your success is all but guaranteed. In the following example, who do you think is most likely to accomplish the goal of losing weight?

- The person who wants to lose weight (a goal)

- The person who wants to lose weight (goal) and writes down their goal (written goal)

- The person who wants to lose weight (goal), writes down their goal (written goal), and outlines a plan for achieving it (written goal with an action plan)

- The person who wants to lose weight (goal), writes down their goal (written goal), outlines a plan for achieving the goal (written goal with an action plan), and reviews it regularly (goal reviews)

- The person who wants to lose weight (goal), writes down their goal (written goal), hires a personal trainer to help outline a specific fitness and diet plan for achieving the goal (written goal with an action plan), and meets the personal trainer at the gym three days a week to weigh in and work out (goal reviews with accountability)

Figure 1

Double Your Money

HOUSEHOLD INCOME	MEDIAN SAVINGS (WITHOUT A PLAN)	MEDIAN SAVINGS (WITH A PLAN)
$20,000-$39,999	$14,300	$28,500
$40,000-$99,999	$41,500	$89,650
$100,000 and up	$201,100	$325,500

Source: Consumer Federatiotn of America and Nations Bank Survey

The answer is obvious. Which person most resembles your approach to accomplishing your financial goals? Needless to say the last person is at least a hundred times more likely to accomplish the goal than the first.

These same rules apply to financial planning. According to a recent report released by the Consumer Federation of America, U.S. households earning less than $100,000 with financial plans reported having twice as much money in savings and investments as those without plans.[2] Households with more than $100,000 of income with financial plans had 62 percent more money than those without plans. (See Figure 1.) One report went so far as to say, "People who stick with written plans to govern their investments, on average, wind up with five times as much money during retirement as those who don't have a plan."[3]

 Only 3 percent of American's have written goals.[1]

To illustrate how a "map" can help you reach your destination, see how you do in the following exercise. The goal of this exercise is to spot as many numbers as you can in the allotted time. Take a look at the random numbers placed from 1 to 100 in Figure 2. Time yourself for 30 seconds and see how many numbers you can find in succession, beginning with the number 1, moving on to 2, then 3, and so on.

Start timing yourself now....and go!

Figure 2

How far did you get? Remember your score.

Now, we're going to try the exercise again, with a "map" to guide you to see if you can improve upon your first score. The strategy is simple: In Figure 3 below, a line has been placed down the center and across the middle of the chart, dividing it into four quadrants. The number 1 is located in the top right quadrant. The number 2 is in the bottom right quadrant. Number 3 is in the bottom left, and number 4 is in the top left. The numbers are sequentially located clockwise, moving from quadrant to quadrant.

Now, time yourself for another 30 seconds to see if you can beat your first score.

Figure 3

You improved, didn't you?

In many cases, people find they can double their score in the second exercise, and it's all because they have a map spelling exactly how to get from point A to point B. In the same way, having a financial strategy will dramatically help you improve your financial situation.

Surprisingly, despite all the evidence, only one of three savers has a plan to guide his or her financial decisions. You would do well to be part of that savvy one-third.

Developing a Plan: The Best Time to Start Is Now
Regardless of whether you are retiring soon, changing jobs, or simply looking toward your future, now is a good time to develop a comprehensive financial plan that addresses every component of your financial portfolio.

These components include:

- Retirement
- Investments
- Taxes
- Liabilities
- Budgeting

- Insurance
- Asset Protection
- Estate Protection
- Children's Education
- Long-Term Care

A comprehensive financial plan will help you establish goals in each of these areas and outline strategies for accomplishing each of them.

To develop a financial plan, begin by taking inventory of your current financial portfolio. Include the details of all of your assets and liabilities. Then think about your financial goals and write them down! You can purchase software or use Web calculators that will provide you with some components of a comprehensive financial plan. Be aware, however, that these do-it-yourself programs, in most cases, will fall short of completely meeting your needs. While many programs will crunch the numbers for you and spit out endless pages of analysis, they often don't outline specific strategies, make specific recommendations, or help you implement your plan. These are the most important components of the planning process. For example, your plan may conclude that "you need to save an extra $200 per month to reach your retirement goals." While this recommendation is helpful, there is much more to it. A good financial planner, who understands all aspects of planning, will prove invaluable when it comes to all the specifics of implementing your strategy. For instance, a good advisor may add the following specifics to the recommendation to increase your retirement savings and provide you with the applications necessary to put it all in motion:

RECOMMENDATIONS

1) Cut $200 out of your monthly dining and entertainment budget to squeeze out an extra $200 per month to meet your savings goal.
2) Open a Roth IRA at a discount brokerage firm like Fidelity or Charles Schwab.
3) Purchase the Vanguard 500 Index mutual fund.
4) Link your bank account to your Roth IRA and have $200 automatically withdrawn each month to fund your Roth.
5) After building a $3,000 position in the Vanguard 500 Index Fund, re-direct your monthly investment into the Dreyfus Mid Cap Index Fund until the balance reaches $2,000. As time goes on, add a small-cap fund, an international fund, and a bond fund.

While a do-it-yourself software package is a good starting point for a less sophisticated financial situation, in most cases you should seek the assistance of an experienced fee-only financial advisor.

Find a financial advisor to help you develop a financial plan – one who can provide objective advice and has a system in place to ensure that your progress in monitored. Avoid advisors who work on commission.

Most people will have more success in achieving their financial goals by hiring a financial planner to help them in their planning than by going it alone. As you'll find, setting your financial goals and developing a written plan for accomplishing them is the easy part. The hard part is having the discipline to stick to the plan, and this is where a good advisor will be a tremendous help.

73 percent of consumers with a written plan used some type of financial professional for its preparation. Certified Financial Planner Board of Standards Inc, 2002 Consumer Survey

But don't rush to hire the first financial planner who offers to develop a financial plan for you. Financial advisors love to talk about the importance of developing a comprehensive financial plan. But be careful. Some advisors use financial plans for the sole purpose of pushing specific products (often insurance). In these cases, once the plan is complete, products sold, and the commission has been paid, clients are often neglected and the plan is never again reviewed. This type of once-and-done financial planning is a waste of your time and money. Financial planning is an ongoing process. If an advisor has no system in place to regularly review your finances and can't give objective advice because of the way he or she is compensated, HIRE SOMEONE ELSE! To find a good financial advisor follow the seven steps outlined in detail in Chapter 3.

Do you think the odds of accomplishing your goals would increase if you met with your financial advisor and did the following?

- Analyzed your current financial status.
- Outlined clear and precise short-term and long-term financial goals (set goals).
- Developed a written financial plan (written goals).
- Outlined a specific plan for accomplishing each goal (action plan).
- Implemented the plan by completing each action step (begin taking immediate action).
- Received a call from your advisor every six months to meet, update your plan, review your progress, and continue to check off items on the action plan (goal reviews with accountability).

38 percent of consumers who have a written financial plan review their financial plan annually. Certified Financial Planner Board of Standards Inc, 2002 Consumer Survey

Once you record your goals and objectives and map out a strategy to accomplish each goal, you will immediately and dramatically increase your chances of reaching them. If you would like to double your money, develop a written financial plan. You'll do much better financially with a plan than without one. You can't afford not to take this important step, especially at retirement.

Dear Mr. or Mrs. Prospective Client,

I understand you will be retiring soon and have accumulated a ton of money in your company retirement plan and I would like a piece of it. I am under tremendous pressure to sell investments and insurance to hit the lofty sales quotas my firm requires me to reach. I need your help.

I work for a big firm and can offer you a lot of expensive financial products: mutual funds, annuities, life insurance, you name it. In fact, I've got a couple of investments in mind that will pay me a huge commission. Funny thing, most of the products I offer I wouldn't sell to my mom or buy myself, but if you don't know any better, I think you'll like them.

I don't have a whole lot of experience, but I would like to cut my teeth on your money. I call myself a financial planner, but I don't really do any planning; I am a product-pushing salesman. Although well meaning, I really don't have the skills and training to give you the advice you need as you retire.

I am confident I can help you make me money. Could we meet soon? I have a mortgage payment coming due. I'll call you to arrange a time to meet.

Sincerely,

Joe Advisor
Financial Consultant

THREE

Fire Your Broker!

✓ RETIREMENT DECISION #3: *Should I fire my broker and hire a financial advisor who can be objective and isn't pitching products?*

As you approach retirement, you will be hunted down by stockbrokers, insurance agents, bank investment representatives, and financial planners who would all like a piece of your nest egg. You may even get a sales letter like the one on the previous page.

You may laugh at this advisor's brash but honest marketing approach. But if you read between the lines of the sales letters you receive from advisors (or the seminars you attend sponsored by advisors), they most always say exactly what this letter says: "I don't have enough experience, I offer expensive products, I am under tremendous pressure to sell you something, and if given the choice *for myself,* I'd buy a no-load investment or insurance product from another company before buying the one I am selling you."

After this bleak introduction to financial advisors, the question still remains. Should you hire an advisor? I believe that unless you have the tools, inclination, and experience to confidently address *every* topic in this book and then adhere strictly to the resulting financial strategy throughout retirement, you definitely need to hire a financial advisor. But be careful, while good advice from a good advisor can mean the difference of hundreds of thousands of additional dollars during retirement, I wouldn't trust most advisors with my own money and I don't think you should either.

You're the Boss

Hiring a good advisor is similar to hiring a good employee. Consider, for instance, the steps Max Sontag took to find a new president to run his 200-employee manufacturing company when he retired.

He started by listing the qualifications the new president would be required to have. He then advertised the job and begin accepting resumes. Max sifted through the resumes and narrowed his search down to a few finalists. These people were called in for interviews. During these interviews, Max asked probing questions about their experience, background and what kinds of things they would do to continue the success of his company. Of course, Max had to make sure he could trust and work with the person he would hire. After deciding on a new president, he drew up a contract to outline the salary he would pay and what expectations the new president was required to meet. Max also set up a schedule of meetings where he could give his input and the new president could report on the progress of the company. Max was careful to hire the right person to manage an asset he had worked his whole life to create.

Essentially, you, like Max, are the boss, and the financial advisor you hire is your employee. You should undertake the job of finding an advisor with the same seriousness as Max did in his search for a president. Like Max, you will trust someone with an asset that has taken a lifetime to build.

Figure 1

How do people select their financial advisors?

Asked A Friend/ Family 56%

Asked Another Professional 31%

Searched on the Internet 0%

Called Company/ Advertised 7%

Phone Book/ Directory 2%

Other 2%

Called Professional Body 2%

Source: http://www.cfp-ca.org

Finding and Hiring a Financial Advisor: A Seven-Step Process

This chapter will help you know what to look for in an advisor, how to conduct an interview, how to spell out what is expected of your advisor over time, and how to outline what fees are involved. If you are already using an advisor, read this chapter to determine if your advisor can make the cut. If not, fire him or her, and find an advisor who can.

Step 1: Find an advisor with at least 10 years' experience

At retirement, Jack Rice attended a seminar taught by a young financial advisor who'd been working as an advisor for less than three years. The advisor was sharp, professional, and seemed to know his topic well. Jack was impressed. Since he knew no other advisors he decided to hire this young rep for assistance in rolling over his $250,000 401(k) to an IRA. The advisor recommended Jack purchase an index annuity. Jack didn't know at the time that this annuity purchase made his advisor a 10 percent commission ($25,000).

One year later, Jack realized he had made a mistake. The problem was that he needed to withdraw more money from the annuity than he had originally planned, which would trigger a hefty 10% surrender charge. What Jack had missed in the glitzy sales presentation was that he was locked into the annuity for 15 years before he could withdraw the balance of his investment without incurring penalties. Jack's inexperienced advisor was well-versed in just one product (annuities), didn't have any financial planning expertise, and wasn't knowledgeable about the many other investment options. The advisor sold the one product he knew and made out like a bandit. As often occurs, the advisor has since left the firm. Jack was stuck holding the bag. In hindsight, Jack should have sought out an advisor who was not so wet behind the ears.

Let the young advisors cut their teeth on others' money, not yours. If you work with an advisor who is new to the financial services business, it is likely he or she won't be in business five years from now. The turnover of financial advisors in the first five years in the business is extremely high. American Express, one of the nation's largest brokerage firms, boasting more than 11,000 financial advisors, reports that 50 percent of its advisors leave the business in the first four years.[1] While the failure rate is high for brokerage firms, the insurance industry fares even worse. According to LIMRA, only 15% of agents make it to the four-year mark. To avoid hiring an advisor who will leave you behind for another career, consider advisors with at least 10 years of experience.

Step 2: Find an advisor with a CFP designation

Advisors come in all shapes and sizes. There are stockbrokers, life insurance agents, bank investment representatives, and independent financial planners. An estimated 800,000 people use the title "financial advisor."[2] The requirements for carrying that title, unfortunately, are minimal. Of all of the stockbrokers, insurance agents, and others who call themselves financial advisors, less than one out of every 10 has earned the Certified Financial Planner™ (CFP) mark. The CFP title is awarded by the International Board of Standards and Practices for Certified Financial Planners. Certified Financial Planners must undergo two years of intensive training followed by a rigorous two-day examination. A code of ethics must be adhered to and participation in a continuing- education program is required. CFPs are trained in many aspects of the financial-services industry, including investment, insurance, retirement, tax, estate planning, and more.

There are 800,000 people calling themselves financial planners. However, only 40,000 have earned the designation of Certified Financial Planner™.

Step 3: Hire a fee-only advisor, not one who works on commission

Can your advisor be objective? Objectivity largely depends on how he or she is compensated. Financial advisors are paid by either fee or commission. The advice and investment products you receive will depend on how your advisor is compensated.

Commissioned Advisors

The majority of advisors are paid via the commissions they receive from the products they sell to their clients. Most advisors at brokerage firms, insurance companies, and banks (stockbrokers, insurance agents, and bank investment reps) fall into this category. You won't have to pay a penny for their services out of your pocket and will never

write them a check for their services. The financial products you purchase from these advisors have built-in investment and insurance expenses designed to compensate your advisor. Although you will likely
never see these fees, you are paying them indirectly, and often too much.

　　Figure 2 outlines common commissions paid out for different types
of financial products. Most products pay an up-front commission to the
advisor when you make your initial investment and a trailing, or ongoing,
commission each year thereafter. The commissions paid are generally
split by your advisor and his or her firm. There is nothing wrong with
working with a commissioned advisor as long as you know exactly what
you are paying, and you are getting an equivalent amount of service.
Discuss this with your advisor at the onset, before investing any money.

Figure 2

Commissions Advisors Are Paid
From Financial Products
$500,000 Investment

Product Type	Up-Front Commission		Annual Ongoing Commission	
Mutual Funds				
Class A Shares	5.00%	$25,000	0.25%	$1,250
Class B Shares	4.00%	$20,000	0.25%	$1,250
Class C Shares	1.00%	$5,000	1.00%	$5,000
Variable Annuities				
Payout Option 1	5.00%	$25,000	0.25%	$1,250
Payout Option 2	1.00%	$5,000	1.00%	$5,000
Index Annuities (up-front commission from 5-10%)	10.00%	$50,000	0.00%	$0
Life Insurance- **Premium $7,000** (VUL, 500k, 45 year old)	80.00%	$5,600	10.00%	$700

Note: chart doesn't take into account possible breakpoints

Beware of Up-Front Commissions

It is usually not a good thing if your advisor receives an up-front commission when you purchase an investment. Why? Not only could you be locked into back-end sales charges for five to 10 years, you run the risk of getting poor service from your advisor for years to come. Here's why.

 Don't buy products that pay your advisor big up-front commissions.

When an advisor receives a big up-front commission (see Figure 2), he or she may be keen on servicing you initially while the big commission is still fresh on his mind. Five years from now, however, when your account is not generating any income for the advisor and the promises of great service forgotten, your advisor may be less interested in managing your investments and financial plan.

Also, the more a fund company pays an advisor up front, often the longer you'll have to hold the fund before you can sell it without incurring the back-end sale charges and penalties. Then, to add insult to injury, many advisors persuade clients to sell an investment as soon as the back-end charges have expired. Clients then get pressure to buy another investment with a high up-front commission. This, of course, generates another commission for the advisor and extends the years of back-end charges.

 Don't buy investments and insurance with back-end sales charges. If you need to make changes to your plan within five to seven years you will live to regret it.

Helping your advisor pay his or her mortgage every few years by buying a high commission product is not often in your best interest.

It is better that your advisor is paid something each year from the products you own, so there is continued incentive to service your accounts.

Commissions will skew your advisor's recommendations toward the financial products that pay the largest commissions, not necessarily those best suited for you. To show you what I mean, let's look at the products Wendy Forsgreen, a commissioned financial advisor, can offer her clients. She works for a large brokerage firm and can only offer clients loaded mutual funds and annuities, as well as stocks and bonds. While she can make a lot of money selling you these products, you would never have to write her a check to pay for her advice. As we'll discuss in Chapter 15, each loaded financial product builds into its price an added expense to pay a commission to the advisor who sells it.

What advice do you think she would give you when you ask her how to invest the $100,000 in your IRA? Do you think the advice would be objective or slanted toward specific products? The only way to know is to see how she is compensated. Wendy earns a 4 percent ($4,000) commission on most funds she sells. However, if she sells you funds sponsored by her company she will make 5 percent ($5,000). If she sells you a variable annuity she will make 6 percent ($6,000). Stocks and bonds will pay her about 1 percent per transaction ($1,000). In addition, you should know that Wendy has to meet an annual production quota to keep her job, and her company has recently been pushing advisors to sell the funds and annuities they sponsor. Also, in any month she reaches $20,000 in commission she qualifies for a trip to a nice resort. Knowing all of this, how objective do you think she can be?

Fee-Only Advisors

Fee-only advisors get paid by the hour, the project, or as a percentage of the assets they manage for clients. These fees are negotiated and agreed upon in a contract. Unlike the fees that are built in to commissioned products that clients never see, the fees fee-only advisors charge, by law, are fully disclosed and regularly reported to clients. Hourly fees range between $100 to $300 an hour. Projects, like preparing a financial plan, may cost between $500 and $5,000.

Figure 3 is a sample fee schedule outlining the annual fees advisors charge if they work for you for a percentage of the assets you invest with them (asset management fees). Many fee-only advisors also have account minimums of $100,000 or more.

Now consider the advice you could receive from Stephen Bryer, a fee-only financial advisor. Stephen will prepare a financial plan for you for a flat fee of $1,000 and as part of that plan, recommend specific strategies to help you meet your goals. Once the strategies are outlined he will recommend specific products and implement the plan for you. Since Stephen doesn't work on commissions he is paid only what you agree to pay him. He uses only no-load products (mutual funds, annuities, life in-

Figure 3

Average Fees as a Percentage of Assets Being Managed	
Account Size	**Annual %**
$0 - $249,999	1.20%
$250,00 - $499,999	1.10%
$500,000 - $999,999	1.00%
$1,000,000 - $2,999,999	0.85%
$3,000,000+	0.75%

surance, etc.) which have low built-in expenses and no front- or back-end charges. He buys stocks and bonds for his clients through a discount brokerage firm to keep transaction costs down. Because the products you buy from Stephen don't pay him anything he doesn't have a bias to sell you one product over another. After completing the plan you can retain Stephen's services on an ongoing basis by paying him an annual retainer which could be a flat fee or a fee based on a percentage of the assets he manages for you. It doesn't matter to Stephen's bottom line whether you buy an annuity or mutual funds or any other product since the only payment he will receive is from you.

 Fees you pay for financial planning my be tax deductible as a miscellaneous itemized deduction on Schedule A (Form 1040) (See IRS Publication 550).

Commissions or Fees: Which Is Better?

Let's compare a $500,000 mutual fund investment made with a commissioned advisor and one made with a fee-only advisor. Let's assume the commissioned advisor receives a 1 percent commission and the fee-only advisor receives a 1 percent asset management fee. Both advisors will receive $5,000 annually from this investment. Although the total fee is the same, the fee-only advisor still may be your best bet for several reasons:

1)   You may be able to negotiate a lower asset management

fee. In addition, your fee may automatically be lowered as your portfolio grows larger. On the other hand, you can't negotiate the fees that are built in to commissioned products, and these fees are not reduced as your portfolio grows.

2) The investment advisory fee you pay is often tax-deductible; mutual fund expenses are not.

3) Fee-only advisors use no-load financial products, which do not carry back-end sales charges. With many commissioned funds, you could be slapped with a significant fee if you sell within five to 10 years.

4) Your fee-only advisor can be objective in his or her recommendations by not having to worry about meeting commission and product quotas.

5) Your fee-only advisor may be able to find funds with expenses much less than commissioned funds.

Whatever you do, do not pay both commissions *and* fees. Some "fee-based" advisors, for example, sell mutual funds that pay them big up-front commissions, which stick their clients with built-in fund expenses that are often double their no-load counterparts (maybe two percent annually). These advisors then charge an investment advisor fee of another 1 percent or more of your assets on top of that. In this case, your total annual fees would total 3 percent per year. That's a big hurdle for your investments to overcome. Before you make a dime, you must make 3 percent to pay your fees.

The Federal Administration on Aging warns investors of the dilemma faced by commission-only advisors:

"A financial planner who collects commissions is open to the criticism that he or she has an incentive to select or recommend investments partly on the basis of the commission offered — not solely on the quality of the investment." It advises, "While competence and performance should be the primary considerations in selecting a planner, compensation should also be considered — especially in cases where commissions are involved."

This is not to say that you should not consider an advisor who works on commissions. The administration concludes, "The fact that commissions or other payments are made does not necessarily mean the investment is a bad one. Rather, it indicates that your planner may be faced with choosing between what is best for him or her and what is best for you."

Fee-only advisors, who charge a flat fee, hourly rate, or a percentage of the assets they manage, work independent of brokerage firms, banks, and insurance companies. By not getting paid from the companies whose products they sell, they have put themselves in a better position to provide objective advice and have *your* best interest in mind.

Step 4: Insist on a plan and a well-defined investment strategy

In Chapter 2 we discussed the importance of having a written financial game plan. Several studies suggest that people with plans have twice as much money as those without plans. You need a plan to provide you with a big picture framework to make all of your financial decisions. Your advisor can't possibly give you advice in line with your goals without seeing the big picture. In the same way, you also need a well-defined investment strategy to spell out exactly how to allocate and diversify your money. As we'll discuss in Chapters 9-18, the investment strategy will also outline the type of investments you are going to buy and how you are going to evaluate and manage those investments. Both a carefully monitored plan and an investment strategy will help you stick to your financial game plan.

Research indicates that individual investors, left to their own devices, are fickle and rarely disciplined when it comes to sticking with an investment strategy. As Benjamin Graham, the legendary American investor, said, "The investor's chief problem — and even his worst enemy — is likely to be himself."[3]

Let's look at the evidence: Figure 4 illustrates the total returns of various market indexes compared with the total returns achieved by the average investor. If an investor had invested money in the S&P 500 Index from 1984 to 2003, he or she would have earned an annualized return of over 12 percent. Unfortunately, during this same period, the average *investor* purchasing equity mutual funds earned just 2.57 percent per year!

Figure 4

Average Annual Total Returns (1984 - 2003)

Why did investors do so poorly during a period when the stock market did so well? One reason was their inability to hold investments and adhere to a strategy over the long term. The average investor holds a fund for less than three years. People who use financial advisors hold their funds longer than those who don't. The job of your advisor is to provide needed encouragement and to help you stick steadfastly to an investment discipline, even when thundering market volatility and the media is tempting you to act out of panic.

According to a DALBAR study, investors who do not seek advice are more likely to panic and sell when stocks dive.[4] With the advice, knowledge, and experience of a financial consultant, investors are more likely to hold on to their investments for the long run.

An advisor can guide you through the turbulence of the financial markets and help you adhere to your strategy. By sticking to a fundamentally sound strategy, you will increase your chances of obtaining better investment performance.

If your advisor doesn't develop a financial plan for you or fails to craft a well-defined investment strategy you should hire someone who will. These documents are your financial constitution and will dictate what to do as the financial winds change direction over time.

Step 5: Insist your advisor has an action plan for servicing your account

You shouldn't have to call your advisor; your advisor should have a system in place to make sure you are consistently being contacted. Find out your advisor's plan of attack to monitor your financial plan and review your investments over time before you begin investing your money. If your advisor is not willing to meet with you semiannually to review and update your financial and investment plan, go elsewhere.

About half of all investors who work with advisors meet with their advisor less than once per year, and half of those people *never* meet with their advisor.[5] This means only half of all advisors are providing even a minimal level of customer service.

Outline the amount of service you expect to receive in writing before investing any money with your advisor.

Only half of all advisors meet with their clients more than once per year.

Step 6: Shop at the supermarket (avoid proprietary products)

One of the reasons stores like Wal-Mart and The Home Depot are so successful is that they offer an enormous number of products under one roof. Customers can compare many different brands of the same types of products before making a decision to purchase. Would you shop at these stores if they carried only one brand of the products you buy?

There are both, narrow one-brand financial advisors and advisors who offer a Wal-Mart-type mega selection of financial products. The more products and services your advisor can offer, the more likely it is you'll get a financial plan and products customized to specifically fit your needs. Make sure your advisor can provide the following products and services:

- Comprehensive financial plan
- A no-load mutual fund supermarket (at least 5,000 funds)

- No-load fixed and variable annuities from multiple companies
- Individual stocks and bonds with low commission rates
- Separate accounts from multiple managers
- No-load life insurance from multiple companies
- Online account access
- Banking features

Avoid advisors who primarily recommend proprietary products (products developed by your advisor's company). This one-brand approach will often leave you with mediocre investments. If the advisor puts together an investment proposal for you outlining seven or eight mutual funds that are mostly proprietary, beware. What are the chances, when compared with the more than 16,000 funds available, that all the proprietary funds the advisor can offer are among the best in each of their respective asset categories? Not very likely.

In fact, in January 2005, I conducted a study of the 63 mutual funds offered by one of the nation's largest brokerage companies. I found that not even one of the 63 funds the firm offers had performed better than its respective asset category average for the past three, five, and 10 years. Not one of their funds met a basic performance screen. If you bought several funds from this company, you would end up with a bunch of below- average investments. In contrast, when I applied the same performance criteria to all 16,000 funds, I found 2,263 with above-average performance. In fairness, just because a product is proprietary doesn't necessarily mean it's bad. Just make sure that if you buy proprietary products they can pass the performance test outlined in Chapter 14.

Avoid financial advisors who push their company's proprietary financial products.

TIP

Step 7: Investigate the advisor's practice

Once you have narrowed your selection to a handful of individuals, be sure to undertake an in-depth investigation of each advisor's background and credentials. Remember, this is the person who will be handling your money and your future for potentially the next 30 years. The Forum for Investor Advice recommends, "Spend time to thoroughly check out your advisor's credentials, experience, investment philosophy, specialties and client references to make sure you find someone whom you can trust and will give you valuable advice."

The majority of investors who hire a financial advisor fail to investigate the advisor's background.

With What Type of Clients Does the Advisor Work?

Ask your prospective advisor the age of his or her average client. If most of the advisor's clients are between the ages of 55 to 70, the advisor has likely handled many retirement transitions like yours. Because you are retiring, ask your prospective advisor how many retirements he or she has handled during the past year. Ask for copies of financial plans the advisor has done for other people who have retired.

Does Your Advisor Have Time for You?

How many clients does your advisor have? If your advisor has too many clients he or she may be spread too thin and not be able to devote enough time to you. A large practice may also mean you end up working with your advisor's staff more than with your advisor. Let's look at this logically. If an advisor must devote 10 hours each year to only you, then how many clients can the advisor service each year? We'll assume your advisor spends 35 hours per week working for clients and five hours per week doing administrative and marketing activities. If your advisor works 49 weeks per year, he or she could successfully work with a total of 171 clients (35 hours multiplied by 49 weeks, divided by 10 hours). As a general rule, you should not hire an advisor with more than 200 clients.

But don't automatically run to advisors with very small practices. They may be more interested in obtaining new clients rather than servicing the clients they already have.

The Final Interview

First, use the Web resources at the end of this chapter to

locate experienced advisors in your area. Then simply call the advisors you feel are the most qualified. You can explain your situation and get some initial feedback on what types of things they may suggest you do. If you like what you hear, arrange for a face-to-face interview. The questionnaire below, provided by the Forum for Investor Advice, will give you a sampling of questions you can ask during this meeting.

Qualifications:

1. What is your educational background? College degree and area of study? Financial-planning education?
2. What financial planning certifications or designations do you hold?
3. What securities licenses do you hold?
4. What is your professional experience? How many years have you been a financial advisor?
5. How do you keep your financial knowledge base and planning skills current?

Services:

1. How would you prepare my financial plan? Do you recommend specific investments or investment products?
2. Can I see a sample financial plan? (Make sure that the plan is clear and comprehensive.)
3. What is your investment philosophy? What types of investments do you favor? Get a sense of the types of investment products (load or no-load, etc.) and methodology that the advisor uses.
4. Do you have certain areas of expertise: insurance, estate planning, retirement planning, education planning, and tax issues?
5. Do you collaborate with professionals in accounting, law, and insurance to offer specialized services?

Clientele:

1. What is the minimum and maximum asset value of your clients? (Make sure your assets fall within this range.)

2. Do most of your clients have financial situations similar to mine?

Accessibility:

1. Describe how you and I will work together.
2. Will I be working with only you, or do you have an assistant?
3. How often will we meet or talk? Can I reach you by e-mail? Can I view my accounts and research online? How often will I receive reports?
4. How do you help clients implement their financial plans? Do you only give advice or do you also make the transactions? Will you have discretionary power to buy and sell assets in my account?

Compensation:

1. What are your fees? Do you operate on a fee-only, fee-based, commission-only, or fee-plus-commission basis?
2. If fee-only, is the fee based on an hourly rate, a flat fee, or a percentage of assets?

Other:

1. Can you provide me with references from long-term clients and professional associates?
2. Is your business registered with the SEC? With the state's securities office?

Interviewing candidates is the most important step in selecting your financial advisor. Keep in mind that *you're the boss*, so act as if you are interviewing a potential employee, an employee who will have a huge impact on your financial success or failure.

You are the boss!

Choosing to work with a qualified financial advisor can dramatically increase your odds of success. Investors who employ the services of a good financial advisor are much more likely to reach their retirement goals and thus improve the long-term outlook of their retirement future. Set the bar high so you end up with an advisor who is ethical, competent and reasonably priced. The information included in this chapter will help you select an advisor who can meet your needs. Don't forget, you're the boss and the advisor you hire is your employee. Be sure to hire a good employee to guide the assets you've worked a lifetime to accumulate.

Perform an Online Search for a Financial Advisor in Your Area

Fee-Only Advisors

• National Association of Personal Financial Advisors, www.napfa.com

• Garrett Planning Network: www.garrettplanningnetwork.com

• Myfinancialadvice: www.myfinancialadvice.com

CFPs (Commissioned and Fee-Only)

• Financial Planning Association: www.fpanet.org

Commissioned Advisors

• Financial Advisor Match: www.financialadvisormatch.com

FOUR

More Life than Money

✓ RETIREMENT DECISION #4: *How much can I safely withdraw from my portfolio?*

There's a critical question you must answer by the first day of your retirement: How much can you withdraw from your retirement savings each year without incurring the risk of running out of money? A miscalculation could mean you outlive your assets and have to live on Social Security alone. This chapter will review four withdrawal methods to help you choose a withdrawal rate that will be as safe as possible in the face of unknown life expectancies and ever-changing economic conditions.

 People rank "outliving their savings" as their greatest retirement fear.[4]

When calculating a safe withdrawal rate, you face two major obstacles: First, there is no way to know exactly how long you will live. Second, it is impossible to predict the exact rate of return your portfolio will generate during retirement. You must also consider the effect inflation and taxes will have on your withdrawals.

Bottom line? In most cases, you should withdraw no more than between 4 to 6 percent of your savings per year. Any more than this and you run the risk of running out of money.

For most of us to obtain the returns we need to maintain an acceptable income level, we must invest a portion of our retirement assets in stocks and bonds. A retiree expecting to be in retirement for 30 years will need more money invested in stocks than the retiree planning for only 20 years. Either way, investing in stocks and bonds brings unpredictability into the equation. But if we make conservative assumptions and err on the side of safety, we can calculate a cautious rate of withdrawal that will ensure our retirement savings last.

There are all sorts of strategies and theories out there on how to determine a safe withdrawal rate. You've probably already heard some, especially if you've sought advice from financial planners. I've boiled them down to the five most common methods. Review each, then choose the method that best fits your goals and objectives.

The Withdrawal Myth

On the surface, it doesn't seem like it should be that difficult to determine a safe withdrawal rate. Since 1926, the annual rate of return of stocks is about 11 percent. If you invest 100 percent of your retirement portfolio in stocks, you should be able to withdraw any amount less than 11 percent and never dip into your principal. It sounds so simple it must be effective, right? Well, as many inexperienced financial advisors and their clients have found, this approach can lead to disastrous results.

For example, if a $500,000 portfolio provides a constant 10 percent annual return and we withdraw just 7 percent of the principal each year, the results are astonishing (Figure 1). We don't even come close to touching our investment principal. There's one problem with this simple scenario, however; stocks do not provide consistent returns. While stocks may average 10 to 11 percent growth over the long run, they often take investors on a very bumpy ride along the way.

For example, the annual investment results for the portfolio in Figure 2 would also provide a 10 percent *average*

Figure 1

Withdrawal Myth	
$500,000 portfolio growing at 10% annually, investor withdrawing 7% ($35,000) annually.	
Year	**Portfolio Value After Withdrawals**
1	$515,000
5	$770,255
10	$1,261,871
15	$2,053,624
20	$3,328,750
25	$5,382,353
30	$8,689,701

annual return over five- and 10-year periods. However, notice what happens to the $500,000 portfolio if the return varies from year to year and if the same 7 percent per year is withdrawn.

Figure 2

Withdrawal Reality

Hypothetical Portfolio Year 1 through 10
$500,000 portfolio growing at a 10% average annual return, investor withdrawing 7% ($35,000) annually

Year	Portfolio Return	7% Annual Withdrawal	Portfolio Value at Year End
1	-25%	$35,000	$340,000
2	35%	$35,000	$424,000
3	-15%	$35,000	$325,400
4	25%	$35,000	$371,750
5	30%	$35,000	$448,275
6	-25%	$35,000	$301,206
7	35%	$35,000	$371,628
8	-15%	$35,000	$280,884
9	25%	$35,000	$316,105
10	30%	$35,000	$375,936

"Post War" 1946-1995 adjusted for inflation

After only a couple of years, these annual withdrawals are already eroding the principal. In year eight, the nest egg that was supposed to last 30 years has been cut nearly in half. By year 10, the balance is $375,936, a far cry from the $1.2 million balance remaining in the first scenario.

While it seems perfectly logical to base your withdrawal rate on average annual returns of stocks and bonds, these assumptions could lead to the total depletion of your investment assets. Actual returns, as opposed to average returns, vary from year to year. Taking this variance into account when deciding how much you can safely withdraw each year is crucial to your retirement planning.

Method 1: Too Fixed on Fixed-Rate

It's 1981, and David and Iris Meredith just retired with a nice $500,000 nest egg. They think their portfolio is large enough that they can live solely off the interest and dividends it kicks off each year. This way, they'll never have to touch their principal. After all, it's 1981 and interest rates are topping 15%. Rates will go down, the couple knows, but they can't possibly drop too much, right?

David and Iris decide to put their retirement savings in ultra-conservative six-month certificates of deposit (CDs). Their plan is simple: They'll continue to buy six-month CDs as each matures and withdraw the interest they earn each year. They'll be able to sleep well at night knowing that their principal is FDIC guaranteed.

Their plan worked great—initially. Their CD earned a whopping 15.79% in 1981, providing David and Iris with a healthy $78,950 of income before taxes. From then on, however, things went down hill. It turns out that interest rates were at their peak in the early 1980s. In 1991, their yearly income before taxes was just $29,550. By 2003, their CD was paying just 1.17%, earning them a scant $5,850.

Of course, the nice thing about this method is that David and Iris' $500,000 principal is still intact. The downside is severe, as many retirees like David and Iris have found out. Their results are summarized in Figure 4 (Method 1). Falling interest rates and falling incomes don't work for long in the world of rising costs. Over the long term, most fixed-rate investments just won't provide the income retirees need as costs increase.

Method 2: In Distributions We Trust

It's 1970, and Jeff and Marci Reynolds are retiring with a savings of $500,000. They want to maintain a fairly lavish lifestyle, so they'll need more income than David and Iris' short-term CDs can provide. They decide to invest their $500,000 into a mutual fund made up of 50% stocks and 50% bonds and cash. Their choice is a reputable, inexpensive mutual fund called Dodge & Cox Balanced. They plan to withdraw just the fund's distributions (dividends, interest, and capital gains distributions) at the end of each year. They know that their income will be volatile, but it will likely be much higher than the CD alternative. In addition, their $500,000 principal would also have a chance to appreciate and keep up with inflation.

Jeff and Marci were prepared for a bumpy ride; they just didn't anticipate how extreme it would be. Their income in 1971 was $21,845 before taxes; in 1986, it hit $115,247. In 1992, it fell to $40,124 and shot up to $260,588 in 2000, before sliding back to $51,939 in 2003. Best of all, however, even after withdrawing all distributions from the fund since 1970, their $500,000 portfolio appreciated to a balance of $1.6 million by the end of 2003.

As Jeff and Marci discovered, retirees using this method are unlikely to deplete their portfolio. See Figure 4 for a summary of their year-to-year results (Method 2). But few people have the luxury to be flexible enough to live on an ever-changing income level. For this approach to work, retirees must have the means to roll with the punches. Most do not.

Method 3: Playing the Percentage

Jeff and Marci weren't the only retirees in 1970 to invest their savings in Dodge & Cox Balanced Fund; Jorge and Felicia Becerra likewise put their $500,000 nest egg in the fund at the exact same time. Jorge and Felicia, however, decided to use a different strategy to withdraw their money. They set a withdrawal rate at a level lower than what they expected the fund would annually produce. They figured the fund's annual total return would be about 8 percent. So they set their withdrawal rate at 6 percent. To determine how much money they deduct from their portfolio, they would simply take the balance of the portfolio at the end of each year and multiply it by 6 percent.

Jorge and Felicia's first-year withdrawal was $30,847 before taxes, leaving them with a portfolio worth $483,274. Because of a severe market downturn in 1973 and 1974, their 6 percent annual withdrawals earned a lot less cash. Their balance in the mutual fund at the end of 1974 dropped to $339,796, providing them with an income of a mere $25,189 (6% of $339,796). The couple and their strategy continued to struggle during the 1970s, as the market struggled. Then came the bull market in the 1980s. By the end of 1990, the portfolio topped $1 million and produced a withdrawal of $65,809; in 2003, it was worth more than $2.3 million and provided $150,879 in income.

As Jorge and Felicia learned, retirees who use this constant-percentage strategy will earn a bigger paycheck when their investments do well and vice versa. In up markets, they will receive a larger income; in down markets, they will have to live on less. Their results are summarized in Figure 4 (Method 3). This method can also be effective in keeping pace with inflation. A fixed percentage of a rising dollar amount equals increased income.

The danger of this method is using a too-high withdrawal rate. Consistently withdrawing more than the portfolio is earning will slowly decrease income, and annual withdrawals won't keep pace with inflation.

This strategy provides a volatile income stream, but with the right investments and a conservative withdrawal rate, retirees should be able to keep their growth rate ahead of their withdrawal rate and see their income rise in most years.

To defer taxes as long as possible, withdraw the money you need for income from your taxable investments first and then from your tax-deferred investments.

Method 4: Playing It Safe with Monte Carlo

The first four methods all had serious drawbacks that will probably discourage you from using them. But what if there was a method in which you could earn predictable and increasing income while knowing that regardless of market conditions you won't likely run out of money? This type of retirement is possible, but it requires testing your portfolio and various withdrawal rates in numerous historical market conditions. We refer to this exercise as a Monte Carlo analysis.

Using Monte Carlo, you will determine a withdrawal rate based on your initial investment balance that you are confident can be maintained through even the worst market conditions. Every year, you will simply withdraw that amount and give yourself a 3 percent raise to keep pace with inflation. Whether your investments are up or down in value, annually you will continue to take 3 percent more than the year before.

Studies have been conducted to help retirees determine a safe withdrawal rate. In what is known as the Trinity Study, three Trinity University faculty members back-tested the effect of various withdrawal rates on five different portfolios of stocks and bonds over 15-, 20-, 25-, and 30-year rolling time frames.[2] They used actual year-to-year returns of stocks and bonds rather than average returns. A success rate was calculated for each portfolio, time frame, and withdrawal rate. One hundred percent success was defined as having money remaining in the account at the conclusion of the specified withdrawal period in every period back tested. The following chart (Figure 3) summarizes their research.

For example, a retiree starting with a $500,000 portfolio consisting of 50 percent stocks and 50 percent bonds who plans to be in retirement for 30 years should be 95 percent successful if he withdraws less than 4 percent, or $20,000, annually. (See Figure 3, Portfolio Composition: 50% Stocks and 50% Bonds.)

Using this method, what is your "safe" withdrawal rate? The table in Figure 3 will help you answer that question. To use this table, first determine what percentage of your portfolio will be invested in stocks and bonds during retirement. Second, estimate how many years you will be in retirement (payout period). Finally, choose a withdrawal schedule that has been successful at least 80 percent of the time. After examining the chart, you will notice that most of the portfolios could sustain a 4 percent withdrawal rate. Higher withdrawals will usually deplete the portfolio assets before your retirement period is over.

Notice what happens if you plan to be in retirement for 30 years and withdraw 7% each year as we discussed earlier. Even with a portfolio consisting of 100 percent stocks, your success rate is only 59 percent. Do you like those odds, running a 41 percent chance of completely running out of money?

Okay. Monte Carlo sounds good on paper, but how would it work in the real world? James and Arlene Reed retired in 1970 and invested $500,000 in Dodge and Cox Balanced Fund. They decided to withdraw 4% annually ($20,000) at the end of each year. They felt

Figure 3

Portfolio Success Rate: Percentage of all past payout periods from 1946 to 1995 supported by the corresponding portfolio after adjusting withdrawals for inflation and deflation

Portfolio Composition: 100% Stocks and 0% Bonds

Payout Period	Withdrawal Rate as a % of Initial Portfolio Value									
	3%	4%	5%	6%	7%	8%	9%	10%	11%	12%
15 Years	100%	100%	100%	91%	79%	70%	63%	55%	43%	34%
20 Years	100%	100%	88%	75%	63%	53%	43%	33%	29%	24%
25 Years	100%	100%	87%	70%	59%	46%	35%	30%	26%	20%
30 Years	100%	95%	83%	68%	59%	41%	34%	34%	27%	15%

Portfolio Composition: 75% Stocks and 25% Bonds

Payout Period	Withdrawal Rate as a % of Initial Portfolio Value									
	3%	4%	5%	6%	7%	8%	9%	10%	11%	12%
15 Years	100%	100%	100%	95%	82%	68%	64%	46%	46%	27%
20 Years	100%	100%	90%	75%	61%	51%	37%	27%	27%	12%
25 Years	100%	100%	85%	65%	50%	37%	30%	22%	22%	2%
30 Years	100%	98%	83%	68%	49%	34%	22%	24%	7%	0%

Portfolio Composition: 50% Stocks and 50% Bonds

Payout Period	Withdrawal Rate as a % of Initial Portfolio Value									
	3%	4%	5%	6%	7%	8%	9%	10%	11%	12%
15 Years	100%	100%	100%	93%	79%	64%	50%	32%	23%	13%
20 Years	100%	100%	90%	75%	55%	33%	22%	10%	0%	0%
25 Years	100%	100%	80%	57%	37%	20%	7%	0%	0%	0%
30 Years	100%	95%	76%	51%	17%	5%	0%	0%	0%	0%

Portfolio Composition: 25% Stocks and 75% Bonds

Payout Period	Withdrawal Rate as a % of Initial Portfolio Value									
	3%	4%	5%	6%	7%	8%	9%	10%	11%	12%
15 Years	100%	100%	100%	89%	70%	50%	32%	18%	13%	7%
20 Years	100%	100%	82%	47%	31%	16%	8%	4%	0%	0%
25 Years	100%	93%	48%	24%	15%	4%	2%	0%	0%	0%
30 Years	100%	71%	27%	20%	5%	0%	0%	0%	0%	0%

Portfolio Composition: 0% Stocks and 100% Bonds

Payout Period	Withdrawal Rate as a % of Initial Portfolio Value									
	3%	4%	5%	6%	7%	8%	9%	10%	11%	12%
15 Years	100%	100%	100%	71%	39%	21%	18%	16%	14%	9%
20 Years	100%	90%	47%	20%	14%	12%	10%	2%	0%	0%
25 Years	100%	46%	17%	15%	11%	2%	0%	0%	0%	0%
30 Years	80%	20%	17%	12%	0%	0%	0%	0%	0%	0%

Note: Numbers in the table are rounded to the nearest whole percentage. The number of overlapping 15-year payout periods from 1946 - 1995, inclusively, is 56; 20-year periods, 51; 25-year periods, 46; 30-year periods, 41, Stocks are represented by Standard and Poor's 500 index, and bonds represented by long-term, high-grade corporates.

Source: The Trinity Study
"Post War" 1946 - 1995 adjusted for inflation

pretty confident that they wouldn't run out of money because a portfolio of 50 percent stocks and 50 percent bonds has historically had a success rate of 95%. So, how'd they do? In the first year of their retirement, their income was $20,000, the second year $20,600, the third year $21,218, and so on increasing their withdrawals by 3% each year for inflation. Thirty-three years later, after enjoying a steady and increasing income, their annual income hit $53,045. This was a period when the markets enjoyed phenomenal growth. Their fund balance at the end of 2003 reached an eye-popping $7.6 million (See Figure 4, Method 4). This was possible due to the low withdrawal rate and a rapidly advancing market.

Harvard University uses a similar strategy. In 1973, Harvard was interested in determining how much of its endowment portfolio could be withdrawn each year without depleting its principal. University researchers determined that a portfolio made up of 50 percent stocks and 50 percent bonds could safely support a 4 percent annual withdrawal rate, adjusted for inflation.[3]

A moderate investment portfolio should safely be able to sustain a 4% withdrawal rate without the risk of running out of money during retirement.

In summary, determining a safe withdrawal rate will help you avoid every retiree's worst nightmare — the premature exhaustion of portfolio assets during retirement. In this chapter, we have examined a number of ways to determine that rate in light of fluctuating personal and economic conditions. Regardless of the method you choose, be conservative.

Monte Carlo Calculator: www.troweprice.com (Individual Investors, Investment Planning & Tools, Retirement Planning, Retirement Income Calculator)

Figure 4

Four Withdrawal Methods from 1970 to 2003
$500,000 Initial Investment

	Method 1 6 Month CD		Method 2 Balanced Mutual Fund		Method 3 Balanced Mutual Fund		Method 4 Balanced Mutual Fund	
	Withdraw Interest Only		Withdraw Dividends and Captital Gains Distributions Only		Withdraw a constant percentage (6% of year end balance)		Withdraw a constant dollar amount (4% of initial balance) inflated annually	
Year	Year End Balance	Year End Withdrawal	Year End Balance	Year End Withdrawal	Year End Balance	Year End Withdrawal	Year End Balance	Year End Withdrawal
1970	$500,000	$38,200	$479,938	$32,099	$483,274	$30,847	$494,121	$20,000
1971	$500,000	$26,050	$510,031	$21,845	$504,537	$32,204	$528,189	$20,600
1972	$500,000	$25,050	$545,921	$21,176	$528,301	$33,721	$567,151	$21,218
1973	$500,000	$45,250	$460,544	$32,544	$448,006	$28,596	$489,796	$21,854
1974	$500,000	$50,100	$348,417	$25,189	$339,796	$21,689	$372,694	$22,510
1975	$500,000	$34,500	$429,113	$20,731	$413,523	$26,395	$459,325	$23,185
1976	$500,000	$28,150	$514,044	$22,291	$487,661	$31,127	$552,367	$23,881
1977	$500,000	$29,550	$472,358	$24,966	$443,513	$28,309	$509,829	$24,597
1978	$500,000	$43,000	$468,569	$31,208	$442,332	$28,234	$515,593	$25,335
1979	$500,000	$57,100	$498,217	$32,768	$472,654	$30,169	$560,007	$26,095
1980	$500,000	$64,700	$562,416	$38,341	$539,757	$34,452	$653,453	$26,873
1981	$500,000	$78,950	$491,306	$57,957	$494,826	$31,584	$609,611	$27,684
1982	$500,000	$62,850	$561,748	$48,371	$586,338	$37,425	$739,943	$28,515
1983	$500,000	$46,400	$609,229	$45,251	$644,689	$41,150	$836,141	$29,370
1984	$500,000	$53,550	$577,798	$57,066	$635,039	$40,534	$845,945	$30,251
1985	$500,000	$41,200	$711,770	$46,142	$790,856	$50,480	$1,089,597	$31,159
1986	$500,000	$32,500	$727,151	$115,247	$885,448	$56,517	$1,265,693	$32,093
1987	$500,000	$35,050	$684,797	$97,413	$896,372	$57,215	$1,330,039	$33,056
1988	$500,000	$39,550	$715,337	$47,703	$940,054	$60,003	$1,449,839	$34,048
1989	$500,000	$45,400	$821,444	$55,060	$1,086,286	$69,337	$1,747,239	$35,069
1990	$500,000	$40,850	$780,874	$47,703	$1,031,015	$65,809	$1,728,068	$36,121
1991	$500,000	$29,550	$893,669	$45,697	$1,168,703	$74,598	$2,046,671	$37,205
1992	$500,000	$18,800	$946,054	$40,124	$1,214,656	$77,531	$2,224,598	$38,321
1993	$500,000	$16,400	$1,034,329	$60,856	$1,323,438	$84,474	$2,539,068	$39,471
1994	$500,000	$24,800	$1,007,802	$47,258	$1,269,822	$81,052	$2,551,052	$40,655
1995	$500,000	$29,900	$1,217,120	$68,880	$1,527,419	$97,494	$3,222,549	$41,875
1996	$500,000	$27,350	$1,333,482	$59,741	$1,647,231	$105,142	$3,654,026	$43,131
1997	$500,000	$28,650	$1,488,631	$122,380	$1,875,498	$119,712	$4,381,518	$44,425
1998	$500,000	$27,200	$1,453,856	$133,080	$1,880,673	$120,043	$4,628,294	$45,758
1999	$500,000	$27,300	$1,464,779	$160,499	$1,979,876	$126,375	$5,136,303	$47,130
2000	$500,000	$32,950	$1,413,732	$260,588	$2,142,186	$136,735	$5,863,559	$48,544
2001	$500,000	$18,300	$1,458,315	$93,401	$2,214,940	$141,379	$6,399,678	$50,000
2002	$500,000	$9,050	$1,354,213	$61,524	$2,020,712	$128,981	$6,159,658	$51,500
2003	$500,000	$5,850	$1,628,177	$51,939	$2,363,781	$150,879	$7,612,298	$53,045

FIVE

Tapping Your IRA Early

✓ RETIREMENT DECISION #5: *If I retire early how can I get the money out of my IRA without penalty?*

Michael Henderson's company is experiencing some corporate downsizing. At age 54, he is offered an early retirement package. The offer includes a one-time, $500,000 lump-sum distribution from the company's pension plan. With that money and the $500,000 balance he has accumulated in his 401(k) plan, he decides to retire and live off his $1 million portfolio.

It's easy street for Michael now, right? Well, hold on. Because he is not yet age 59 ½, distributions from his retirement plans will be subject to a 10 percent early withdrawal penalty. Right out of the gate, Michael's retirement savings, which needs to support him for 30 years, will take a big hit.

All is not lost, I'm happy to report. If Michael follows the formula allowed by the IRS, he *can* avoid the penalty and begin enjoying his riches far into retirement.

If, like Michael, you're fortunate enough to be able to retire before age 59 ½, a hearty congratulations to you! Early retirement, however, can throw some challenges your way for which you need to be prepared. This chapter will address those challenges and how to effectively deal with them without penalty.

 One out of three people continue to work during retirement (30%).[1]

The Road to Penalty-Free Withdrawals: Section 72T

Gaining access to the investment assets you have locked up in qualified retirement accounts, such as IRAs, 401(k)s, and profit-sharing plans, is usually the biggest issue to consider if you're planning to retire early. Each of these retirement plans carries a 10 percent penalty on withdrawals made before age 59 ½. This puts you, the early retiree, in a predicament: You've accumulated enough money to retire comfortably, but all, or at least a large part, of that money is invested in retirement plans that limit access to your money.

Don't worry. There's a way out of this problem. If you retire before age 59 ½, here's how to avoid early withdrawal penalties.

There's a section in the Internal Revenue Code (IRC) called 72T. Follow it to a T, and your early withdrawals will be exempt from penalties. Anyone who has not yet reached age 59 ½ and who has an IRA is eligible for penalty-free distributions. Distributions can begin at any age and for any reason. The 72T distributions can even begin while you are still employed. In fact, many people trim their work hours back to part time as they approach retirement. They then begin using 72T distributions to supplement their part-time income.

FACT *You can withdraw IRA money before reaching age 59½ without inccuring penalties.*

To qualify for 72T, roll your money to an IRA and then strictly adhere to the following rules:

1. The distributions must be a part of a "series of substantially equal payments" made regularly, at least annually.[2]

2. The amount withdrawn each year must be calculated using one of three IRS-approved distribution formulas: amortization, annuitization, or life expectancy.

3. Distributions must continue for five years or until the recipient is 59 ½, whichever is longer.[3]

This penalty-free withdrawal strategy also works with deferred annuities (non-qualified variable or fixed) as outlined in the IRC section 72Q.

Taking the Distributions

The annual distribution amount you're allowed to withdraw is based largely on the size of your retirement account and your life expectancy (or if married, your joint life expectancy, if you choose). Consequently, 72T distributions are typically better suited for those nearing retirement (between ages 50 and 59 ½) with large retirement balances. If you're younger than 50 or have a small account balance, your annual distribution amounts will be low.

To determine how much you can withdraw annually from your IRA without penalty, you must choose one of three approved formulas: life expectancy, amortization, or annuitization. Each calculation will produce a different result.

The best way to determine which formula to use is to plug several combinations of variables into a 72T distribution calculator and compare the results side by side. One of the most user-friendly 72T calculators on the Web is offered by KJE Computer Solutions at http://www.javacalc.com. (Go to the Retirement Savings and Planning section on the home page and click More. Scroll down to find the 72T calculator.) Your tax or financial advisor also can perform these calculations for you.

Method One: Life Expectancy

This formula will produce the lowest annual payment. To calculate the life expectancy distribution amount, simply take your previous year-end retirement account balance and divide it by your life expectancy or joint life expectancy. Life expectancy tables can be found on the IRS Web site http://www.irs.gov. (Search for Publication 590.) A 72T calculator will do this number crunching for you automatically. If you use this method, you must recalculate your distribution annually; thus, your yearly distributions will vary somewhat from year to year.

As you get older and your life expectancy decreases, your annual distribution will typically increase. This occurs, however, only if your IRA grows faster than the rate at which you are taking money out of your account.

Method Two: Amortization

This formula provides a substantially higher distribution amount than the life expectancy method. This method amortizes your IRA balance over your life expectancy and assumes your account will grow at a reasonable interest rate. In addition, the annual withdrawal amount is determined in the first year before the first payment is made and remains fixed for the remaining distribution years. You cannot increase the amount to combat inflation or reduce it to offset the negative impact of a down year in the stock or bond market; doing either will trigger penalties.

Method Three: Annuitization

This method typically provides the highest annual payout. The formula computes payments using a different life expectancy table, the Annuity 2003 Mortality Table, and a reasonable assumed interest rate. With this method, the retirement account balance is divided by an annuity factor to determine the penalty-free distribution amount. As in the amortization method, the withdrawal amount is fixed in year one and does not change from year to year.

Reasonable Interest Rate

What is a reasonable interest rate assumption? The IRS allows some flexibility in determining this. It approves using any rate under 120 percent of the federal midterm rate. For example, as of December 2003 the federal midterm rate was 4.26 percent; any interest rate under 5.1 percent, which is 120% of the midterm rate, would be acceptable. The midterm rate can be found at http://www.irs.gov. (Search for federal midterm rate.) This is usually built-in to most 72T calculators.

If you use an interest-rate assumption that is too high and deplete your IRA before completing your required withdrawals, there are severe penalties. These include both an interest penalty and the 10 percent early withdrawal penalty you had tried to avoid. These penalties are retroactive on *all* previous 72T distributions.

An Example of a 72T Distribution

Let's return to Michael Henderson. Remember, he's 54 and received an early retirement package that included $500,000 from the company's pension plan. He also has $500,000 in his 401(k) plan for a total of $1 million.

Because he is not yet age 59 ½, distributions from his retirement plans would normally be subject to a 10 percent early withdrawal penalty. However, if Michael follows the formula outlined in Section 72T, he can avoid the penalty and begin taking withdrawals now.

Michael decides to use a 5 percent interest-rate assumption. After running the numbers using a 72T calculator, he discovers he could withdraw between $16,393 and $64,583 annually from his million-dollar portfolio without incurring penalties. Figure 1 outlines how much he could take out annually under each IRS-approved distribution formula.

Figure 1

72T

Age at Year End	Life Expectancy Payout	Amortization Payout	Annuitization Payout
54	$16,393	$64,583	$63,896
55	$17,240	$64,583	$63,896
56	$18,133	$64,583	$63,896
57	$19,072	$64,583	$63,896
58	$20,062	$64,583	$63,896
59	$21,104	$64,583	$63,896

IRA balance $1 million, Single Life Expectancy, 5% Interest Rate Assumption

As you manipulate the interest-rate assumptions, you can vary the annual distribution amounts. This flexibility is available only when you initially perform the calculations. Remember, when using the amortization and annuitization methods, you cannot change the amount once you begin receiving distributions.

Stick to Your Schedule

The method you choose to calculate your distributions isn't as important as adhering to your set schedule. To satisfy the "substantially equal payment" rule, you must choose one of the three methods discussed above and withdraw the calculated amount at least annually.

Failure to withdraw the calculated amount will result in a 10 percent early withdrawal penalty tax, plus an interest penalty. The tax and penalty are imposed, retroactively, on all withdrawals received. Additionally, if you have been receiving payments and suddenly take a distribution amount that either exceeds or is below your annual distribution requirement, you will be penalized on every distribution you have received to date.

There is one-time exception to this rule. In 2002, the IRS ruled that early retirees can change their distribution payout calculation one time from the annuitization or amortization methods to the life expectancy method. For example, if due to market losses, your IRA is being depleted too quickly, this exception will allow you to change to an option that will reduce the amount you must withdraw each year.

Although the IRS' distribution structure is very rigid, it is very easy to automate your withdrawals by setting up a systematic withdrawal program from your IRA. Most financial institutions will allow you to establish automatic monthly, quarterly, or annual distributions from your IRA for a set number of years. By setting up a systematic withdrawal plan, you will not need to worry about breaking IRS rules by deviating from the required distribution amounts or how frequently you receive them.

Again, once you begin taking distributions, you must continue to do so for the next five years, or until you are 59 ½, whichever is longer. For example, if you begin taking distributions at age 52, you must continue for seven and a half years. If you begin taking distributions at age 57, you must continue for five years until you are 62. With this in mind, if you're 40, you would not be wise to begin taking distributions. Many changes could occur in your financial life in the years before reaching age 59 ½. For example, if you decide to go back to work and you no longer need the income generated from distributions, you cannot stop them without incurring the 10 percent early withdrawal penalty. Of course, you could redirect your 72T distributions into a non-retirement investment account and simply earmark the funds for retirement.

Once you fulfill the five-year or age 59 ½ requirement (which ever is applicable to you), you can withdraw any amount without incurring penalties.

Tax Considerations

The distributions from your IRA are penalty-free if you follow the guidelines outlined above. They are not, however, free from income tax. IRA distributions regardless of when they are taken are subject to income tax and will be taxed as ordinary income.

Each year after receiving distributions, you will receive a Form 1099R from your IRA provider indicating the amount of taxable withdrawals taken during the previous year. A distribution code 2 will be placed on the Form 1099R. This indicates that the distributions are part of early withdrawals with a known exception — "substantially equal payments." If the code 2 does not appear on your 1099R form, the IRS will view your distributions as premature and apply penalties. In situations where this occurs, don't be alarmed. Simply file a Form 5329 along with your 1040, indicating that you are taking a series of substantially equal payments according to the rules set forth in Section 72T of the IRS code. These forms and the instructions for completing them can be found at http://www.irs.gov.

Additionally, when you begin taking distributions from your IRA, you should, in most cases, request that taxes be withheld. Otherwise, you'll be facing a large tax bill when you file your taxes at year-end. Withholding taxes from your distribution is similar to the taxes withheld from your payroll check while working. Your IRA provider has a tax withholding form that allows you to specify the percentage of your distributions you want to withhold to pay federal and state income taxes. When determining your distribution amount, consider up front how much money you will need for taxes and living expenses.

Future Flexibility: Splitting Your IRA

Before you begin taking distributions, consider the following important questions. First, do you anticipate needing to take withdrawals from your IRA in future years larger than your calculated 72T payments? And second, will your scheduled 72T distributions require you to continue taking withdrawals past age 59 ½ to satisfy the mandatory five-year withdrawal period? If the answer is "yes" to either of these questions, you may want to consider the following strategy.

If you have a large enough portfolio balance, split your IRA into two separate IRA accounts before starting 72T distributions. Both accounts will be in your name but will have different account numbers. There are no limits to the number of IRA accounts you can open. In fact, you can have multiple IRA accounts at the same financial institution.

In the first IRA account, deposit only the amount necessary to provide you with the income you will need during the time you take 72T distributions. Using a 72T calculator, manipulate the account balance and the interest-rate assumption in the distribution formulas discussed above to determine the minimum amount to deposit into this IRA account. Be conservative; deposit a little more than is needed to lessen the risk of depleting your IRA before completing your scheduled distributions.

Let's return to Michael Henderson again to see how this strategy works. Michael, who's retiring at age 54, figures he needs only $40,000 before taxes each year to maintain his lifestyle until age 59 1/2. If he deposits $625,000 of his $1 million portfolio into one IRA and uses a 5 percent interest rate assumption and the amortization method, he could receive distributions of up to $40,364 per year penalty free. He could then deposit his remaining $375,000 into a second IRA and not take any withdrawals from this account until he's 59 ½ (see Figure 2).

However, in the second year of his retirement (age 55), Michael decides he needs $12,000 more income annually. Because he set up a second IRA account, he can simply follow the same process above to tap

Figure 2

Splitting Your IRA

	Year 1	Year 2
IRA #1:	Deposit $625,000. Begin taking 72T distributions of $40,364 per year. This could be accomplished using the amortization method and an 5% interest rate assumption.	Continue taking $40,364 annual 72T distributions
IRA #2:	Deposit $375,000. No distributions will be taken in the first year.	Transfer $190,000 from IRA #2 to IRA #3. With remaining $185,000 in IRA #2 begin 72T distributions of $12,000 per year. This could be accomplished using the amortization method and an 5% interest rate assumption.
IRA #3:		IRA #3 Now has a $190,000 balance. No distributions are being taken from this account.

into his second account penalty free. He has $375,000 in his second IRA but calculates he only needs $190,000 to generate the extra income he desires. He then directs the remaining $185,000 into a third IRA account, which is available for future needs.

Splitting his IRA before taking 72T deductions gave Michael income flexibility in the future. If Michael had kept all his money in one IRA account and had begun taking 72T distributions, he would not be able to make any changes until he turned 59 ½.

Splitting an IRA into two or more accounts also makes sense if you will turn 59 ½ during the mandatory five-year distribution period. Remember, normal IRA distributions can begin at age 59 ½ without penalty. Let's say you begin taking distributions at age 57; you must continue doing so until you reach age 62 — the mandatory five-year period — to avoid the penalty. Three years after you start taking your 72T distribution, you decide to purchase a condo and need a lump sum of money. What can you do? With only one IRA, your options are limited because of the 72T rules. You can't take any additional withdrawals beyond the 72T distributions for two more years. Had you split your retirement money into two IRAs, the first account would have provided your 72T distributions and the second would be available after age 59 ½ for your condo, without penalty. Remember, you must split the IRA before beginning any 72T distributions.

If you die during the distribution period, your beneficiary is not required to continue receiving distributions. If the IRA beneficiary is your spouse, he or she has the option to roll the money into his/her own IRA account.[4]

 • 72T Calculator: KJE Computer Solutions, www.javacalc.com.
• 72T Information: 72T on the Net, www.72t.net.

More Penalty-Free Distribution Strategies...

Lump-Sum Distributions for Those Over Age 55

If you are 55 or older and leave your company, you are eligible for a one-time, lump-sum cash distribution (entire balance) from your employer-sponsored retirement plan without incurring the 10 percent early withdrawal penalty.

This exception to the early withdrawal penalty only applies to distributions taken directly from an employer-sponsored plan, not from an IRA. The employer must, however, withhold 20 percent of the distribution amount for taxes.

This distribution strategy works particularly well if you know you're going to need a large sum of money immediately upon leaving your company to do things such as launch your own business or buy resort property. In these cases, a penalty-free, lump-sum payment can be especially useful.

Upon leaving your company, you can request to have all or part of the lump-sum distribution sent directly to you free from penalty. Any portion not distributed directly to you can be rolled over into an IRA to avoid taxes and penalties on money you don't need immediately.

Be aware, however, that even though the early withdrawal penalty is avoided, there are disadvantages to this distribution method. First, the amount you withdraw will be taxed as ordinary income, and a large distribution may launch you into a higher tax bracket. Second, your employer is required to withhold 20 percent of your distribution amount to pay taxes. If you owe more, you will be required to pay additional taxes when you file.

The biggest disadvantage, though, is the loss of tax deferral and future compounded interest on both the amount you withdraw and spend, as well as the portion of the distribution that goes to pay taxes. The severe impact of this approach is discussed in the Cash Distribution section of Chapter 24. A cash distribution early in retirement that greatly reduces the size of your retirement nest egg may hamper your ability to reach your long-term retirement goals. It is highly recommended you seek professional advice before taking a cash distribution to make sure you have enough money to fund your retirement goals. Most investment advisors will recommend you take out as little as possible in the form of a lump sum, so you don't undermine your ability to enjoy your golden years.

In-Service Withdrawals

To maintain company benefits, especially health insurance, many people work part-time as they ease their way into retirement. This move from full- to part-time employment usually means a significant drop in income. To compensate, many employees take "in-service withdrawals" from their company-sponsored retirement plans to supplement their income and maintain an acceptable standard of living.

As the name suggests, this distribution method allows an employee to take a withdrawal from the company's retirement plan while still an active plan participant. This distribution can initially be rolled over into an IRA to avoid taxes and penalties. Once in the IRA account, distributions can provide additional income. Remember, the usual taxes and penalties will apply to your IRA distributions. Consequently, if you are not yet age 59 ½, you should consider implementing a 72T distribution plan to avoid the 10 percent early withdrawal penalty.[5]

This is a sound strategy if a substantial portion of your retirement savings is invested in your company-sponsored retirement plan and you need additional income. In-service withdrawals are not permitted by all company-sponsored retirement plans. If, however, the plan allows in-service withdrawals, plan provisions will specify the portions of the plan available for distribution. Contact your retirement benefits administrator to determine if this withdrawal method is available and to determine the portion of your plan balance that can be withdrawn.

Conclusion

If you're thinking of retiring early, don't be intimidated by the penalties associated with withdrawals from retirement plans. By applying the strategies and tactics discussed in this chapter, you can avoid pitfalls that often harm early retirees. With foresight and savvy financial planning, you can develop a strategy to minimize the impact of penalties on your hard-earned nest egg.

SOURCES OF
RETIREMENT INCOME

—Social Security
—Company Pensions
—Personal Savings

SIX

Tax Refunds Every Year for Life

✓ RETIREMENT DECISION #6: *When should I begin taking Social Security?*

You've been paying Social Security taxes all of your working life. Now it's time for a tax refund. Those retiring want to know two things about their Social Security benefit: how much will their benefit be and when should they begin taking it. You'll know the answer to these questions by the end of the chapter.

Figure 1

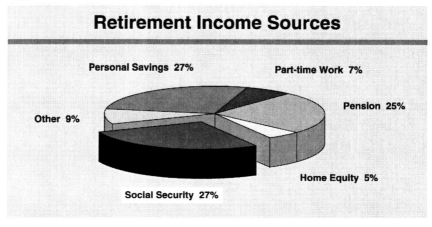

How much will Social Security really contribute to your income when it comes time to retire? Some people assume that because FICA taxes seem to take such a notable chunk out of their paychecks that they will be able to count on Social Security as their sole source of retirement income. Others mistakenly suppose that Social Security benefits will be so insignificant that they will have almost no affect on their long-term retirement income. In truth, neither assumption is accurate.

Statistics show that 27 percent of the average retired American's income is derived from Social Security; another 27 percent comes from investments (personal savings, IRAs, 401(k)s, etc.); and 25 percent from pensions. The other 21 percent is obtained through part-time work, home equity, and other sources, as illustrated in Figure 1.

Social Security was never intended to be a reliable single source of retirement income. Still, it will likely make up more than one-fourth of your retirement income pie and is, therefore, worth taking the time to understand.[1]

Who Qualifies For Social Security?

If you think that simply being a U.S. citizen qualifies you for Social Security benefits, think again. As you work and pay FICA taxes, you earn Social Security credits. You must earn 40 credits to be eligible for benefits. In 2005, you have to earn $920 in income during the year to obtain one credit. You can earn a maximum of four credits per year, earning them all in the first month or over 12 months. You must work at least 10 years to be eligible for retirement benefits.

These credits simply qualify you to receive benefits. Most people will earn more credits than the minimum 40 they need to be eligible for benefits. Extra credits will not increase the amount of benefits you receive; however, you won't receive any benefits if you don't have the minimum 40 credits.

How Much Have You Paid In?

If you earn $90,000 or less annually in 2005, you contribute 6.2 percent of your income into the Social Security trust fund; your employer pays an additional 6.2 percent of your salary into the fund. Any income over $90,000, however, is not taxed for Social Security. Thus, the more you make above this level, the smaller the percentage of your annual income goes into the fund.

How Social Security Determines Your Benefit Amount

The average earnings over your working life determine how much your monthly Social Security benefits will be in retirement. The government uses the following elements to determine your benefit:

- Your earnings are adjusted to account for inflation. For example, if a 3 percent inflation rate is used, the $10,000 you earned in 1985 would be equivalent to a little more than $18,000 in 2005.

- Your total earnings during the 35 years in which you earned the most income are averaged to determine your average monthly "indexed" earnings. The maximum earnings used per year is $90,000 in 2005.

- A formula is applied to these earnings to arrive at your basic benefit or primary insurance amount. This is the amount you receive at your full retirement age. For most people preparing to retire in the near future, full retirement age is 66. (See upcoming section on age requirements for more details.)

The benefit computation is complex, and there are no simple tables published by the Social Security Administration (SSA) to show exactly how much you will receive. However, the SSA sends a Social Security estimate statement to all participants older than age 25. You should receive this statement each year about three months before your birthday.

Participants can request a Social Security estimate via the Web by logging-on to www.ssa.gov and clicking *Calculate your benefits.*

Figure 2

Maximum Social Security Benefit

	2004
Retirement at age 62:	**$1,422/month**
Retirement at age 65:	**$1,784/month**
Retirement at age 70:	**$2,111/month**

Source: Social Security Administration, 2004

Figure 3

Average Social Security Benefit

Type of Benefit	Average Monthly Benefit
All retired workers	$922
Aged couple	$1,523
Widowed mother & 2 children	$1,904
Aged widow(er) alone	$888
Disabled worker, spouse, & one or more children	$1,441
All disabled workers	$862

Source: Social Security Administration, 2004

Full Retirement Age

Full retirement benefits are available when you reach full retirement age, which for many years was age 65. In the past few decades, however, that age has been gradually raised to reduce the strain on the Social Security system caused by increased life expectancy in the United States. As Americans continue living longer, it's reasonable to expect that the retirement age will continue to increase. The table in Figure 4 displays the Social Security Administration's definition of full retirement.

Figure 4

Full Retirement Age

Year of Birth	Full Retirement Age
1937 or earlier	65
1938	65 and 2 months
1939	65 and 4 months
1940	65 and 6 months
1941	65 and 8 months
1942	65 and 10 months
1943-1954	66
1955	66 and 2 months
1956	66 and 4 months
1957	66 and 6 months
1958	66 and 8 months
1959	66 and 10 months
1960 and later	67

Source: Social Security Administration

When to Start Taking Social Security

Not everyone chooses to start receiving benefits at his or her full retirement age. Some people begin as early as age 62, while others postpone receiving benefits until reaching age 70. When should you begin taking your benefit? The answer depends primarily on two factors: how long you live and whether or not you are going to continue to work.

If you continue working after you begin receiving Social Security, your benefit may be reduced. If it is reduced, you likely should not take retirement early.

Let's look closer at each of these determining factors of when you should start taking Social Security.

Life Expectancy

If you knew exactly how long you are going to live, deciding when to begin taking Social Security would be an easy question to answer. You can begin receiving benefits as early as age 62, but your benefit will be less than what it would be if you waited until your full retirement age. Or you can delay receiving benefits until age 70 and receive a benefit greater than your full retirement age amount. The catch is that once you start receiving benefits at a certain rate, that

Figure 5

Social Security Calculator

Life Expectancy Age 70

Age to Start SS	62	66	70
Annual SS Benefit	$7,500	$10,000	$13,200
Years Benefit Paid	8	4	0
Total Benefit (Not Inflated)	$60,000	$40,000	$0

Life Expectancy Age 75

Age to Start SS	62	66	70
Annual SS Benefit	$7,500	$10,000	$13,200
Years Benefit Paid	13	9	5
Total Benefit (Not Inflated)	$97,500	$90,000	$66,000

Life Expectancy Age 80

Age to Start SS	62	66	70
Annual SS Benefit	$7,500	$10,000	$13,200
Years Benefit Paid	18	14	10
Total Benefit (Not Inflated)	$135,000	$140,000	$132,000

Life Expectancy Age 85

Age to Start SS	62	66	70
Annual SS Benefit	$7,500	$10,000	$13,200
Years Benefit Paid	23	19	15
Total Benefit (Not Inflated)	$172,500	$190,000	$198,000

rate is locked for as long as you receive Social Security benefits (adjusted for inflation).

Let's assume you were born in 1943 and are trying to decide whether you should take your benefit at 62 or wait until your full retirement age of 66 or beyond. If your benefit is $10,000 per year at full retirement, it would be reduced to $7,500 if you begin at 62 (a 25% reduction). If you begin taking it at 62, the amount will stay the same for life, it won't adjust back up to $10,000 when you hit 66. (It will, however, adjust annually for inflation.)

So which option will put the most money in your pocket? Well, again it depends on how long you will live. The break-even point when comparing the total benefits you'd receive at age 62 to those at beginning at age 66 is age 78. If you don't make it to age 78, you would receive more money by starting your benefit at age 62. If you live past age 78, you would receive more total benefits if you wait to start until age 66, your full retirement age, to begin receiving Social Security. If, however, you live past age 83, you would receive the most money by delaying the start of your benefit until age 70. Figure 5 outlines the total benefits paid at different ages assuming different life expectancies.

To make an educated guess at your life expectancy, review Figure 5 in Chapter One. Also, consider your current health and future health based on your family medical history.

Receiving Benefits Prior to Your Full Retirement Age

As we saw above, if you choose to receive benefits before reaching your full retirement age, your benefits will be reduced (Figure 6); waiting beyond your full retirement age will increase benefits (Figure 7).

Let's consider the choices facing Edwin, age 62, who would like to retire now before he is eligible for full retirement benefits. Edwin has determined that he will need at least $700 monthly in Social Security benefits to supplement his other retirement income to maintain his desired standard of living. At his full retirement age, 66, his Social Security monthly benefit would be $1,000. Will Edwin's Social Security benefits amount to $700 if he retires at age 62, 48 months before full retirement?

Using the information in Figure 6, we can determine that Edwin will meet his goal: His full retirement benefit would be reduced by

25 percent if he were to retire now (0.52 multiplied by 48 months equals 25 percent). Consequently, his benefit would drop from $1,000 to $750 per month. If he decided to wait to receive benefits until age 65, his benefits would be reduced by only 6 percent (0.52 multiplied by 12 months equals 6 percent). In this case, his monthly benefit would be reduced by only $60 to equal $940 per month.

The Social Security Administration's Web site, www.ssa.gov, offers the following guideline:

"If your full retirement age is 67, the reduction for starting your benefits at 62 is about 30 percent; at age 63, it's about 25 percent; at age 64, about 20 percent; at age 65, about 13 1/3 percent; and at age 66, about 6 2/3 percent."

Every person approaching retirement age should keep in mind one very important point: If you choose to receive Social Security before your full retirement age, your benefit is *permanently* reduced. So do the math before making your final decision.

Figure 6

Social Security Reduction for Early Retirement

Year of Birth	Full Retirement Age	Age 62 Reduction Months	Monthly % Reduction	Total % Reduction
1937 or earlier	65	36	.555	20.00
1938	65 and 2 months	38	.548	20.83
1939	65 and 4 months	40	.541	21.67
1940	65 and 6 months	42	.535	22.50
1941	65 and 8 months	44	.530	23.33
1942	65 and 10 months	46	.525	24.17
1943-1954	66	48	.520	25.00
1955	66 and 2 months	50	.516	25.84
1956	66 and 4 months	52	.512	26.66
1957	66 and 6 months	54	.509	27.50
1958	66 and 8 months	56	.505	28.33
1959	66 and 10 months	58	.502	29.17
1960 and later	67	60	.500	30.00

Note: Persons born on January 1 of any year should refer to the previous year

Source: Social Security Administration

Delaying Social Security Benefits

Depending on your circumstances, it may be beneficial to delay receiving Social Security until after your full retirement age. The longer you wait to begin receiving benefits, up to age 70, the larger your benefit will be. Figure 7 outlines the rate of increase for delaying your retirement benefits.

Let's take the example of Alice Treynor, a 66-year-old who enjoys her job as a sales manager for a pharmaceutical company. Because she likes working and has a comfortable income from her employer, she has decided to delay Social Security benefits until age 68. What will her benefit amount be at 68 if her full retirement age is 66 and her benefit is $1,000 per month (Figure 7)?

In Alice's case, the benefit increase is 8 percent per year. Delaying benefits two years will increase the amount Alice receives by a total of 16 percent. As a result, her benefit at age 68 will be permanently increased by $160, to $1,160 per month.

The Social Security Administration issues the following advice to those who delay retirement. "If you decide to delay your retirement, be sure to sign up for Medicare at age 65. In some circumstances, medical insurance costs more if you delay applying for it."

Figure 7

Social Security Increase for Delayed Retirement

Year of Birth	Yearly rate of increase for each year you delay benefits	Monthly rate of increase for each month you delay receiving benefits
1930	4.5%	3/8 of 1%
1931-1932	5.0%	5/12 of 1%
1933-1934	5.5%	11/24 of 1%
1935-1936	6.0%	1/2 of 1%
1937-1938	6.5%	13/24 of 1%
1939-1940	7.0%	7/12 of 1%
1941-1942	7.5%	5/8 of 1%
1943 or later	8.0%	2/3 of 1%

Source: Social Security Administration

Working and Receiving Benefits

Like Alice, many people simply enjoy working and choose to continue doing so well past their Social Security retirement age. Others continue to work because they need or want extra income. In either case, the good news is that if you work and are at full retirement age you can keep all your Social Security benefits no matter how much you earn. However, if you retire early and continue working, there are limits on the amount you can earn. Exceeding those limits will reduce your benefit. The annual earning limitations are posted at http://www.ssa.gov/pubs/10069.html.

Using 2004 limits, if you are working and collecting benefits between ages 62 and your full retirement age, your benefit will be reduced $1 for every $2 you earn over $11,640. In the year you reach your full retirement age, you will lose $1 for every $3 you earn over $31,080 until the month you reach full retirement age. If you plan to continue working after age 62, these reductions will dictate whether you should begin taking your benefits.

For example, in 2004, Ken Ashton, at age 62, qualified to receive the maximum $17,064 per year Social Security benefit available to those age 62. He earned $45,750 in salary in 2003. He wants to know how much his benefit will be reduced if he continues to work and earn the same amount in 2004. His $45,750 income is $34,110 over the $11,640 earnings limit. His benefit will be reduced by $1 for every $2 he earns over $11,640 (divide $34,110 by 2). Consequently, in 2004 Ken's benefit will be reduced by $17,055, wiping out his entire benefit. Obviously, Ken should not begin taking his benefit at age 62. It should be noted that if you retire and begin receiving benefits early the income your spouse earns will not adversely affect your benefit.

Nearly one out of three people continue to work during retirement (30%).[2]

Diane Jamison, 62, also qualifies for the $17,064 per year maximum benefit. She earns $30,000 per year but decides she needs a little extra money. Her $30,000 salary is $18,360 over the $11,640 earnings limit. Her benefit will be reduced by $9,180 to equal $7,884 per year. By earning

$30,000, her $17,064 benefit will be cut by more than half. Even though adding her income ($30,000) and the reduced Social Security benefit ($7,884) would provide 26% more money each year, Diane should wait to start receiving her benefits.

Don't forget, beginning in the month you reach full retirement age your earnings will not affect your Social Security benefit. You can earn as much as you want.

Applying for Benefits

Deciding when to start taking Social Security benefits can be a difficult decision to make. By now, however, armed with the information in these pages, you are far more knowledgeable on Social Security than the average person. Still, even if you've decided when to start taking benefits, meet with a Social Security representative or professional financial advisor one year before you plan to retire. The rules governing Social Security are complicated, and according to the SSA, "It may be to your advantage to start your retirement benefits before you actually stop working."

When you're ready, you can apply for your benefits in one of three ways:

- Apply online at http://www.ssa.gov/applytoretire/
- Call toll-free: 1-800-772-1213. Hearing impaired:TTY at 1-800-325-0778.
- Apply in person or by phone at your local Social Security office.

Spousal Benefits

Your spouse's Social Security benefits will be calculated in the same manner as your own — by using the number of years he or she has worked and the amount he or she has earned. Your spouse will receive his or her earned benefit or one-half the amount of your benefit, whichever is greater. (This rule also applies to non-working spouses who haven't qualified for their own benefit.) The same rules apply for early or delayed retirement. Additionally, your spouse can qualify for Medicare on your record at age 65, if he or she has not already qualified.

Divorced Spouse

Your divorced spouse (even if you have remarried) may qualify for benefits based on your record, if you are 62 or older, even if you are not receiving benefits yet. There are three main requirements for your ex-spouse to qualify for benefits based on your record:

- The marriage must have lasted at least 10 years
- Your ex-spouse must be at least 62 years old
- Your ex-spouse must currently be unmarried

The amount of benefits your divorced spouse will receive does not affect your benefits nor those of your current spouse.

Taxation of Your Social Security

Whether your Social Security benefits are taxed depends on the level of your income during retirement. If your income is between $25,000 and $34,000 for individual filers, or between $32,000 and $44,000 for joint filers, 50 percent of your Social Security benefit is subject to income tax. If your income is greater than $34,000 for a single filer and $44,000 for joint filers, up to 85 percent of your Social Security benefits are subject to income tax.

Income is calculated by combining all of your wages, earned interest, taxable dividends, tax-free interest, and retirement plan distributions, and then adding half of your Social Security benefit.

At the beginning of each year, the SSA issues a Social Security

Figure 8

Taxation of Social Security Benefits

Filing Status	50% of Benefit is Taxable	85% of Benefit is Taxable
If you file a federal tax return as an "individual"	Income between $25,000 and $34,000	Income above $34,000
If you file a joint return	Income between $32,000 and $44,000	Income above $44,000

Source: Social Security Administration, www.ssa.gov

Benefit Statement (Form SSA-1099), which shows the total amount of benefits you received during the previous year. Use this statement when you complete your federal income tax return.

Strategies for Reducing Taxes on Social Security Benefits

One item that may be pushing your income above the threshold listed in Figure 8 is interest and dividends derived from stocks, bonds, mutual funds, bank accounts, money market accounts, municipal bonds, and other interest-bearing investments. If you are not spending the interest or principal from these investment vehicles and are just reinvesting all of your earnings, you may want to consider repositioning the money into a fixed or variable annuity.

Annuities provide tax-deferred growth. Therefore, your investment earnings are not reported each year for tax purposes and aren't added to your income. If you are not using the money right now, it does not make sense to have the investment earnings increase your income and, thus, the amount of tax you pay on your Social Security benefits.

The Status of the Social Security Trust Fund

Many people are wondering these days, and understandably so, whether Social Security benefits will be available when they are eligible to receive them. Even the Social Security Administration acknowledges that the program is on dangerous ground. The SSA has made the following statement on its Web site:

"Social Security now takes in more in taxes than it pays out in benefits. The excess funds are credited to Social Security's trust funds, which are expected to grow to over $4 trillion before we need to use them to pay benefits. In 2015, we will begin to pay out more in benefits than we collect in taxes. By 2037, the trust funds will be exhausted and the payroll taxes collected will be enough to pay only 72 percent of benefits owed. We're working to resolve these issues."

The main thing that contributes to the depletion of Social Security is Americans' increased life expectancy. We're healthier today than ever before, and life expectancies continue climbing. When the Social Security program first began paying benefits in 1940, the average life expectancy for men and women reaching age 65 was 77 and 78, respectively. Today, life expectancy has increased four years for men, to age 81, and six years for women, to age 84.

In addition, we face a shift in demographics as the baby-boomer generation moves toward retirement. In the future, there will be fewer workers to support each retiree. The ratio of workers-to-retirees has plummeted and will continue to fall (Figure 9).

There is considerable debate today over what the government should do to ensure that Social Security is around for future generations. Several options are currently being discussed. Now more than ever, with the program's future less certain, you should devote significant attention to other sources of retirement income, such as pensions and personal savings.

Despite Social Security's uncertainty, it currently composes more than one-fourth of most retirees' income. Therefore, it requires that you understand how the program works and how to incorporate Social Security into your retirement plan. Using the information presented in this chapter, you should now be better informed about the issues surrounding Social Security and how you can best take advantage of it.

Figure 9

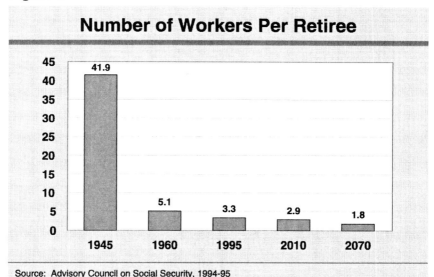

Source: Advisory Council on Social Security, 1994-95

SEVEN

Maxing Your Pension

✓ RETIREMENT DECISION #7: *Which pension payout option should I choose?*

There was a time, not long ago, when most full-time employees could count on their companies to provide a generous pension plan at retirement. But today, the traditional company pension plan is fast becoming an endangered species. More and more U.S. corporations are discontinuing their pension plans to cut costs and are shifting the responsibility of retirement saving to their employees through employee savings programs such as 401(k)s and other types of qualified plans.

Figure 1

Retirement Income Sources

Personal Savings 27%   Part-time Work 7%

Other 9%   Pension 25%

Social Security 27%   Home Equity 5%

Despite this move away from traditional pension plans, 44 million Americans are still covered by these plans.[1] If you are fortunate enough to work for a company that can still afford to offer one and you qualify for benefits at retirement, you will receive a monthly pension check for the rest of your life. This benefit can be an important piece of your retirement income, because statistics show that company pensions currently account for 25 percent of the average retiree's income (Figure 1).

Understanding pensions and their payment options will be important to the overall success of your retirement planning. This chapter is intended to help you better understand these options and to help you learn simple, effective strategies to maximize your pension and ultimately put more money in your pocket during retirement.

How Big Will Your Pension Payment Be?

The formula that determines the size of your pension payments is usually based on your level of income and the length of service with your employer. When you retire, you will be given a statement outlining several pension payout options. Some employers will even provide you with the option of taking a one-time, lump-sum distribution rather than monthly payments. It's important to realize that the decision you make at this time is irrevocable. Thus, you should fully understand your options and make a choice that will help you accomplish your retirement goals.

In addition, make sure you don't retire just before your pension benefit is going to be bumped up. All it takes is a quick call to your human resources benefits coordinator to find out when your benefits are scheduled to increase and at what point your benefits level out. This will help you set your exact retirement date.

Common Pension Payment Options

Figure 2 outlines the most common pension payout options and an example of what each may pay in relation to the other options:

Definitions for each payout option are outlined below. Which should you choose? This is an important decision you will be required to make at retirement. Study your options carefully because once you make your choice, you can't change it.

Immediate Life Annuity: This annuity will pay a monthly lifetime benefit beginning immediately. Benefits cease at your death.

Figure 2

Pension Payout Options (Sample)

	Monthly Benefit During Your Life	Monthly Benefit To Your Spouse Upon Death
Immediate Life/Annuity	$500	$0
Single Life/Annuity	$1,000	$0
Joint and 100% Survivor/Annuity	$850	$850
Joint and 75% Survivor /Annuity	$880	$660
Joint and 50% Survivor/Annuity	$920	$460
Life and 10 Year Period Certain	$950	*$950

One Time Lump-Sum Distribution (not offered by all plans) $150,000.

*Note: This option provides a $950 monthly benefit for your lifetime. However, if you die within the period certain (10 years), payments will continue to your beneficiary for the remainder of the ten-year period.

Single Life Annuity: This option begins at retirement and will provide you with the most money each year. However, benefits cease upon your death, so your surviving spouse and heirs will not continue receiving any income. Thus, if you pass away only weeks after signing the final pension paperwork, all payments will immediately cease.

Joint & 100% Survivor Annuity: At retirement, this annuity pays a pension for your lifetime and continues to pay your surviving spouse the same amount after you die. Benefits will not be paid to your heirs upon your spouse's death. Defined benefit pension plans are required to provide this annuity as an option. If you decide to choose an option other than this one, you must obtain your spouse's consent.

Joint & 75% Survivor Annuity: This option allows you to receive a higher benefit than the Joint and 100% Survivor option. However, your surviving spouse receives only 75 percent of the benefit amount upon your death.

Joint & 50% Survivor Annuity: This option provides you with an even higher benefit than the Joint and 100% and 75% Survivor options. As the name suggests however, your surviving spouse receives only 50 percent of the monthly benefit amount upon your death.

Life Only with 10-Year Period Certain: This annuity provides benefits to you for your lifetime. However, if you die within the period certain (10 years from the time payments commence) payments will continue to your beneficiary (spouse or others) for the remainder of the 10-year period. (Some plans will provide 15- and 20-year period certain payment options, but the longer the period certain, the lower your annuity benefits will be.) If you die after the period certain time frame, benefits will be discontinued.

Lump-Sum Distribution (not offered by all plans): At retirement, the pension will make a one-time distribution. This money can be rolled into an IRA, avoiding taxes and penalties. If you choose this payout option, you must be ready to make your own investment decisions. These include where to invest the money and how much you can take out each year without completely depleting your assets during retirement.

Other Annuity Options: Although not as common, some plans offer additional options such as the Refund option and the Joint with Period Certain option.

Pension Plan Advantages

The biggest advantage of pension plans is the peace of mind that comes with receiving a consistent paycheck for the rest of your life, regardless of how the financial markets or economy perform. Your employer hires a team of professional money managers to handle the portfolio of investments in the pension plan for you, lifting the management burden from your shoulders.

In addition, the Pension Benefit Guaranty Corp. (PBGC) insures most defined benefit pension plans. If your plan does not have sufficient money to pay all of your promised benefits, the PBGC will step in and keep your benefits flowing. Your benefits could be reduced, however, if this occurs.

The maximum benefit paid by the PBGC to participants of defunct company pension plans is $45,614 per year (65 year old).
Source: PBGC 2004

Pension Plan Disadvantages

Even though pension plans have many perks, there are some disadvantages. First, many pensions do not have a cost-of-living adjustment. This means inflation will take its toll on your pension. You will receive the same amount of money every year, even though the prices of goods and services will increase dramatically during your retirement. Prices double every 20 to 22 years. For example, the $35,000 annual pension payment you receive today may be more than adequate to meet your current income needs. However, in 20 years you will likely need $70,000 to buy the same amount of goods and services you're purchasing today. You can overcome this disadvantage with additional income from other retirement investments.

Also, the fact that your choice of an annuity option is irrevocable can be problematic. Let's assume, for example, you choose the Joint and 100% Survivor Annuity option (see Figure 2) and you receive a $850 monthly pension. You would be choosing a lower monthly check than the $1,000 you could have received with the Single Life Annuity. But accepting the reduced amount, you are ensuring that upon your death, your spouse will continue to receive $850 per month during his or her lifetime. What if your spouse passes away first? You will continue to receive this reduced $850 amount for your lifetime and can't change it to reflect your new circumstances. Additionally, if you choose this option and both of you die during the first year, no further benefits will be paid to your heirs.

Pension Maximization Strategy

Selecting the best pension payout option can be difficult. Should you choose the option with the highest monthly payment that will provide a benefit for your lifetime only? Or do you select the option with the largest payout to your surviving spouse?

Believe it or not, there is a way to have your proverbial cake and eat it, too. You can obtain the highest annuity payment and still provide for your spouse upon your death by "maxing" your pension. Before pursuing this strategy, there are a couple of points you need to consider. The younger you are, the better this strategy will work. Most advisors will suggest you implement this strategy before retirement; although, if you're in good health, it may be worth considering even after you've retired.

Here's how it works: At age 60, Nate Strong is considering retiring and taking a Joint and 100% Survivor Annuity to ensure that his wife, Sheila, will be provided for upon his death. Instead of $45,000 a year he could earn with a Single Life Annuity, Nate will receive $35,000 per year, and, after his death, Sheila will continue to collect $35,000 annually. See Figure 3.

Figure 3

Pension Comparison

Payout Option	Income During Your Lifetime	Income to Your Survivor
Single Life Annuity	$45,000 year	$0
Joint and 100% Survivor Annuity	$35,000 year	$35,000

To make sure Sheila is financially protected, Nate is essentially forfeiting $10,000 per year — the difference between the highest-paying Single Life Annuity and the Joint and 100% Survivor Annuity. Like most people, Nate would love to have the best of both options: the higher single life annual payout and the greatest yearly payment to Sheila for the rest of her life at his death. Such an option is possible. Read on.

First, Nate needs to ask himself this question, "How much money would I need in a separate interest-bearing account to produce $35,000 of income per year for Sheila until she reaches age 85?" If Nate had an investment portfolio (in addition to his current investment assets) earning 6 percent per year, he would need $615,000 to produce $35,000 of annual income for 25 years (assumes 3% inflation). A portfolio growing at 8 percent would require a total of about $500,000 to produce the required income.

If Nate had a separate portfolio from which Sheila could draw $35,000 of income each year after his death, he could then opt for the Single Life Annuity and obtain $10,000 more in income per year[2] and enjoy the best of both worlds.

This is possible, but the strategy requires the use of life insurance.

Like most people who are nearing retirement, the idea of purchasing more life insurance isn't too appealing. However, realize that if Nate chooses the Joint and Survivor Annuity, he is, in effect, buying an expensive life insurance policy. He is buying insurance that will pay Sheila $35,000 per year for her lifetime upon his death. This insurance costs Nate $10,000 each and every year. Is that a good deal? Perhaps not.

If Nate could purchase a $500,000 life insurance policy for less than $10,000 per year, then he could opt for the higher $45,000 pension payout of the Single Life Annuity and still protect Sheila. If, for example, a $500,000 insurance policy costs only $5,000 per year, Nate could use some of the additional $10,000 he receives each year to pay his life insurance premiums and still be ahead of the Joint and 100% Survivor Annuity by $5,000. When Nate dies, his Single Life Annuity will cease, but Sheila will receive $500,000 tax-free from the life insurance policy. She can use that money to buy a portfolio of investments that will provide her with an income to replace the pension. In addition, while Nate is alive, he has access to the cash value of the policy as needed.

In hindsight, knowing that he would be receiving a pension in the future, Nate should have purchased the insurance at age 40 or 50 to lock in much lower premiums. Fortunately, he is in good health and can still qualify for a policy at age 60.

Type of Policy

Realize that the sole purpose of the insurance policy is to replace some or all of Nate's pension income at his death. If he dies at age 60 just one day after choosing the Single Life Annuity, then Sheila would need a full 25 years or more of income. As they get older, however, there are less years of income they will need to replace. For instance, at age 70 Sheila would only need income for 15 more years. Consequently, they can reduce their life insurance coverage over time or buy a policy that does this automatically. Buying a policy that automatically reduces the coverage will drop the annual premiums. Universal or variable universal life can provide this flexibility.

The critical question for Nate is determining how much $500,000 of life insurance will actually cost? Age and health are the biggest determinants. Figure 4 illustrates annual universal life insurance price ranges at different ages and compares load (commission) policies to no-load (no-commission) policies. Based on these premium levels, the pension maximization strategy would work well for Nate whether he purchased $500,000 or $600,000 of coverage. Remember, all he needs is an annual premium less than $10,000. If he is comfortable with a little more risk, he could purchase a variable universal life policy and invest the cash value he accumulates in subaccounts (like mutual funds).

WARNING: Do not purchase a life insurance policy from a commissioned agent without comparing the cost to a no-load policy. No-load life insurance often has premiums that are 50 percent to 70 percent lower, which can make buying a policy at retirement much easier to stomach. In addition to lower premiums, no-load policies carry no surrender charges, so your cash value is available immediately. Load policies carry surrender

Figure 4

What Will Insurance Cost?

$500,000 Universal Life Insurance (UL)

Age	Load Premium	Load Cash Value*	No-Load Premium	No-Load Cash Value*
40	$2,720	$0	$1,615	$975
45	$3,620	$0	$2,195	$1,345
50	$5,315	$0	$3,150	$1,991
55	$6,540	$0	$3,910	$2,372
60	$7,780	$0	$4,715	$2,847
65	$10,010	$0	$6,255	$3,564

$600,000 Universal Life Insurance (UL)

Age	Load Premium	Load Cash Value*	No-Load Premium	No-Load Cash Value*
40	$3,264	$0	$1,938	$1,170
45	$4,344	$0	$2,634	$1,614
50	$6,378	$0	$3,780	$2,390
55	$7,848	$0	$4,692	$2,847
60	$9,336	$0	$5,658	$3,417
65	$12,012	$0	$7,506	$4,276

*End of first year cash surrender value.

charges that last 10 to 15 years and will penalize you for withdrawing any money during this period. (See Chapter 15, "No-Load Means Lower Cost.")

How Much Insurance Will *You* Need to Make This Strategy Work?

Okay, Nate figured he needed a $500,000 policy to make his strategy work. How much will you need? The amount of insurance you need depends on four factors: 1) the amount of annual income your surviving spouse will need; 2) the length of time the income is needed; 3) the rate-of-return assumption; and 4) inflation.

Figures 5, 6, and 7 contain tables to help you determine how much life insurance you will need to purchase. Once you know the amount, obtain some no-load life insurance quotes to determine how much

Figure 5

Pension Maximization
How much insurance do you need?

Rate of Return 6%

Amount of Income Needed Annually	Number of years income is needed (Assumes portfolio will be completely depleted)					
	10	15	20	25	30	35
$10,000	$85,684	$120,137	$149,984	$175,839	$198,237	$217,640
$15,000	$128,526	$180,206	$224,976	$263,759	$297,355	$326,459
$20,000	$171,367	$240,275	$299,968	$351,678	$396,474	$435,279
$25,000	$214,209	$300,343	$374,959	$439,598	$495,592	$544,099
$30,000	$257,051	$360,412	$449,951	$527,517	$594,711	$652,919
$35,000	$299,893	$420,481	$524,943	$615,437	$693,829	$761,739
$40,000	$342,735	$480,549	$599,935	$703,356	$792,948	$870,558
$45,000	$385,577	$540,618	$674,927	$791,276	$892,066	$979,378
$50,000	$428,418	$600,687	$749,919	$879,195	$991,184	$1,088,198
$55,000	$471,260	$660,755	$824,911	$967,115	$1,090,303	$1,197,018
$60,000	$514,102	$720,824	$899,903	$1,055,034	$1,189,421	$1,305,838
$65,000	$556,944	$780,893	$974,895	$1,142,954	$1,288,540	$1,414,658
$70,000	$599,786	$840,961	$1,049,887	$1,230,873	$1,387,658	$1,523,477
$75,000	$642,628	$901,030	$1,124,878	$1,318,793	$1,486,777	$1,632,297
$80,000	$685,469	$961,099	$1,199,870	$1,406,713	$1,585,895	$1,741,117
$85,000	$728,311	$1,021,168	$1,274,862	$1,494,632	$1,685,014	$1,849,937
$90,000	$771,153	$1,081,236	$1,349,854	$1,582,552	$1,784,132	$1,958,757
$95,000	$813,995	$1,141,305	$1,424,846	$1,670,471	$1,883,250	$2,067,576
$100,000	$856,837	$1,201,374	$1,499,838	$1,758,391	$1,982,369	$2,176,396

Note: assumes all calculations are adjusted for 3% inflation

it will cost. See Figure 5 in Chapter 15 for a list of insurance companies offering no-load life insurance.

The return-rate assumption you choose will determine which chart you use. For example, Figure 5 assumes when the proceeds of your insurance policy are paid out to your surviving spouse, he or she will invest the money in a portfolio earning 6 percent annually. Figure 6 uses 8 percent, and Figure 7 uses 10 percent. Each chart has a built-in inflation adjustment and assumes your surviving spouse will need 3 percent more income than the previous year. If you are working with an insurance agent, make sure inflation is factored in. Otherwise, your insurance need will be skewed lower and may be insufficient for your spouse.

Here's how to use the charts: Assume you would like to provide your spouse with $35,000 of annual inflation-adjusted income for 25 years

Figure 6

Pension Maximization
How much insurance do you need?

	Rate of Return 8%					
Amount of Income Needed Annually	Number of years income is needed (Assumes portfolio will be completely depleted)					
	10	15	20	25	30	35
$10,000	$77,766	$104,826	$126,175	$143,020	$156,310	$166,795
$15,000	$116,650	$157,239	$189,263	$214,530	$234,465	$250,193
$20,000	$155,533	$209,652	$252,351	$286,040	$312,619	$333,591
$25,000	$194,416	$262,065	$315,439	$357,550	$390,774	$416,988
$30,000	$233,299	$314,478	$378,526	$429,059	$468,929	$500,386
$35,000	$272,182	$366,891	$441,614	$500,569	$547,084	$583,783
$40,000	$311,066	$419,304	$504,702	$572,079	$625,239	$667,181
$45,000	$349,949	$471,717	$567,789	$643,589	$703,394	$750,579
$50,000	$388,832	$524,130	$630,877	$715,099	$781,549	$833,976
$55,000	$427,715	$576,543	$693,965	$786,609	$859,704	$917,374
$60,000	$466,598	$628,956	$757,053	$858,119	$937,858	$1,000,772
$65,000	$505,481	$681,368	$820,140	$929,629	$1,016,013	$1,084,169
$70,000	$544,365	$733,781	$883,228	$1,001,139	$1,094,168	$1,167,567
$75,000	$583,248	$786,194	$946,316	$1,072,649	$1,172,323	$1,250,964
$80,000	$622,131	$838,607	$1,009,403	$1,144,158	$1,250,478	$1,334,362
$85,000	$661,014	$891,020	$1,072,491	$1,215,668	$1,328,633	$1,417,760
$90,000	$699,897	$943,433	$1,135,579	$1,287,178	$1,406,788	$1,501,157
$95,000	$738,781	$995,846	$1,198,667	$1,358,688	$1,484,942	$1,584,555
$100,000	$777,664	$1,048,259	$1,261,754	$1,430,198	$1,563,097	$1,667,953

Note: assumes all calculations are adjusted for 3% inflation

after your death. First, choose the chart that most closely reflects the rate of return (6 percent, 8 percent, 10 percent) you believe your surviving spouse could achieve if required to invest your insurance proceeds upon your death. I recommend selecting the most conservative percentage, 6 percent. Next, go to the row that says $35,000 and the column under 25 years. The intersecting number, $615,437, is the amount of insurance you should consider purchasing to make your strategy work. [3]

If your insurance premiums will be less than the difference between the Life Only Annuity and the Joint and 100% Survivor Annuity you are planning to take, then the pension maximization strategy may work well for you. It is definitely worth obtaining an insurance quote before locking yourself into a lifetime pension payment. It may mean thousands of extra dollars each year during retirement.

Figure 7

Pension Maximization
How much insurance do you need?

Amount of Income Needed Annually	Rate of Return 10%					
	Number of years income is needed (Assumes portfolio will be completely depleted)					
	10	15	20	25	30	35
$10,000	$70,903	$92,264	$107,640	$118,708	$126,675	$132,410
$15,000	$106,354	$138,396	$161,460	$178,062	$190,012	$198,614
$20,000	$141,805	$184,527	$215,280	$237,416	$253,350	$264,819
$25,000	$177,256	$230,659	$269,100	$296,770	$316,687	$331,024
$30,000	$212,708	$276,791	$322,920	$356,124	$380,025	$397,229
$35,000	$248,159	$322,923	$376,740	$415,478	$443,362	$463,434
$40,000	$283,610	$369,055	$430,559	$474,832	$506,699	$529,638
$45,000	$319,062	$415,187	$484,379	$534,186	$570,037	$595,843
$50,000	$354,513	$461,319	$538,199	$593,539	$633,374	$662,048
$55,000	$389,964	$507,450	$592,019	$652,893	$696,712	$728,253
$60,000	$425,415	$553,582	$645,839	$712,247	$760,049	$794,458
$65,000	$460,867	$599,714	$699,659	$771,601	$823,387	$860,663
$70,000	$496,318	$645,846	$753,479	$830,955	$886,724	$926,867
$75,000	$531,769	$691,978	$807,299	$890,309	$950,061	$993,072
$80,000	$567,220	$738,110	$861,119	$949,663	$1,013,399	$1,059,277
$85,000	$602,672	$784,242	$914,939	$1,009,017	$1,076,736	$1,125,482
$90,000	$638,123	$830,373	$968,759	$1,068,371	$1,140,074	$1,191,687
$95,000	$673,574	$876,505	$1,022,579	$1,127,725	$1,203,411	$1,257,891
$100,000	$709,026	$922,637	$1,076,399	$1,187,079	$1,266,749	$1,324,096

Note: assumes all calculations are adjusted for 3% inflation

Pension Max Calculator: www.javacalc.com.

Taking a One-Time Lump-Sum Distribution

What if your company offers you the chance to take a one-time lump-sum distribution instead of a yearly pension?

This recently happened to Craig Lennar, who was given the following choices at retirement: 1) an annual pension payment of $35,000 per year for the rest of his and his wife's life, or 2) a one-time lump-sum distribution of $500,000. What should he do? Is it better to take the lump sum or receive a lifetime of annuity payments?

Lump Sum Advantages

If Craig takes the lump-sum money and transfers it into an IRA, he can gain tremendous flexibility and avoid taxes and penalties in the process. Once in the IRA, he can begin taking withdrawals to obtain the income he and his wife, Linda, need. He can even give himself a "raise" by withdrawing a little bit more each year to compensate for inflation — a benefit not available with his pension.

He can also withdraw principal at any point in time if he ever needs a large cash infusion to buy real estate, for example, or pay for his daughter's wedding. Because the money is in an IRA, he can develop and manage an investment strategy on his own or with the aid of a financial advisor instead of relying on his former employer to do it for him.

Any assets left in his IRA at death can be transferred into Linda's IRA without taxes or penalties and continue to grow tax-deferred. Linda can continue managing the money and taking out income as needed. Upon her death, the remaining balance in the portfolio will pass on to their children or whomever they name as beneficiaries. (Read more about IRA rollovers in Chapter 24.)

Lump Sum Disadvantages

If Craig and Linda invest their IRA money in stocks or bonds (or stock or bond mutual funds), there are no guarantees that they'll obtain the rate of return they need. If they are unsuccessfully managing their portfolio, they could be in danger of depleting their IRA assets prematurely. This risk won't exist if they choose the pension option with the guaranteed monthly payments.

Figure 8

Pension or Lump Sum?

Lifetime Pension Payouts	Lump Sum
Choice of annuity payout option is irrevocable	Flexible and changeable payout schedule
Income is guaranteed	Income is not guaranteed
Recipient does not have to manage an investment portfolio	Investor must manage an investment portfolio
N/A	Investment returns are not guaranteed
Access to investment principal is not available	Investment principal is available at any time
Once annuity has been paid based on terms of option chosen no money is left to heirs	Any money not spent during retirement passes on to heirs

Lump Sum vs. Annual Pension

Before making a final decision, Craig and Linda should run some numbers. Let's go back in time and say Craig got this same offer in 1975. A $35,000 annual pension for the rest of their lives would have sounded pretty good then. Of course, walking away with $500,000 wouldn't have been too bad either. Which turned out to be the best deal? Let's break it down.

An annual payment of $35,000 seemed like a substantial income in 1975. That's $82,000 in today's dollars. But what seemed plush in 1975 is barely cutting it today. A $500,000 lump-sum distribution invested into an IRA, however, would only need to grow 5 percent per year to outperform the pension, assuming they'll be in retirement for 25 years. Let's assume they took the lump sum and put it in an IRA consisting of 50 percent blue-chip U.S. stocks[4] and 50 percent government and corporate bonds[5] — essentially meaning that half of their money is in relatively conservative investments, while the other half is at risk in the stock market.

To make this a fair comparison, let's say they withdrew only $35,000 annually — the same amount they would have received from their pension — from their IRA every year from 1975 to 2000, with no cost-of-living adjustment. How much would be left in their IRA account 25 years later?

Brace yourself. The answer is a whopping $4.49 million. Craig and Linda would have had that much money left over even after withdrawing $35,000 per year ($875,000 in total withdrawals). Their balanced portfolio would have enjoyed an average annual return of 12.98 percent. Even if they had given themselves a 3 percent raise each and every year to keep up with rising prices, increasing their annual income from $35,000 per year in 1975 to $71,148 in 2000, their portfolio would still contain a very substantial $3.02 million at the end of 2000.[6] Had they chosen the annual pension payment, all they could look forward to was their measly annual benefit of $35,000.

Although these numbers look very convincing, it should be noted that this balanced portfolio would have followed the natural ups and downs of the stock and bond markets. During six of the 25 years, Ron and Linda would have taken withdrawals from their portfolio when it produced negative returns. Their success, then, would depend on their ability to tolerate the rough economic circumstances of the mid-1970s, early 1980s, the 1987 stock market crash, and negative markets in 1990, 1994, and 2000, without deviating from their balanced investment strategy. Some people simply do not have the ability to weather this kind of volatility. Plus, it is unlikely that another 25-year span, which included the longest stock bull market in history, will produce the same returns. The lesson to learn here, however, is that if you have the choice between a lump sum and a pension, it's not a choice you should make lightly. Look at both options very carefully, work through the different scenarios you could pursue, and then make the decision that will best help you reach your retirement objectives. Who knows with results like these, you may just end up with a large amount of money in your portfolio after 25 years of retirement.

Conclusion

After reading this chapter you should be more familiar with the various pension payment options and the risks and benefits associated with each. With a more firm understanding of the way your pension will be paid out, you can now use the maximization strategies outlined in this chapter to help you make the most of those payments at retirement.

Pension Tips from AARP
1. Make sure you get credit for the last year you work. You may need to work a certain number of hours during the year or continue working until a specified date. Quitting at the wrong time could mean being credited for 19 instead of 20 years. This would severely affect your total lifetime benefit.
2. Find out if your plan uses "Social Security Integration" to calculate your benefits. If it does, your pension may be reduced by up to 50% when you start receiving Social Security benefits.
3. Calculate your own benefit. Mistakes are made. Find out how your benefit is calculated and double check your company's math.
4. Determine if any of your past employers had pensions. If so, you may be entitled to a benefit. If you don't have record of a pension benefit from a former employer, call the Pension Guaranty Corp.'s Pension Search Program at 1-800-400-7242 or visit www.pbgc.gov.

EIGHT

Avoiding the 10 Most Common Investor Mistakes

✓ RETIREMENT DECISION #8: *How should I manage my personal savings?*

Max Haley has been investing in the stock market for the past 20 years. In 1984, at age 40, he started with $55,000. Since then, he has invested in a number of individual stocks and stock mutual funds. Max prides himself on his "investment expertise." To determine what stocks and funds to buy, when to buy, and when to sell, he reads *Money* magazine, subscribes to *The Wall Street Journal*, frequently visits investment Web sites, and tunes into CNBC several times each day to obtain stock prices and reports.

So how's he doing? By the end of 2003, his investment had grown to $99,336. Max's average annual return was only a meager 3 percent. Had Max simply invested his $55,000 in an S&P 500 stock index fund and never looked at it again for the 20 years, he would have had $570,577.[1]

What if Max has to retire now and needs income from his portfolio for the next 30 years? If he annually withdraws 7 percent of his hand-picked portfolio, it will kick off about $8,000 per year. If he had simply invested in the index fund, he could have taken out $46,000 each year at the same withdrawal rate. What's really surprising about his performance is that Max's 3 percent annual return was better than what the average U.S. stock investor earned during this period!

After applying so much effort, why did Max do so poorly? Max, like most individual investors, was guilty of making 10 mistakes. Had he read and applied the lessons when he started in 1984 that you will learn in this chapter, he likely would be sitting on a large nest egg today.

Mistakes Will Cost You

And make no doubt about it: You will need a large nest egg to retire on. Social Security is under pressure as more and more baby boomers start tapping into the system. Companies are eliminating traditional pension plans. More than ever before people need solid returns from their own investment portfolios in order to produce a livable retirement income. Plain and simple, your success as an investor may well dictate whether or not you reach your retirement goals.

Today, the average retiree relies upon personal savings for about one-third of his or her retirement income (see Figure 1). In the future, savings and investments will take on an even greater importance. This is a huge problem for most retirees. Why? Because most people—including, most likely, you—simply don't invest very well.

Figure 1

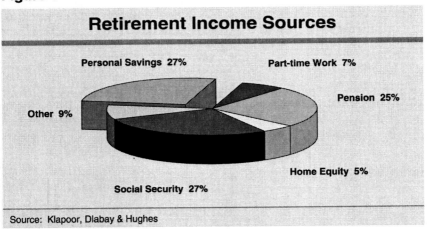

Retirement Income Sources

Personal Savings 27%   Part-time Work 7%

Other 9%   Pension 25%

Home Equity 5%

Social Security 27%

Source: Klapoor, Dlabay & Hughes

A 19-year investor study dramatically illustrates the grim lack of success many investors have experienced. According to the study, the average stock-fund investor achieved returns of only 2.6 percent a year from 1984 through 2002. Had these same investors simply invested their money in the S&P 500 Index (composed of large U.S. company stocks) and forgotten all about it, they would have achieved a 12.2 percent annual gain. Even bonds beat most investors, growing 4.2 percent per year. [2] The stock market provided results almost five times better than those experienced by millions of stock mutual fund investors!

Consider for a moment the difference between an investor earning an average annual return of 2.6 or 4.6 percent as opposed to an investor earning a 12.2 percent return. Compare the results in Figure 2.

We've recently concluded one of the strongest raging bull markets in stock market history. It should have been easy for even the average investor to make substantial sums of money, but many didn't capitalize on this strong market.

Figure 2

$100,000 Invested at Different Growth Rates

	2.6%	4.2%	12.2%
10 Years	$129,263	$150,896	$316,175
20 Years	$167,089	$227,694	$999,671
30 Years	$215,983	$343,582	$3,160,718

Over the long run, even during bull markets, most investors struggle to obtain performance better than low-yielding investments like money markets and certificates of deposit because they make common investor mistakes. How is it that investors do so poorly at times when investments are doing so well? No single mistake explains this poor performance. Rather, there are a combination of errors repeated over and over — mistakes that can be overcome by simply implementing and adhering to a disciplined investment strategy. (Developing a strategy is discussed in Section Three, Chapters 9 through 18.)

In this chapter, you will learn that it's possible to obtain good long-term returns by avoiding the obstacles that plague so many investors. By avoiding common mistakes, you will be in a better position to reach your retirement goals. Here are the 10 most common investor mistakes.

Mistake 1: Excessive Buying and Selling

Like the amateur chef that continually seasons food until it's inedible, investors who are overactive in their trading undermine their goals.

A study of more than 66,000 households with investment accounts at a well-known brokerage firm found that investors who traded most frequently underperformed those who traded the least. For the study, the investors were split into five groups based on their trading activity. The returns achieved by the 20 percent of investors who traded the most lagged behind the least active group of investors by 5.5 percentage points annually. The study also showed that men trade 45 percent more actively than women, and consequently, women outperformed men.[3]

Many investors make the mistake of thinking that the more often they trade, the better their returns will be. The advertisements aired by many discount brokerage firms promoting active trading want you to believe this is true. However, the evidence suggests exactly the opposite. So sit back and relax!

 From 1984 to 2002 the average stock investor held their positions for a short 2.5 years while bond investors held their positions for 2.9 years.

Mistake 2: Information Overload

Too much information can be dangerous to your wealth.

Not long ago at the beginning of an investment seminar, I asked the audience how many knew the previous day's closing level of the Dow Jones Industrial Average. Many hands went up, and these "smart" investors had no difficulty citing the index's closing value.

Then I asked who in the audience didn't have a clue where the market had closed. Timidly, a woman with very little investment experience raised her hand. The crowd was surprised as I handed her a $20 bill. I explained that investors who rarely check the market and the value of their investments keep more of their money invested in stocks, thus, they often obtain better long-term results. Those who monitor the market too closely have a tendency to undermine their portfolios with self-destructive behavior.

What role should information play in your investment decisions? Recently, University of Chicago Professor Richard Thaler and three other professors specializing in investment behavior studied the decisions investors made over a 25-year period. The professors focused on the amounts people invested in stocks.

Three groups of investors were studied. Group A was bombarded every six weeks with reports on market gyrations and investment performance. Group B received performance information about their investments just once each year. Group C received investment updates only once every five years. Which group do you think did the best?

The investors who received the most performance information allocated the smallest amount of their portfolios — about 40 percent — to stocks. They not only maintained the lowest equity exposure but tended also to sell stocks immediately after a loss.[4] The group that only received updates every fifth year devoted 66 percent of their portfolios to stocks. And, as we all know, based on the history of the market, investors with greater exposure to the equity markets have enjoyed far better long-term performance than those with lesser exposure.

The bottom line: The more closely investors follow the market, the more tentative they become about investing in stocks, which ultimately hurts their returns.

Figure 3

25 Years of Information Overload

	Group A	Group C
Total Reports:	200+	5
Report Frequency:	6 weeks	5 years
Stock Allocation	40%	66%

Source: Richard Thaler, University of Chicago, 1996

The solution? Develop a fundamentally sound investment strategy and maintain your stock allocation through up and down markets. Stay away from financial sites on the Internet, turn off CNBC, consider canceling *The Wall Street Journal*, and quit worrying about your investments every day. Prof. Thaler said it best, "My advice to you is to invest in equities, and then don't open the mail."[5]

Mistake 3: Market Timing

History has shown that the stock market rises about 70 percent of the time. The danger, when investing, is in finding yourself out of the market during the 70 percent of the time it is going up, all because you're trying to avoid the 30 percent of the time the market is falling.

Trying to choose the right times to jump in and out of the market is an impossible task. Too many investors make the mistake of thinking they can do it. Investors attempting to time the ebbs and flows of the market tend to jump in too late, missing major upswings, and jump out after the market has fallen. Consequently, many investors end up buying high and selling low, yielding poor results that often lead to the kind of frustration that keeps investors out of the stock market altogether.

If you had invested in the S&P 500 from 1991 to 2003, covering 3,278 trading days, you would have enjoyed an 11.9 percent annualized return. If you had missed the market's 30 best days, your annualized return would have been cut to a scant 2.1 percent! There's a dramatic difference between an investor who spent 3,248 days invested in the stock market and another who stayed invested all 3,278 days (Figure 4).[6] There is a huge price to pay if you mistime the market. Research shows that poor market timing has cost investors more than $1 trillion since late 1993.[7]

Figure 4

Staying in the Game!
S&P 500 Annualized Return 1991 - 2003

Source: S&P 500 Index

Mistake 4: Chasing Returns

Individual investors are notorious for buying last year's winners. Guess which mutual funds attract the most new money each year? You got it; money flows into mutual funds that have just enjoyed the greatest performance in the *previous* year. In 2000, for example, investors poured more than $60 billion into the 10 funds that had the greatest performance during the previous year. The returns of these 10 funds, on average, was triple the performance of the stock market in 1999. In 2000, however, these same funds reported returns less than half that of the stock market.[8] In other words, investors who chased market-beating returns in 2000 got soundly beaten by the market.

It shouldn't be surprising that chasing returns is a very common investor mistake. There's an entire financial media industry built around one simple theme: "Don't Miss Out on the 10 Hottest Stocks," or some variation of it. For many investors, the lure of phenomenal past returns is just too tempting to pass up; this allure leads to critical mistakes.

Figure 5

Nicholas-Applegate Global Tech I Fund

Source: Morningstar Principia Pro, December 31, 2002

For example, in 1999, the Nicholas-Applegate Global Tech I Fund posted an unbelievable 494 percent return, and investors saw instant riches parading before their eyes. An individual investing in this fund at the start of 2000, however, experienced the following returns: -36.37 percent in 2000, -49.26 percent in 2001, and -44.96 percent in 2002 (Figure 5).[9] At the end of three years, a $10,000 investment was worth just $1,777.

When the fine print says "Past performance is no guarantee of future returns," believe it!

Mistake 5: Believing Persuasive Advertising Messages

Many brokerage firms advertise in order to convince you how easy, fun, and inexpensive it is to delve into the stock market and make big money. In fact, the brokerage industry spends hundreds of millions of dollars each year on TV commercials convincing us that it's easy to be a success in the market.

Remember Stuart? He was that red-headed, punk rocker made famous in the late 1990s through a series of commercials for a large discount brokerage firm. He taught us and his boss how easy it is to make money in the stock market. Stuart advised that all you had to do was open an online account, start trading, and watch the money roll in. As Stuart said in the commercial:

> "I don't want to beat the market. I wanna grab it, sock it in the gut a couple of times, turn it upside down, hold it by the pants, and shake it 'til all those pockets empty out the spare change."[10]

Although the Stuart commercials, like many ads for the investment houses in the late 90's, were hilarious, they did more damage than good. We don't see Stuart talking about investing anymore because he probably lost his shirt in 2000. He learned the hard way that there is more to developing a solid investment strategy than merely opening an online brokerage account and trading.

No question about it, buying and selling stocks can be exhilarating. Many investors roll up their sleeves and play with their money, checking stock prices and market values throughout each day. While this may be a great form of entertainment, most discover it's also a successful formula for losing money.

Rarely a day passes when a brokerage firm isn't telling Americans that they can trade stocks for as little as $5 to $8 per transaction. Think about it. By offering such cheap trades, these firms have to make up for it by dealing in quantity. Their goal is to have you trade as often as possible without concern for cost. What they don't tell you is what it's *really* costing you. As we've seen, hyperactive trading equals poor performance.

Mistake 6: Poor Diversification

Investors tend to be concentrated in one or two companies or sectors of the market. Overconcentration can hurt a portfolio whether the market is performing well or poorly. Poor diversification leads to excessive volatility, and excessive volatility causes investors to make hasty, poor decisions.

Suppose you had placed the bulk of your portfolio in a company like Lucent Technologies, Enron, WorldCom, Qwest, or Adelphia Communications. From 2000 to 2002, you would have watched your portfolio head into an unrecoverable tailspin. People who had concentrated the bulk of their portfolios in these companies saw values drop to almost zero. Many were left with no other option but to start from scratch and begin rebuilding an entirely new portfolio.

Many investors who got caught up in the technology craze of the late 1990s suffered the same fate. Staggering amounts of money poured into technology mutual funds as investors bulked up their investments in this single market sector. This lack of diversification proved fatal for technology investors when the average tech fund fell 30.7 percent in 2000, another 35.2 percent in 2001, and another 42.73 in 2002.[11]   By comparison, a well-diversified growth portfolio consisting of 80% stocks and 20% bonds would have fallen just 4 percent in 2000, 8 percent in 2001, and 13 percent in 2002. [12] When volatility is controlled, it's easier for investors to maintain a long-term investing outlook.

Poor diversification even takes its toll during bull markets. In 1999, the S&P 500 Index recorded a 21 percent return. However, just eight of the 500 stocks in the index accounted for half of its 21 percent gain. The odds were stacked against the investor who bought just a few S&P stocks during 1999. The chances of an investor successfully choosing those eight big winners out of 500 would be a little better than winning the lottery.[13]   Most would be far more successful by simply diversifying, buying an S&P 500 Index fund, and owning stakes in all 500 companies.

Mistake 7:   Lack of Patience

Most mutual fund investors hold their funds for only two or three years before impatience gets the best of them. Individual stock investors are even less patient, turning over about 75 percent of their portfolios each year.[14]   You simply can't realize good returns from the stock market if you only invest for weeks, months, or even a couple of years. When investing in stocks or stock funds, investors must learn to set their investment sights on five- and 10-year periods.

Investors would do well to study the example of the fund with the best 10-year annual return for the period ending December 31, 2003: Calamos Growth-A. During that decade, this midsized company stock fund provided investors with a stunning annual return of 20.79 percent. A $10,000 investment in the Calamos Growth A fund would have grown to $66,158 during this period. Most investors, it's safe to say, would be very happy with this performance. However, it didn't deliver huge returns every single year. In fact, during that 10-year period, three years were pretty rough. The fund lost 5.7 percent in 1994, fell 7.68 percent in 2001, and dropped 15.88 percent in 2002.[15] An investor would have had to endure these three negative years (years when a FDIC bank account would have done much better) to gain the 20.79 percent long-term average annual return. Investors who sold the Calamos fund during one of these downturns left money on the table. Patient investors were rewarded.

Anne Scheiber is a model of patience that all investors should emulate. She retired from her $3,150-per-year IRS auditor job in 1943. At that time, she invested $5,000 — a little over one year's salary — into a portfolio of stocks. Over the years, she bought and held mostly blue-chip U.S. stocks and some municipal bonds. She didn't worry about daily market fluctuations and rode out the difficult market periods. When Anne died in 1995, at age 101, her $5,000 had grown to more than $22 million, which she donated to a Jewish university. Patience was at the core of Anne's stunning investment success.[16]

Mistake 8: Not Understanding the Downside

Many investors are just convinced that their investment portfolios should always go up. When returns don't meet these unrealistic expectations, they tend to throw in the towel and give up. It's a mistake to sell *good* investments just because they are having a sluggish year or struggling through a bear market. You need to invest with your eyes wide open knowing beforehand what to expect from your investments in both bull and bear markets. In most cases when your investments take near term dips or fluctuate with the market, you should stay invested and hold on.

Most investors ask only one question before buying a portfolio of investments, "What will my return be?" Usually, they answer this by looking at recently posted one-year returns. Stopping at this question will likely leave you disappointed at some point during your investment journey.

In addition to knowing what the returns of your investments have been recently, be sure to ask the following:

- What has the portfolio returned on average over the past one, three, five and 10 years?
- What was the *best and worst* three-month period during the past 10 years?
- What was the *best and worst* one-year period during the past 10 years?
- What was the *best and worst* three-year period during the past 10 years?
- How has the investment performed during past wars, bear markets, terrorist attacks and elections?

Once you know the answers to these questions, you can now ask yourself an even more significant question: "If I want the long-term returns this investment or portfolio can produce, can I withstand the volatility?" Without understanding this risk from the onset, volatility will likely get the best of you somewhere down the road. See the asset allocation chart in Chapter 9 (Figure 7) to examine the ups and downs of various mixes of stocks, bonds, and cash.

Let's investigate the markets' ups and downs during different periods. Figure 6 shows the worst one-year results for different segments of the stock and bond markets from 1975 to 2000. You need to take downturns in context. For example, the chart shows the worst year for large-company stocks was -9%. An investor would have been shortsighted to sell a portfolio of large-company stocks after this poor performing year. A $10,000 investment into a stock index fund starting in January 1975 would have grown to $262,479 by December 2000. Figures 7, 8, 9 and 10 review the stock market's performance during various bear markets, wars, terrorism, and elections.

Figure 6

Risk and Return of the Stock and Bond Markets
1975 - 2000

Market Sector	Average Annual Return	Worst One Year
Large Company Stocks	16%	-9%
Small Company Stocks	19%	-22%
Long-Term Corporate Bonds	10%	-7%
Long-Term Government Bonds	10%	-9%
Intermediate-Term Government Bonds	9%	-5%
U.S. Treasury Bills	7%	-3%

Despite all the recessions, wars, terrorist attacks, and market crashes, the stock market has been an excellent investment over the long term. The key is to stay invested through thick and thin. When you invest in a portfolio of stocks and bonds, be aware of the potential upside *and* downside associated with your investments. If you don't understand the risks at the outset, you are more likely to react poorly during periodic market setbacks and get scared out of the market.

Figure 7

Bear Markets
S&P 500

Bear Market Begin	End	Total Months	Total Return S&P 500	Total Return First Year After Decline	Months to Break-Even (from end of bear market)
Jul '48	May '49	11	-9.8%	42.4%	4
Jan '53	Aug '53	8	-8.7%	35.0%	5
Aug '57	Dec '57	5	-14.9%	43.6%	7
Jan '60	Oct '60	10	-8.4%	32.6%	2
Jan '62	Sep '62	9	-19.4%	31.7%	7
Feb '66	Sep '66	8	-15.6%	30.6%	6
Dec '68	Jun '70	19	-29.2%	41.9%	9
Jan '73	Sep '74	21	-42.9%	38.1%	21
Jan '77	Feb '78	14	-14.1%	16.6%	5
Dec '80	Jul '82	20	-16.9%	59.4%	3
Sep '87	Nov '87	3	-29.5%	23.2%	18
Jul '90	Sep '90	3	-14.7%	33.5%	3
Feb '94	Jul '94	5	-8.0%	26.0%	3
Mar '00	Oct '02	30	-47.6%	29.4%	*27+
Average		**12**	**-20.0%**	**34.6%**	**8**

*As of 12/13/04 the S&P 500 still had not reached the break-even point

When you buy an investment, you should plan on worst-case scenarios occurring when you invest. If you understand the risk from the onset, you are more likely to stay invested for the long term and realize solid long-term gains. It is true that past performance isn't guaranteed to repeat, but it does give us an indication of what to expect.

Figure 8

War
Dow Jones Industrial Average (DJIA)

War	War Start/Finish	Total Months	Change In DJI
World War I	Apr. 1917- Nov. 1918	20	-19%
World War II	Dec. 1941 - Aug. 1945	45	41%
Korean War	Jun. 1950 - Jul. 1953	37	20%
Vietnam War	Aug. 1964 - Jan. 1973	102	21%
Gulf War	Jan. 1991 - Feb. 1991	2	15%
IRAQ War	Mar. 2003 - Present*	22	29%
Average		38	18%

Source: Consulting Group, Dow Jones, BigCharts.com

Figure 9

Terrorism September 11
— S&P 500

Attacks of September 11	Days After Attack	Total Return S&P 500
Initial Market Reaction Septmeber 17, 2001	7	-4.9%
Market Bottom After Attack September 21, 2001	11	-11.6%
One Month After Attack October 11, 2001	30	0.4%
Two Months After Attack November 10, 2001	60	2.5%
Three Months After Attack December 10, 2001	90	4.3%

Figure 10

Election-Year Returns

Year	S&P 500	President Elected
1960	-3.0%	John F. Kennedy
1964	13.0%	Lyndon Johnson
1968	7.7%	Richard Nixon
1972	15.6%	Richard Nixon
1976	19.1%	Jimmy Carter
1980	25.8%	Ronald Reagan
1984	1.4%	Ronald Reagan
1988	12.4%	George H.W. Bush
1992	4.5%	Bill Clinton
1996	20.3%	Bill Clinton
2000	-10.1%	George W. Bush
2004	10.87%	George W. Bush

Mistake 9: Focusing on Individual Investment Holdings Rather Than Your Portfolio as a Whole

During the 2000-2002 bear market, I had a client, Marcus Ramsey, who each time we met to review his investments was convinced that he was going to go bankrupt due to the market's tumble. Why was Marcus so concerned? One of his brokerage accounts was invested in some fairly aggressive individual stocks that were routinely getting beat up. He watched the value of this account drop 50 percent. Because of this one account, he was ready to sell every stock investment he owned and move to money markets and CDs. However, when we evaluated his overall portfolio, including the money he had in his bank, 401(k), IRA, brokerage accounts, and an annuity, we discovered just how well he was weathering the bear-market storm.

When we viewed Marcus' total investment portfolio, we saw that only 30 percent of it was invested in stocks and stock funds; 40 percent of his money was invested in municipal bonds; and 30 percent was in money markets and CDs. The single aggressive account that caused him so much heartburn (and nearly persuaded him to give up on the stock market entirely) represented less than 1% of his overall portfolio.

So how did Marcus do? Not only did his complete portfolio handle the market downturn well, it actually made a little money. In 2000, when the stock market as measured by the S&P 500 was down 9.1 percent, and the Nasdaq dropped a whopping 39.29 percent, Marcus *made* 4 percent. In 2001 and 2002, when the stock market dropped 12 and 22 percent, respectively, his portfolio stayed afloat, making 1%. While everyone else seemed to be losing money, Marcus gained. Then, in 2003, because he had stayed invested in stocks, he participated in the markets' rally, climbing more than 14 percent.

If you are properly diversified, I can guarantee you that each year some of your investments will do poorly, lagging behind others in your investment portfolio. If you look at investments in isolation rather in context of your overall portfolio, you will be tempted to make poor decisions. You may get yourself into trouble by getting rid of investments when they're low in value and replacing them with those that just experienced success. This leads to buying high and selling low. This is often a mistake made by investors who gauge their entire portfolio by the performance of just one account or one investment.

So remember, evaluate your portfolio as a whole rather than by its individual pieces.

Mistake #10: Lack of a Clearly Defined Investment Strategy

Let's imagine for a moment that you are in charge of investing the $100 million in your state's retirement pension plan. The money will be used to provide pension incomes and other benefits to thousands of employees who have diligently worked for the state. These employees are counting on you to make good investment decisions to help secure their financial futures. What steps would you take to make sure this money was managed properly?

Most likely you would begin by developing an investment strategy that outlines your objectives and the parameters you will follow as you make investment decisions and manage the money. Then you would use the services of institutional money managers to handle the day-to-day buying and selling of stocks and bonds. You would likely interview many financial professionals, hire the best ones, and then monitor their performance very closely.

Picture yourself in one of these interviews. You would no doubt ask lots of specific questions about each manager's investment strategy and how successfully they have managed money. How much confidence would you have in a candidate who answered your question with this statement?

> *"Well, our investment management company doesn't really have a strategy. We usually read Money magazine and look for hot tips. We always watch CNBC and often get good investment ideas there. Sometimes we even look on the Internet for investment ideas. On occasion, I talk to my doctor or father-in-law to get their thoughts and ideas. We buy a little here and a little there and hope the investments work well and compliment each other. Once we purchase the portfolio of investments, we go to the Internet to obtain stock quotes several times each day. When it feels right, we sell. It's kind of a gut feeling we get. I think you will be happy with our investment management services."*

How much of your state's $100 million are you going to trust with this money manager candidate? It's safe to say you would usher him out of your office as quickly as possible.

You are the money manager of your own money. Now, put yourself in the hot seat. How would you respond if asked, "What strategy do you follow in managing your own portfolio?" All too often, investors respond the same way the money manager did in our previous example. If your investment strategy consists of hot tips from television, the Web, and the guy next door, how successful will it be? Can you effectively manage your own money? Not without a well-defined and disciplined investment strategy.

Just as you wouldn't hire a money manager without a clearly defined investment strategy to oversee your state's pension, you shouldn't manage your own money without developing a similar disciplined strategy. A strategy doesn't work unless it has structure and is carried out with discipline. Investors who do not follow a disciplined investment strategy continue to repeat the same costly mistakes mentioned in this chapter.

Now, more than ever, the size of your retirement nest egg will heavily depend on your ability to turn yourself into a good investor. By following the steps for developing a successful investment strategy that will be outlined in the subsequent chapters, you will significantly magnify your chances of attaining sound returns and living a secure retirement!

■ SECTION THREE ■

DEVELOPING A SUCCESSFUL INVESTMENT STRATEGY

—Asset Allocation
—Diversification
—Buying the Best Investments
—Ongoing Portfolio Management

NINE

The Most Important Investment Decision You'll Make

✓ RETIREMENT DECISION #9: *How much should I invest in stocks, bonds, and cash?*

While playing high school basketball, I developed a bad habit of throwing showy behind-the-back passes to my teammates. This made my coach crazy, especially considering the number of times I threw the ball out of bounds or to the other team. My coach insisted I stop my unpredictable passing habits and focus on the fundamentals or join him on the bench.

Many investors take a behind-the-back-pass approach to investing. They skip the fundamentals and focus on gimmicky or speculative investing. The volatility often associated with this approach to investing lands many retirees on the bench, or in the case of investing, on the sidelines in a money market or certificate of deposit (CD) paying 1 or 2 percent. Sitting on the bench earning little to no return will reduce your chances of reaching your retirement goals.

A fundamentally sound investment portfolio can control unwanted volatility. It can help keep you in the game earning good rates of return, so your money will last for the next 25 to 30 years. Retirees would do well to develop a four-step investment strategy that focuses on the fundamentals: asset allocation, diversification, prudent investment selection, and strategic ongoing management. Leave the behind-the-back passes of investing to those who still have time to earn back big losses.

Before we start constructing your retirement portfolio with the first step, one that most people skip, let's take a one-question quiz:

What is the most important variable in determining your investment success?

A. Accurate market timing — the ability to be in or out of the market at the right time.

B. Asset allocation — establishing an appropriate mix of stocks, bonds, and cash.

C. Selection of securities — the ability to uncover the next Microsoft.

The correct answer is B, and it's not even a close race. A recent study of accounts managed by institutional money managers (those who invest money for state pension accounts, large retirement plans, and endowment money) revealed that 91.5 percent of their total account performance was attributed to the money manager's asset-allocation policies. Only 8.5 percent of their returns was a result of security selection and market timing combined.[1] Accordingly, if a money manager produced a 10 percent rate of return, that return was almost entirely a result of how assets were allocated. Thus, the most important variable in determining investment success is how you divide your money among stocks, bonds, and cash.

Figure 1

What Has the Most Impact on Returns?

Asset Allocation

Asset Allocation 91.5%

Security Selection 4.6%

Market Timing 1.8%

Other 2.1%

Source: Financial Analysts Journal. May/June 1991

Most people don't realize what Figure 1 proves and, consequently, approach the investment process backward. Rarely do investors call their brokers or financial advisors and ask about the fundamentals—

what percentage of their money should be invested in stocks, bonds, and cash. In most cases, the first question an investor asks is, "What stock is hot?" The second is, "When should I buy?" Most investors are concentrating on security selection and market timing, the two variables that are the most fun to talk about but that matter least in investment success.

If more than 90 percent of your portfolio return is determined by how well you allocate your money, it makes sense that your asset-allocation policy should be your primary focus and ultimately the most important investment decision you'll make.

A landmark study of institutional money managers indicated that over 91% of investment return is attributed to asset-allocation decisions. Market timing and security selection accounted for only 6.4 percent combined.

Asset-Allocation Methods

Figure 2 outlines the annualized investment performance of stocks, bonds, and U.S. Treasury bills from 1925 to 2003. Stocks provide the highest returns but, of course, also carry the greatest risks. What percentage of your portfolio should be invested in each of these asset classes? There is not a "one size fits all" answer to this question. You must factor in your time frame, age, income requirements, level of risk tolerance, and desired rates of return. Let's examine several asset-allocation methods based on each of these variables, and then depending on your priorities, determine your personal asset-allocation policy.

Figure 2

Stocks, Bonds, and Bills
Annualized Returns 1925-2003

Stocks	10%
Bonds	6%
Cash	4%

Age-Based Allocation Method

An age-based approach is a conservative one, and the way it works is simple. Take the number 110 and subtract your age. The result is the percentage of your investment portfolio you should invest in stocks or stock mutual funds. For example, if you're 60, 50 percent of your money should be invested in stocks and the rest in bonds and cash. An 80-year-old, by this formula, should invest 30 percent of his/her portfolio in stocks. Why at that age would you continue to invest money in securities with a higher risk factor? Is there a chance an 80-year-old could live another 20 years? Yes, there is, and due to this possibility, a portion of the portfolio needs to be growing at a higher rate to provide a hedge against inflation.

If you follow this formula and adjust your portfolio each year, your investment strategy will slowly become more conservative as you get older. Although this formula is a good general guideline, it's probably a little too conservative for most people.

The chart in Figure 3, using the age-based formula, outlines asset-allocation mixes at different ages with their corresponding historical returns.

Figure 3

Asset Allocation at Various Ages

Age	Stock %	Bond %	Cash %	Average Return
20	90%	0%	10%	11.8%
30	80%	10%	10%	10.7%
40	70%	20%	10%	10.0%
50	60%	30%	10%	9.4%
60	50%	40%	10%	8.7%
70	40%	50%	10%	8.0%
80	30%	60%	10%	7.4%
90	20%	70%	10%	6.7%

Source: Ibbottson Associates1926-2002

Income-Needs Allocation Method

This formula can be more aggressive than the age-based formula. With this method, you simply allocate your money based on when you are planning to spend it.

Picture three buckets in front of you. The first bucket contains money you plan on spending during the next year or two. The second bucket contains money you will need for income from year three to year seven, and in the third bucket, you place money you don't plan on spending for more than seven years.

Figure 4

The money in Bucket 1 is invested in cash-type investments that protect your principal (CDs, money markets, Treasury bills, bank savings accounts). This is your short-term money and is not put at risk by being invested in the stock or bond markets.

In Bucket 2, intermediate-term money is invested in bonds (corporate, government, municipal). You can structure your bond portfolio by purchasing bonds that mature each year from "year three through year seven." This is known as a "bond ladder." As each bond matures, money is available to provide income during the upcoming year. Bonds are guaranteed by the bond issuer and typically pay a higher rate of interest than cash-type investments. Although bonds will fluctuate in value, the volatility is usually far less than that of stocks.

Your long-term money in Bucket 3 is invested in stocks (individual stocks or stock mutual funds). This money won't be spent for at least seven years. This is the growth portion of your portfolio and will naturally increase or decrease with the fluctuations in the stock market.

When handled properly, the pieces of this strategy fit together perfectly to ensure you a steady flow of retirement income. As you spend and deplete the money in your cash accounts, a bond will mature to replenish your cash reserves and provide the income needed during the upcoming year. To maintain your allocation, you will occasionally need to sell some stock positions to replenish your bond portfolio as bonds mature. If the stock market has a poor year, you can wait to transfer money from stocks to bonds, so you're not selling stocks in a down market.

At any point, you are ensured to have income for seven years (two years via cash and five years via bonds). Consequently, you don't need to worry excessively about a down year in the stock market because you're not going to be spending any of your stock investments for at least seven years. In that lengthy timespan, your stock portfolio has plenty of opportunity to regain any losses from a down year or two.

Let's consider Catherine Dalton, a 60-year-old retiree who has accumulated $500,000 and has an income need of $25,000 per year. Following the income-needs allocation method, she has decided to invest $50,000 in secure cash investments to provide income during her first two years of retirement; $125,000 in bonds to provide income in years three through seven; and the remaining $325,000 in stocks to help meet her long-term retirement goals (see Figure 5):

Figure 5

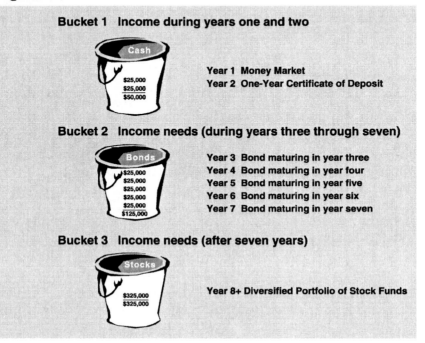

Bucket 1   Income during years one and two

Cash
$25,000
$25,000
$50,000

Year 1 Money Market
Year 2 One-Year Certificate of Deposit

Bucket 2   Income needs (during years three through seven)

Bonds
$25,000
$25,000
$25,000
$25,000
$25,000
$125,000

Year 3 Bond maturing in year three
Year 4 Bond maturing in year four
Year 5 Bond maturing in year five
Year 6 Bond maturing in year six
Year 7 Bond maturing in year seven

Bucket 3   Income needs (after seven years)

Stocks
$325,000
$325,000

Year 8+ Diversified Portfolio of Stock Funds

Investing $325,000, or 65 percent, of her money in stocks may be too aggressive for Catherine. If this is the case, she can adjust her portfolio very easily, making it more conservative by simply reducing her stock exposure and adding a little more money to bonds.

Now, let's look at the case of Darin Zimmerman, age 30, who plans to retire at age 60. So far, he has accumulated $50,000 in his company's 401(k) plan. Because retirement is far into the future, his primary goal is to see his money grow. He has a regular paycheck and doesn't require income from his investment portfolio. Choosing to use the income-needs allocation approach, he allocates his portfolio as shown in Figure 6.

Figure 6

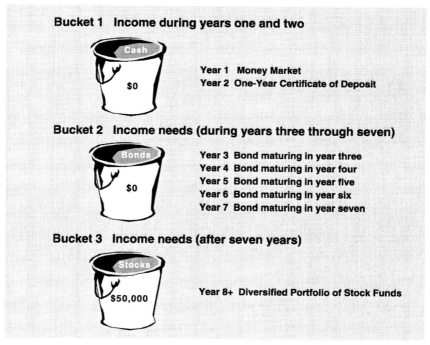

Bucket 1 Income during years one and two

$0

Year 1 Money Market
Year 2 One-Year Certificate of Deposit

Bucket 2 Income needs (during years three through seven)

$0

Year 3 Bond maturing in year three
Year 4 Bond maturing in year four
Year 5 Bond maturing in year five
Year 6 Bond maturing in year six
Year 7 Bond maturing in year seven

Bucket 3 Income needs (after seven years)

$50,000

Year 8+ Diversified Portfolio of Stock Funds

As you can see, Darin has allocated 100 percent of his portfolio to stocks. This approach is much more aggressive than the age-based strategy, which would have allocated just 80 percent of Darin's money to the stock market. Darin eschews the age-based approach because his priority is growth rather than income.

Risk-Tolerance Allocation Method

How much volatility can you endure? That's the central question in the risk-tolerance allocation method.

Many investors are overconfident and choose an investment mix because they like the high potential rate of return. They often fail to consider, however, the potential downside. When the markets go south, these investors frequently run for the hills, selling their most volatile investments at the worst possible time, losing sight of their long-term objectives. Obviously, selling is not a wise option when investments are down in value. By simply examining the potential downside of your asset-allocation mix *before* initiating your investment strategy, you can avoid unfortunate decisions down the line.

The average rate of return for different mixes of stocks, bonds, and cash from 1926 through 2002, is illustrated in Figure 7. The chart also outlines how often each portfolio lost money and the magnitude of the average loss. Most importantly, it shows the worst-case scenario for each mix.

Determining your asset allocation using this method is simple and involves a question only you can answer: "What is my breaking point?" Determine how far your portfolio can drop before you decide you want out. If your portfolio starts at $100,000, and market losses take it down to $90,000, $80,000, or even $70,000, at what point do you begin losing sleep at night?

Locate the Largest Loss column in Figure 7, and review the worst-case scenarios for the different asset-allocation models. How much downside can you tolerate? For example, if you could handle a 25 percent loss in the worst-case scenario — without modifying your investment strategy — then a mix of 50 to 60 percent stocks would be suitable for you. Although you may never see the worst-case scenario occur, this method of asset-allocation prepares you in advance for the downturns that may occur in the markets.

Target-Rate-of-Return Allocation Method

What annual rate of return is required for you to reach your retirement goals? Once you've determined that rate by developing a retirement plan, you can also use Figure 7 to determine an appropriate

Figure 7

Asset Allocation - Risk & Reward
Annual Returns (1926 - 2002)

Portfolio	Average Return	Largest Annual Gain	Largest Annual Loss	Positive Years	Negative Years
90% Stocks 0% Bonds 10% Cash	11.36%	48.62%	-38.90%	53	23
80% Stocks 10% Bonds 10% Cash	10.70%	43.40%	-34.79%	54	22
70% Stocks 20% Bonds 10% Cash	10.04%	38.19%	-30.69%	57	19
60% Stocks 30% Bonds 10% Cash	9.78%	32.97%	-26.59%	57	19
50% Stocks 40% Bonds 10% Cash	8.72%	27.76%	-22.49%	58	18
40% Stocks 50% Bonds 10% Cash	8.06%	24.17%	-18.39%	60	16
30% Stocks 60% Bonds 10% Cash	7.40%	24.94%	-14.29%	63	13
20% Stocks 70% Bonds 10% Cash	6.74%	25.70%	-10.18%	67	9
10% Stocks 80% Bonds 10% Cash	6.02%	26.47%	-6.08%	71	5
0% Stocks 90% Bonds 10% Cash	5.13%	27.24%	-4.24%	68	8

Ibbotson Associates. Stocks-S&P Index, Bonds-U.S. Inter. Term Govt. Bonds, Cash- 30 Day Treasury Bill

asset-allocation mix. This will help you create a portfolio that has historically produced the rate of return you've targeted. If, for example, you've determined that you need an 8 percent annual return on your investments, then your portfolio should consist of at least 40 percent stocks, 50 percent bonds, and 10 percent cash according to historical market returns from 1926 to 2002 (see the Average Return column in Figure 7).

Combining All Four Allocation Methods

Each of these asset-allocation methodologies — age, income needs, risk tolerance, and target rate of return — is useful. In your allocation strategy, you can follow one of these methods alone or blend them together. One way to determine which allocation strategy you should use is to complete an investment questionnaire like the one that follows.

These questions are a sampling of those that most financial advisors will ask their clients before making asset-allocation recommendations. Your answers will help you select the most appropriate asset-allocation model for your goals and circumstances. Corresponding points are listed next to each question. After you finish the questionnaire, you'll total the points of the answers you selected to determine which mix of stocks, bonds and cash fits you.

Asset-Allocation Questionnaire

Investment Objective

1.   What is your primary purpose for investing?

    A.   Preserve investment capital (2)

    B.   Emphasis on current income (4)

    C.   Emphasis on income with some growth (6)

    D.   Emphasis on growth with some income (8)

    E.   Maximum growth (10)

Time Horizon

2.   When do you plan on spending the money you are investing?

    A.   0-2 Years (2)

    B.   3-7 Years (4)

    C.   8-15 Years (6)

    D.   16+ Years (10)

Risk Tolerance

3. Which statement best describes your feelings about risk?

    A. I am willing to take a lot of risk to obtain maximum growth. (8)

    B. I am willing to take some risk to obtain moderate growth. (6)

    C. I am willing to take a little risk realizing that my potential for growth will be less. (4)

    D. I am not willing to risk my investment principal. (2)

4. I can endure periods of principal erosion and volatility if my portfolio has potential for high returns.

    A. Strongly Agree (10)

    B. Agree (8)

    C. Somewhat Agree (6)

    D. Somewhat Disagree (4)

    E. Disagree (2)

5. Review the risk and returns of the following hypothetical investment portfolios. Choose the portfolio that most accurately reflects your long-term return requirements and risk tolerance.

		Average Year	Worst Year	Best Year	
A.	Portfolio A	12%	-27%	53%	(10)
B.	Portfolio B	10%	-17%	36%	(8)
C.	Portfolio C	9%	-11%	26%	(6)
D.	Portfolio D	7%	-3%	25%	(4)
E.	Portfolio E	6%	-2%	12%	(2)

6.   What would your reaction be to a 15 percent drop in the value of your investment portfolio?

   A.   I would consider this an opportunity to buy more investments at lower prices. (8)

   B.   I am investing for the long term. I would not alter my strategy if the market fell 15 percent. (6)

   C.   This would make me very anxious. I would consider repositioning my portfolio more conservatively in attempts to cut any further losses. (4)

   D.   I would sell my volatile investments. (2)

Scoring

   After answering each of these six questions add up the numbers found at the end of each of your answers. Then find the portfolio below that corresponds with your score.

Scoring Point Range	Portfolio	Percent of Portfolio to Invest in Stocks
12 to 21	Conservative	0-25%
22 to 30	Conservative to Moderate	25-50%
31 to 40	Moderate	50-70%
41 to 50	Moderate to Aggressive	70-85%
51 to 56	Aggressive	85-100%

   Review Figure 7 again, and locate the portfolio that consists of stock exposure that most closely fits your score. Figure 7 will also help set your expectations for your target portfolio.

Don't Forget Emergency Reserves

   In addition to investing to cover your long-term income needs, you also need to allocate some of your money to an emergency fund. When you need a new furnace, the roof begins to leak, or your car breaks down, you'll need sufficient money to cope with the problem without having to disrupt your long-term investment strategy. As a general guideline, you should have three to six months worth of living expenses set aside. For example, if you need $5,000 each month to cover your expenses, your reserve fund should contain between $15,000 and $30,000.

Most of your reserves should be placed in cash investments, so you can withdraw the money immediately. Depending on how comfortable you are with risk, a portion could also be invested in stocks and bonds in a non-retirement investment account. Stocks and bonds can be sold and turned into cash within three business days. As a general guideline, the older you are, the more money you want to have in cash and bonds and the less in stocks.

Conclusion

Step 1 of the investment process, as outlined in this chapter, was designed to help you see the importance of having a wise asset-allocation policy; the different methods of asset allocation discussed here will help you determine how much of your money should be allocated to stocks, bonds, and cash. Allocating your portfolio properly can help you develop a successful investment strategy that will aid in the overall strength of your retirement plan. Don't bypass the most important step of the investment planning process.

 Asset Allocator: www.javacalc.com has an easy-to-use asset allocation calculator.

Step 2 of the investment process, which is covered over the next three chapters, will help you understand the reasons for diversifying your portfolio within each asset class, the various components of a diversified portfolio, and how various portfolios have performed in the past.

TEN

Investment Consistency

✓ RETIREMENT DECISION #10: *How should I diversify my investment portfolio?*

Even the most casual baseball fan knows that a winning team doesn't put all nine of its players in the same position. How good would the New York Yankees be if most of the players stood in left field?

Figure 1

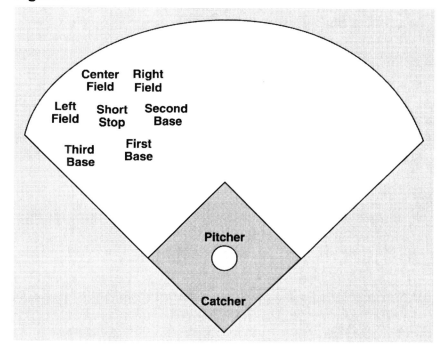

There's an obvious reason why coaches position their players all over the field: They have no way of knowing where the batter will hit the ball. With some players in the infield and some in the outfield, there is a good chance, as shown in Figure 2, of having someone in the right place to field the ball.

Figure 2

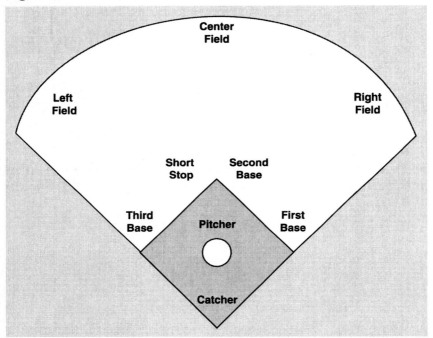

Step 2 of the investment process is determining how to diversify your portfolio. The stock and bond markets are much like a batter in a baseball game. When the "market" steps up to the plate, nobody knows exactly where the ball is going to fly. Will the markets go up or down? Will interest rates rise or fall? Will the economy see expansion or recession? Will there be tax reforms? Will the nation experience a change in leadership? Will there be inflation? What will foreign economies do?

There is no way of knowing the answers to these questions with absolute certainty. You can try to project the future, but you can't guarantee an accurate prediction. However, if you have properly covered the field with your investments, you will be able to take advantage of market conditions, whatever they may be. It is crucial that you are properly diversified so that no matter what occurs in the market, some of your investments do well.

Did this hold true even during the bleak bear market of 2000, 2001 and 2002? Did some investments actually do well? If your portfolio was properly diversified, then yes, you would have seen growth in many of your investments even during some of the worst stock market conditions in decades.

During the 2000 – 2002 bear market, large-company U.S. stocks, as measured by the S& P 500 Index, were down 9 percent in 2000, 12 percent in 2001, and 22 percent in 2002, respectively. More aggressive U.S. companies, as measured by the Nasdaq Index, fell 39 percent, 21 percent, and 32 percent, respectively.

If you were diversified and owned bonds and value stocks in your portfolio during these three difficult years, you may have made money when everyone else was losing money. For example, mid-cap value stocks rose 30 percent in 2000.[1] In 2001, small-company value stocks gained 20 percent[2], and in 2002, while most sectors of the stock market lost money, international bonds made 22 percent[3], and long-term government bonds rose 17 percent.[4] It's true that if you were diversified some pieces of your portfolio likely struggled during this period. If you were properly diversified, however, many of your investments did well and greatly softened the blow of the biggest stock market downturn since the 1970s.

Although baseball managers would never consider the thought of positioning all their players in left field, many investors make this very mistake. Too often, investment portfolios are positioned like the team in Figure 1. This was certainly the case in 2000 and 2001. Many investors accumulated a long list of hot-performing investments in 1998 and 1999, only to find out that every investment they owned was concentrated in one or two asset classes, typically large and mid-sized company growth stocks. Many technology stocks fell into these categories. This strategy worked fine in 1998 and 1999, when the market routinely enjoyed good performance, whacking the ball to these two areas of the growth market. However, in 2000 and 2001, the market changed directions and hit the ball the other way, to value stocks and bonds. Investors who didn't own value stocks and bonds experienced dramatic losses.

Many investors get confused about what it means to be properly diversified, falsely believing that diversification can be achieved by owning 10 different stocks or mutual funds. This, however, doesn't guarantee true diversification. For example, it is possible to own 10 mutual funds and still end up with a portfolio that looks like the baseball team in Figure 1. How? If each of your funds buys high-tech growth stocks, you are not diversified. If high tech does well, you'll feel like you hit a home run; if it does poorly, your portfolio strikes out. Many technology-fund investors were ecstatic in 1999 when the average technology fund rose 128 percent. A $10,000 investment made on Jan. 1, 1999, in the average tech fund grew to more than $22,800 by year-end; that would definitely be considered a grand slam home run. However, in 2000, 2001, and 2002, this sector of the market plummeted back to earth, losing 32 percent, 36 percent, and 43 percent, respectively.[5] The portfolio that grew so quickly to $22,800 nose-dived below the original amount invested, finishing at $5,656. This inconsistent performance and high volatility often lead investors to make frequent portfolio changes and ultimately earn poor returns.

There are three major reasons why diversification is so important to successful long-term investing.

1)   Diversification lowers portfolio risk by reducing volatility.
2)   Diversification protects the overall portfolio from one or two poor performing investments.
3)   Diversification provides investors with more consistent returns and helps them stay invested for the long term.

Diversification allows investors to purchase investments that alone may be very volatile, but when combined with other investments actually reduces the volatility of the portfolio as a whole. *In essence, diversification is a way of covering the entire field to make sure all of those hits get caught.*

Lowering Portfolio Risk By Reducing Volatility

Compare the two hypothetical investments in Figures 3 and 4. Assuming the two investments experience the ups and downs depicted in the charts, and over time, both provide an average annual return of 10 percent, which would you choose? As you can see, regardless which investment you select, an investment of $100,000 would grow to $259,274. Notice, that although the average return for each investment is identical over the long run, Investment A and Investment B experienced ups and downs at different times.

Figure 3

Figure 4

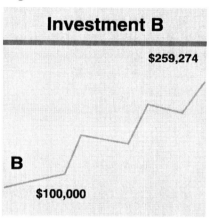

Now let's say that you split your $100,000 investment equally between Investment A and B (see Figure 5). Your $100,000 would still grow to $259,274 in 10 years. However, from year to year, your performance would be much more consistent. In fact, in this example, your portfolio would never encounter a down year. In years when one investment does poorly, the other picks up the slack. In other words, when one investment is "zigging" the other is "zagging." The key to develop-

Figure 5

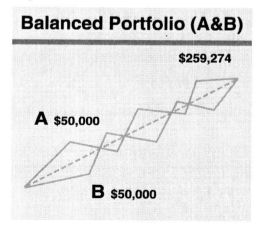

ing a portfolio that reduces volatility is to buy investments that complement each other as Investment A and B do in Figure 5. Proper diversification will reduce portfolio volatility.

Protecting Your Portfolio from the Risk of a Bad Investment Choice

Have you ever made a really bad investment? One or two bad investment decisions could dramatically reduce the returns of your overall portfolio. Diversification will protect you from this possibility.

Twenty years ago, Edward Brantley rolled $100,000 into his IRA and decided to diversify into five investments equally. Unfortunately, Edward made a couple of poor investment choices. Figure 6 shows his results.

Figure 6

Five $20,000 Investments

Value After 20 Years

Investment #1: $20,000 lost 100%	$0
Investment #2: $20,000 broke even	$20,000
Investment #3: $20,000 gained 5% per year	$53,066
Investment #4: $20,000 gained 10% per year	$134,550
Investment #5: $20,000 gained 15% per year	$327,330
Total Initial Investment	$100,000
Total After 20 Years	$534,946
Compounded Annual Rate of Return	8.74%

Although Edward's team didn't have a perfect game, they still won. His portfolio still produced a respectable 8.74 percent annual return, even though three of the five investments performed very poorly.

Edward could have taken a big chance, invested all of his money in just one or two of these investments and hoped for great returns. If he guessed right, he'd have ended up with an average annual return of 10 to 15 percent; if he guessed wrong, however, he would have been stuck with a meager growth rate of 5 percent or less.

Diversification protected Edward from the risk of having a majority of his assets in losing investments. If he had placed all his money in poorest-performing investment, his portfolio at retirement, instead of being valued at $534,946, could have been worthless.

Poor diversification often occurs with investors who have their money invested too heavily in their company's stock. There are far too many examples of people losing their nest egg because they bet too heavily on their employer's stock. (Handling company stock will be discussed in Chapter 13.) Diversification can protect your nest egg from this disastrous possibility.

Let's take a look at an example. Linda Monson retired from her company in 1999. At retirement, she had more than $1 million invested in her former employer's stock. In the past, the stock had generated huge profits, helping Linda accumulate a substantial sum for retirement. At retirement, she had to choose between leaving the shares alone in hopes of similar returns in the future, or selling some or all of the shares in order to diversify her portfolio. She made the decision to sell the stock and diversify, realizing that a drop in her employer's stock could keep her from accomplishing her retirement goals.

Linda's decision was a good one. Shortly after retirement, the market went south and her company's stock dropped from a high of $49 per share in 1999 to $1 per share in 2002, a price drop of 98 percent.[6] Had she stayed invested in the stock, her $1 million nest egg would have fallen to $20,000. Although it's true that the diversified portfolio of investments she chose to replace her company stock suffered a 15 percent drop during this same period, this loss won't stop her from accomplishing her retirement goals. In fact, the 15 percent loss was quickly recovered in 2003. A 98 percent loss, however, would have required growth of an impossible 4,900 percent for her to break even.

If your portfolio loses 20 percent of its value, how much does it need to earn to get back to even? It seems logical that 20 percent of growth would offset a 20 percent loss; this is not the case. If a $100,000 portfolio dropped 20 percent to $80,000, it would require a 25 percent gain to get back to $100,000. If the same portfolio dropped 50 percent to $50,000, it would require a 100 percent return to climb back up to $100,000.

Importance of Performance Consistency

How important is performance consistency? We can best deter-mine that by studying the examples of Grant Monson and Ann Schilling, two people who each have $100,000 to invest. After reviewing the re-turns each achieved in Figures 7 and 8, who do you believe will accumu-late the most money over the five-year period?

Figure 7

Performance Results For Grant

Year 1	20%
Year 2	40%
Year 3	20%
Year 4	-50%
Year 5	40%
Five-Year Average Annual Return	14%

Profile of Investor One: Grant

Grant is an aggressive in-vestor whose goal is to take ad-vantage of the big moves in the market. All of Grant's money is concentrated in one sector of the stock market. Consequently, he experiences very high "highs" and very low "lows." Figure 7 illustrates his results over the past five years.

Figure 8

Performance Results For Ann

Year 1	9%
Year 2	9%
Year 3	9%
Year 4	9%
Year 5	9%
Five-Year Average Annual Return	9%

Profile of Investor Two: Ann

Ann is a moderate inves-tor whose goal is to obtain good, consistent returns. She has split her money into two different in-vestments. Each investment moves in a typical cycle of ups and downs. The two invest-ments, however, have a zig-zag relationship. When one is zigging, the other is zagging. The result is consistent performance. Her diversified portfolio does not produce returns as high as Grant's, but it doesn't drop as low as his does either. Figure 8 illustrates Ann's results.

Who experienced better performance, Grant or Ann? Whose results would you rather have? Not only did Ann's portfolio perform much better (see the results in Figure 9), but her portfolio was also far less volatile than Grant's. One also can't help but wonder how many bad decisions Grant made due to the additional volatility in his quest to capture the big moves. Higher returns coupled with lower risk are the magic combination that every investor should seek. This can often be accomplished with proper diversification. Remember consistency is the key.

It is also interesting that Grant's average annual return was 14 percent, compared to Ann's 9 percent (add up the returns for each year and divide by five). Ann's actual *compounded* annual rate of return was 2 percentage points higher than Grant's. Be careful not to be misled by *average* annual rates of return.

Figure 9

Initial Investment of $100,000

Year	Investor: Ann		Investor: Grant	
	% Change	Dollar Value	% Change	Dollar Value
1	9%	$109,000	20%	$120,000
2	9%	$118,810	40%	$168,000
3	9%	$129,502	20%	$201,600
4	9%	$141,158	-50%	$100,800
5	9%	$153,863	40%	$141,120

In this chapter, we have discussed the vital importance of having a properly diversified portfolio. The goal is to invest so that no matter what occurs in the market, some of your investments will perform well. As we continue our discussion of Step 2 of the investment process in the following chapter, the various components of a well-diversified portfolio will be outlined.

ELEVEN

Know Your Team

✓ RETIREMENT DECISION #10 (continued): *How should I diversify my investment portfolio?*

Many years ago, I played Little League baseball. We practiced every day and our coach became very familiar with our individual talents and abilities. Because my coach knew his players well and what to expect from each of us, he was able to position each player on the field according to his talents, giving us the best chance at winning games.

By the end of this chapter, you will know how to manage your retirement portfolio in the same manner my Little League coach ran our team. To build a sound retirement portfolio (your team of investments), you need to properly diversify. It is important to understand each asset class and how each has performed historically in relation to the others. Once you understand each investment's pluses and minuses, you will be better equipped to position them to your portfolio's advantage.

Figure 1 illustrates the components of a well-diversified investment portfolio. Remember that, like the fielders on a baseball team, each asset class covers a different part of the market field. You want to be in position to take advantage of favorable market conditions, wherever they may be. Therefore, some of your money should be invested in each asset class.

However, what do we mean when we say "small and mid-cap growth," "large-cap value," and "government bonds"? What attributes do these different styles of stocks and bonds have? How has each asset class traditionally performed during bull and bear markets? How will rising interest rates affect bond funds? Learning the answers to these types of questions will make you better equipped to manage your retirement portfolio. Let's begin by talking about stocks, then, we'll cover bonds and cash.

Figure 1

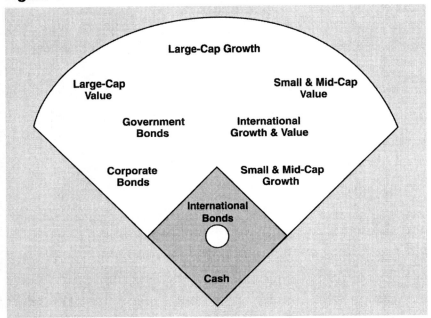

Stocks

Stock Size

Stocks are categorized as large, mid-sized, or small based on their market capitalization. Market capitalization is simply the price of a stock multiplied by the number of outstanding shares. For example, a stock that is priced at $50 per share with 100 million shares outstanding has a market capitalization of $5 billion, which makes it a mid-cap stock. Here's what you should know about each stock size.

Large U.S. Stocks

Large-cap U.S. stocks are usually defined as companies with market capitalizations of more than $10 billion. The market capitalization for the average large-cap U.S. stock mutual fund is $31 billion. The largest U.S. company stocks with their respective market capitalizations are listed in Figure 2.

Figure 2

Largest U.S. Company Stocks

Company Name	Ticker	Industry	Market Cap
General Electric	GE	Electric Equipment	$354 Billion
ExxonMobil	XOM	Oil/Gas	$314 Billion
Microsoft	MSFT	Business Applications	$300 Billion
Pfizer	PFE	Drugs	$231 Billion
Citigroup	C	International Banks	$229 Billion
Wal-Mart Stores	WMT	Discount Stores	$227 Billion
American International Group	AIG	Insurance (Property)	$177 Billion
IBM	IBM	Computer Equipment	$144 Billion
Intel	INTC	Semiconductors	$129 Billion
Cisco Systems	CSCO	Data Networking	$123 Billion

Source: Morningstar Principia Pro, December 31, 2003

Mid-Cap U.S. Stocks

Mid-cap U.S. stocks are defined as companies with market capitalizations usually between $1.5 billion and $10 billion. The market capitalization for the average mid-cap U.S. stock fund is $4 billion. Examples of mid-cap U.S. stocks with their respective market caps are listed in Figure 3.

Small U.S. Stocks

Small-cap U.S. stocks are defined as companies with market capitalizations below $1.5 billion. The market capitalization for the average small-cap U.S. stock fund is $894 million. Examples of small-cap U.S. company stocks with their respective market caps are shown in Figure 4.

Which market cap has provided the best returns? Over the long run, small- and mid-cap stocks have outperformed large-cap stocks. From 1926 through 2003, small-company stocks had an average annual return of 12.7 percent, while large-company stocks returned 10.4 percent.[1] Large companies tend to hold up better in market downturns because of their financial strength and stability. Although small and mid sized company stocks offer more potential growth, they also possess more potential for loss — to obtain higher returns, you must be willing to endure more risk.

Figure 3

Mid-Cap U.S. Stocks

Company Name	Ticker	Industry	Market Cap
H & R Block	HRB	Personal Services	$9.9 Billion
Archer Daniels Midland	ADM	Agriculture	$9.8 Billion
Unocal	UCL	Oil/Gas	$9.5 Billion
Pitney Bowes	PBI	Office Equipment	$9.5 Billion
Limited Brands	LTD	Clothing Stores	$9.3 Billion
Adobe Systems	ADBE	Development Tools	$9.1 Billion
Estee Lauder	EL	Household/Personal Prod	$8.9 Billion
Mattel	MAT	Toys/Hobbies	$8.2 Billion
Apple Computer	AAPL	Computer Equipment	$7.8 Billion
Washington Post	WPO	Media Conglomerates	$7.5 Billion

Source: Morningstar Principia Pro, December 31, 2003

Figure 4

Small-Cap U.S. Stocks

Company Name	Ticker	Industry	Market Cap
Gateway	GTW	Computer Equipment	$1.5 Billion
MONY Group	MNY	Insurance (Life)	$1.5 Billion
Reader's Digest Association	RDA	Publishing	$1.4 Billion
Goodyear Tire & Rubber	GT	Rubber Products	$1.4 Billion
Dillard's	DDS	Department Stores	$1.4 Billion
Tommy Hilfiger	TOM	Apparel Makers	$1.3 Billion
Callaway Golf	ELY	Recreation	$1.3 Billion
Pep Boys	PBY	Auto Retail	$1.2 Billion
Sylvan Learning Systems	SLVN	Education	$1.2 Billion

Source: Morningstar Principia Pro, December 31, 2003

Figure 5 shows the performance of large-, mid-, and small-cap stocks for the past one-, three-, five-, 10-, and 15-year periods (ending December 2003). Mid-cap stocks were the best performing asset for the past 10 and 15 years, while small-cap stocks led the way during the past one, three, and five years.

Figure 5

Asset Class	1-Year Average Return	3-Year Average Return	5-Year Average Return	10-Year Average Return	15-Year Average Return
Large-Cap Stocks	28.7%	-4.1%	-0.6%	11.1%	12.2%
Mid-Cap Stocks	35.6%	4.8%	9.2%	13.9%	15.8%
Small-Cap Stocks	38.8%	8.1%	9.7%	11.4%	12.0%

Wilshire market indexes were used to measure each asset class.
Source: Morningstar Principia Pro, December 31, 2003

While smaller stocks have provided higher returns than larger stocks over the long term, don't be fooled into thinking this is a consistent rule. During some periods, large caps have outperformed their small- and mid-cap counterparts. The main point here is that there are no hard and fast rules to indicate which size will perform best in the future. Therefore, it is important to diversify your portfolio and own an array of large-, mid-, and small-cap stocks.

 Half of all households own stock either directly or indirectly through mutual funds.[1a]

Investment Styles — Growth and Value

A stock's market-cap size is an important tool to use when determining how diversified your portfolio is, but you need to drill down deeper. After all, not all large-company stocks perform exactly the same way. We can further categorize stocks, whether they are large, mid sized, or small, based on their investment "style," or how fast the companies that issue the stocks are growing. A stock can be classified as either growth or value. This is an important distinction because growth and value stocks have a lead and lag relationship over time (see Figure 6). If your portfolio contains both types of stocks, you can reduce your overall portfolio risk and volatility.

Figure 6

And The Winner Is . . .

Year	Growth	Value	Winning Style
1979	15.72%	23.16%	Value
1980	39.40%	23.59%	Growth
1981	-9.81%	0.02%	Value
1982	22.03%	21.04%	Growth
1983	16.24%	28.89%	Value
1984	2.33%	10.52%	Value
1985	33.31%	29.68%	Growth
1986	14.50%	21.67%	Value
1987	6.50%	3.68%	Growth
1988	11.95%	21.67%	Value
1989	36.40%	26.13%	Growth
1990	0.20%	-6.85%	Growth
1991	38.37%	22.56%	Growth
1992	5.07%	10.53%	Value
1993	1.68%	18.60%	Value
1994	3.13%	-0.63%	Growth
1995	38.13%	37.00%	Growth
1996	23.98%	21.99%	Growth
1997	36.38%	29.99%	Growth
1998	42.15%	14.68%	Growth
1999	28.25%	12.72%	Growth
2000	-22.08%	6.08%	Value
2001	-12.72%	-11.71%	Value
2002	-23.59%	-20.85%	Value
2003	25.66%	31.79%	Value

Source: S&P 500 Barra Growth Index and S&P 500 Barra Value Index

Growth Stocks

Buying a growth stock is similar to shopping at a trendy store and purchasing fashions that are in *vogue*. Because these items are in such high demand, you will be required to pay "up" for them — maybe even more than they are worth.

Growth stocks are typically in high demand due to their high earnings growth rates and their tendency to outperform the market when the economy is strong and robust. Because of investor demand, prices of growth stocks are often bid up to astronomical levels, as occurred in 1998 and 1999. Growth investors buy high in hopes that the company's earnings momentum will carry the price even higher. When the stock market falters, growth stocks tend to fall harder than their value stock equivalents. Conversely, in strong bull markets growth stocks usually outperform value stocks. For example, the American Century Ultra Fund, one of the most popular U.S. large-cap growth funds, posted a 40.75 percent return during its best three-month period and a dismal –22.86 percent during its worst three-month stretch of the past 10 years. By comparison, the Dodge and Cox Stock Fund, one of the most popular U.S. large-cap value funds, finished its best three-month period up 20.13 percent and its worst three months at –17.92 percent.[3] Another thing to know about growth stocks is that they typically pay no or low dividends.

According to a NASD financial literacy survey, only 14 percent of Americans can tell the difference between a growth and a value stock, while 63 percent of Americans know the difference between a halfback and a quarterback.[2]

Value Stocks

Like buying growth stocks, buying value stocks is similar to shopping at your favorite store. In this case, though, instead of buying the high-priced, trendy items, you're sifting through the discount racks and purchasing only items that are marked down. Value companies are considered "on sale" in the stock market because they have temporarily fallen out of favor and sell for less than their true value. Their prices are low because of their relative standing in categories like earnings, book values, and sales. These companies are often located in industries that have fallen out of favor or have profitability or management problems. Investors who buy value stocks buy low, patiently wait, and hope the company rebounds. Because value stocks are already trading at low prices, there is less room to fall if the stock market turns sour. Also, value companies usually pay dividends.

Distinguishing Between the Two

There are many technical measurements to help investors distinguish between growth and value stocks, the most common being the price to earnings ratio (P/E). A company's P/E ratio is determined by dividing its stock price (the "P") by the previous 12 month's earnings per share (the "E"). The P/E ratio measures how much investors are willing to pay for each dollar of the company's profit.

Other characteristics to look for are price/sales ratios and price/book ratios. The higher these ratios, the more growth oriented they are. You can also use these ratios when comparing mutual funds. Funds list their portfolio's average P/E, price/sales, and price/book ratios. These figures are used to categorize a fund as growth or value. The average large-company growth and large-company value mutual funds had the following technical measurements (Figure 7). The dividends that mutual funds pay are measured by yield.

Figure 7

Comparing Growth and Value

Technical Measure of the Average Large Company Growth & Value Mutual Fund							
	Price-to-Earnings Ratio	Price-to-Cash Flow Ratio	Price-to-Book Ratio	Yield	Volatility Standard Deviation	Total Return Best Year	Total Return Worst Year
Large-Cap Growth Fund	24	11	4	0%	21%	39%	-28%
Large-Cap Value Fund	15	6	2	1%	16%	31%	-17%

Morningstar Principia, 12/31/04

Figure 8 shows specific examples of large-company growth and value stocks and their P/Es and yields.

Which Style is Better?

Although the performance for growth and value stocks varies dramatically from year to year, over the long run they have provided about the same returns.

A $10,000 investment in large-company growth stocks made on

Figure 8

Growth Stocks			Value Stocks		
Company	**P/E**	**Yield**	**Company**	**P/E**	**Yield**
Microsoft	33	0.60%	Exxon	15	2.30%
Walmart	26	0.80%	Citigroup	13	3.20%
Intel	29	0.40%	Bank of America	12	3.80%
Coca-Cola	27	1.90%	SBC Communications	15	4.90%
Dell	36	0%	Wachovia	13	3.40%
Cisco Systems	39	0%	BellSouth	12	3.70%
06/30/2004					

Dec. 31, 1978, grew to $265,936 by the end of 2000.[4] Similarly, a $10,000 investment made into large-company value stocks[5] over the same period grew to $287,167. The average compounded rate of return of *growth* stocks was 16.08 percent, while *value* stocks grew at 16.48 percent. Although the investment performance was about the same, growth stocks experienced more volatility than value stocks.

There is no crystal ball to predict exactly when growth stocks will be in favor and value stocks out of favor. Rather than making futile attempts at guessing, it is better to have a portfolio balanced between both styles. This is referred to as "style neutral." A well-diversified stock portfolio will be balanced between growth and value stocks and include large-, mid-, and small-cap U.S. stocks, as well as international stocks.

Let's compare two hypothetical investors to examine how growth and value stocks can complement each other and reduce volatility.

On Jan. 1, 1990, Gene Howard put all his eggs into one basket and invested $100,000 into large-company growth stocks. By the end of 2003, 14 years later, Gene's $100,000 had grown in value to $379,095, an average compounded rate of return of about 10 percent (see Figure 9). That doesn't sound too bad, does it? However, notice the extreme volatility Gene experienced when the markets fell in 2000, 2001, and 2002. He watched his portfolio drop from a high mark of $674,833 at the end of 1999 to $302,430 at the end of 2002. That represents a loss of $372,404, or 55 percent. While large-company growth stocks were the single best performing asset class from 1990 to 1999, they were the single worst investment from 2000 to 2002.[6] Not many investors could sustain such dramatic losses and stick to their long-term investment strategy. Many investors, shaken by market downturns, sell when the market is near the bottom, and they don't return until the market has bounced back. Sound familiar? It's called buying high and selling low.

Figure 9

Gene Howard's Portfolio:
100% Large-Cap Growth Stocks

Annual Portfolio Performance		
Year	Annual Return	Growth of $100,000.00
1990	0.34%	$100,340.00
1991	46.62%	$147,118.00
1992	4.48%	$153,709.00
1993	3.26%	$158,720.00
1994	1.69%	$161,402.00
1995	34.10%	$216,441.00
1996	22.46%	$265,053.00
1997	32.78%	$351,938.00
1998	42.32%	$500,878.00
1999	34.73%	$674,833.00
2000	-24.99%	$506,192.00
2001	-20.36%	$403,131.00
2002	-24.98%	$302,429.00
2003	25.35%	$379,095.00
Portfolio Performance (1990-2003)		
Average Annual Rate of Return		12.70%
Average Compounded Rate of Return		9.99%
Best Year		46.62%
Worst Year		-24.99%
Number of years positive		11
Number of years negative		3

Source: Wilshire Large-Cap Growth Index

Now let's look at our second hypothetical investor, Renee William, who followed a different strategy than Gene during the same time frame.

Renee invested 50 percent of her money into large-company growth stocks and 50 percent into large-company value stocks. Her portfolios performed better than Gene's, and she experienced much less volatility (see Figure 10). Her balanced growth and value portfolio dropped from its high water mark of $546,946 at the end of 1999 to $324,179 at the end of 2003—a loss of $222,767, or 40.73 percent, compared with the 55 percent drop in Gene's growth portfolio. Which investor is more

Figure 10

Renee's Blended Portfolio:
Large-Cap U.S. Growth Stocks   50%
Large-Cap U.S. Value Stocks   50%

Annual Portfolio Performance

Year	Annual Return	Growth of $100,000.00
1990	-3.63%	$96,375.00
1991	36.13%	$131,195.00
1992	7.81%	$141,441.00
1993	10.11%	$155,734.00
1994	0.45%	$156,427.00
1995	37.65%	$215,314.00
1996	22.19%	$263,092.00
1997	33.02%	$349,965.00
1998	28.63%	$450,161.00
1999	21.50%	$546,945.00
2000	-11.95%	$481,585.00
2001	-14.27%	$412,887.00
2002	-21.49%	$324,178.00
2003	28.52%	$416,618.00

Portfolio Performance (1990-2003)

Average Annual Rate of Return	12.48%
Average Compounded Rate of Return	10.73%
Best Year	37.65%
Worst Year	-21.49%
Number of years positive	10
Number of years negative	4

Source: Wilshire Large-Cap Growth Index & Wilshire Large-Cap Value Index likely to adhere to their investment strategy? Chances are it will be Renee, who had comparably more stability.

International Investing

International stocks are also a key ingredient of a well-diversi-fied portfolio, but investors too often overlook their benefits. Most port-folios should contain international exposure of between 5 and 20 percent. There are several important reasons not to overlook the international component of your portfolio.

International Investing Adds More Diversification

An extra layer of diversification can reduce your portfolio's vola-tility and increase your returns. International stocks, like the different styles of U.S. stocks discussed earlier in this chapter, go through cycles of ups and downs. If international stocks are doing well and the U.S. market is struggling, the international portion of your portfolio will help offset the U.S. downturn and lower your portfolio's volatility. In other words, international stocks provide another potential "zigging" investment when other parts of your portfolio may be "zagging."

We've seen this principle played out over the past 30 years. In the 1970s and 1980s, the foreign stock markets outperformed the U.S. market. By owning international stocks during those two decades, you would have increased your portfolio returns. However, in the 1990s, the investment winds changed, as they often do, and the U.S. market domi-nated the global equities marketplace (see Figure 11).

Again, because there is no way of knowing exactly when one market will take off and another will falter, it is simply best to buy and hold both U.S.-and foreign-based assets. You will enjoy more consistent long-term performance by diversifying rather than trying to supercharge your performance through attempts to be in the hottest market at just the right time.

A Foreign Market Will Outperform the U.S. Market

Virtually every year, the U.S. stock market is surpassed in per-formance by a foreign market. In fact, take a guess at how many times during the last 18 years the U.S. stock market was the best performing

Figure 11

U.S. Versus International Stocks

1970-1979 (10 years)	Cumulative Return
U.S. Market (S&P 500)	77%
Major International Markets (EAFE)	162%
1980-1989 (10 years)	Cumulative Return
U.S. Market (S&P 500)	400%
Major International Markets (EAFE)	678%
1/1/1990-12/31/2000 (11 years)	Cumulative Return
U.S. Market (S&P 500)	424%
Major International Market (EAFE)	89%

Figure 12

The Best Performing Markets in the World
1983-2003

Year	Market	Return	U.S. Market Return
1983	Australia	56%	23%
1984	Hong Kong	47%	3%
1985	Germany	137%	32%
1986	Japan	100%	17%
1987	Japan	43%	2%
1988	France	39%	18%
1989	Germany	47%	29%
1990	United Kingdom	10%	-5%
1991	Hong Kong	50%	34%
1992	Hong Kong	32%	10%
1993	Hong Kong	117%	11%
1994	Finland	52%	.2%
1995	Switzerland	44%	37%
1996	Spain	40%	22%
1997	Portugal	47%	32%
1998	Finland	122%	24%
1999	Finland	153%	21%
2000	Switzerland	6%	-8%
2001	New Zealand	10%	-12%
2002	New Zealand	26%	-23%
2003	Greece	70%	29%

Source: Return Represented by MSCI Country Index

market in the world. The answer, surprisingly, is zero. The United States did happen to finish in second place twice during the past 18 years (1995 and 1997). Figure 12 shows the top performing markets each year from 1983 through 2003. The lesson is clear: by participating in international markets, you can potentially boost your portfolio returns.

Overseas Companies Are Fueled By Our Consumer Purchases

Another reason to own international stocks is that we Americans make foreign companies more profitable each day through our purchasing habits. If you examine your daily purchases, you will find that you buy many products produced by overseas companies. Even companies you may think are tried and true American may be foreign owned. Have you ever purchased any of the products listed in Figure 13? Are your

Figure 13

Foreign Products

Product	Parent Company	Country
Quik Chocolate Milk	Nestle	Switzerland
Gerber	Novartis	Switzerland
Benetton	Benetton Group	Italy
Fila	Fila Holding Sp.	United Kingdom
Aquafresh	GlaxoSmithKline	Italy
Maybelline	L'Oreal	France
Nintendo	Nintendo	Japan
Pioneer	Pioneer Electronic	Japan
Jeep Cherokee	Daimler Chrysler	Germany
Shell	Royal Dutch Petroleum	Netherlands
Game Boy	Nintendo	Japan
Vodafone	Vodafone	United Kingdom
Paine Webber	UBS	Switzerland
Alliance Funds	AXA	France
Sharp	Sharp	Japan
Packard Bell	NEC	Japan
Burger King	Diageo PLC	United Kingdom
Hard Rock Cafe	Rank Group	United Kingdom
Los Angeles Dodgers	News Corporation*	Australia
7-Eleven	Ito-Yokado	Japan
Columbia TriStar	Sony	Japan
Magnovox	Philips Electronics	Netherlands

*2002

daily spending habits making foreign companies more profitable? Why not own some of these companies (outright or through a mutual fund) and participate in that profitability?

Foreign Equity Markets Are Expanding

In the past, most global stock market opportunities, as measured by total market capitalization, existed in the United States. For example, in 1970, 66 percent of the global equity opportunities were found in the U.S., while only 34 percent were in foreign markets. The total global market cap in 1970 was $850 billion. This has dramatically changed. In 2000, only 52 percent of the global opportunities were found in the U.S. and 48 percent were located overseas. The total market cap of the world equity markets in 2000 increased to more than $20 trillion.

Emerging Markets Have Room to Grow

International stocks are categorized by capitalization size (large and small) and style (growth and value) similar to domestic stocks. In addition, foreign stocks can be subcategorized by the maturity of the international market. Overseas stocks are either located in mature stable markets, such as Europe, or in developing emerging markets, such as South America. Our discussion about the international markets up to this point has revolved around the developed markets of the world. Some consideration, however, also must be given to the world's emerging markets.

There are many markets located in parts of the world such as Asia, Latin America, and Eastern Europe that are considered "emerging" because their economies are in the beginning stages of development. There is, of course, more risk when investing in these countries, but there is also more upside potential when an emerging market takes off. The room for growth in these economies is the attractive feature about investing in these markets. It may be hard to believe, but the United States was once considered an emerging country. There may well be future economic powers that have not yet popped up on the radar screen.

Less developed countries have tremendous potential for growth. As the global standard of living improves, millions of people will have more money to spend. As spending increases, financial markets are driven upward. As more people in these emerging countries buy basic items like telephones, cellular phones, and computers, the companies providing these services will likely do very well. Consider the statistics in Figure 14 outlining the number of telephone lines, cellular phone subscribers and computers per 100 people in various countries. How much room there is for future growth?

Figure 14

Room for Foreign Growth

Country	Telephone Lines	Cellular Subscribers	Computers
U.S.	62	54	65
Hungary	33	68	11
Greece	52	78	8
Argentina	22	18	8
Russia	24	12	9
Brazil	22	26	7
South Africa	11	36	7
China	21	21	3
India	5	2	1

Source: World Telecommunications Development Report, 2003

Bonds

Most investors, with the possible exception of very young people in their 20s and early 30s, should own some bonds. Bonds provide diversification, income, and a cushion to soften the blow of a falling stock market. This is important particularly if you are a retiree, since you will not have as much time to make up for sharp market losses. From 2000 to 2003, the stock market fell 38 percent.[7] During this same period, bonds gained 37 percent.[8] Investors with diversified portfolios consisting of stocks and bonds suffered much less than those invested in stocks alone.

While stocks represent a piece of ownership in a company, bonds simply represent the outstanding debt of a company or the government. If you purchase a bond, you are loaning money to the issuer, which could be a corporation, a municipality, or a government entity. In return, the bond's issuer promises to pay you interest, called the coupon, and to repay your principal at a stated maturity date. For example, if you bought a 10-year bond with an 8 percent coupon, you would loan the issuer $1,000, and the issuer would promise to repay you the $1,000 at maturity while paying you $80 of interest each year along the way (see Figure 15). The promise to repay your principal with interest is as sound as the institution that issued the bond.

Figure 15

Like stocks, bonds come in all shapes and sizes, based on such things as credit ratings, maturities, and yields. Some are taxable, others are tax-free. However, most bonds share some common characteristics. First, when interest rates go up, bond prices fall. Conversely, when rates fall, bond prices increase (see Figure 16). Second, long-term bonds are more volatile than short-term bonds. Third, bonds issued by low-quality companies pay higher yields than those issued by high-quality companies.

Interest Rates & Bond Prices

To understand the relationship between movements in interest rates and bond prices, let's look at the actual experience of a bond investor

Figure 16

When interest rates fall, bonds rise in value.   When interest rates rise, bonds fall in value.

named Perry Langford. Perry purchased a 10-year General Electric corporate bond for $1,000 on Jan. 1, 1976, with an 8 percent coupon. The bond paid him $80 of interest per year for 10 years. At the end of 10 years, he received his original investment of $1,000 back. The $80 of interest he received each year and his principal at maturity were guaranteed by the underlying bond issuer, General Electric.

 Only 38% of investors understand that when interest rates go up bond prices usually go down. [9]

Although General Electric guaranteed the interest and principal, the value of Perry's bond fluctuated between 1976 and 1985. Price movements in bonds are largely due to changes in interest rates. This 10-year period was marked by rising interest rates (see Figure 17). After owning the bond for five years, Perry considered selling it. However, there was one problem. Because interest rates had increased, similar newly issued bonds being issued in 1980 were paying 10 percent interest ($100 per year). Consequently, Perry's 8 percent bond wasn't very appealing to other investors. In 1980, why would an investor want to buy Parry's 8 percent bond when a newly issued bond paying 10 percent was available?

Perry asked his broker to put his 8% bond up for sale and see what investors would be willing to pay for it in this higher interest-rate environment. He received offers from investors to buy his bond for $924. (The open market told him that to make his bond attractive to bond buyers he'd have to discount the price of the bond by $76.) A bond purchased for $924 paying $80 of interest per year and maturing in five years at $1,000 would be equivalent to a new five-year bond paying $100 of interest each year (this assumes the bond type, maturity, and credit ratings are similar). Rather than selling the bond for less than he purchased it for, Perry decided to simply hold on to it until maturity and receive his original $1,000 investment back.

 Buy short-term bonds when interest rates are rising and buy long-term bonds when interest rates are falling. In 2003, interest rates hit 50-year lows. (See Figure 18)

Figure 17

Key Interest Rates

6 Month CD		Prime Rate		AAA Corp LT		Fed Funds	
1976	5.63	1976	6.84	1976	8.43	1976	5.05
1977	5.91	1977	6.83	1977	8.02	1977	5.54
1978	8.60	1978	9.06	1978	8.73	1978	7.94
1979	11.42	1979	12.67	1979	9.63	1979	11.20
1980	12.94	1980	15.26	1980	11.94	1980	13.35
1981	15.79	1981	18.87	1981	14.17	1981	16.39
1982	12.57	1982	14.85	1982	13.79	1982	12.24
1983	9.28	1983	10.79	1983	12.04	1983	9.09
1984	10.71	1984	12.04	1984	12.71	1984	10.23
1985	8.24	1985	9.93	1985	11.37	1985	8.10
1986	6.50	1986	8.33	1986	9.02	1986	6.80
1987	7.01	1987	8.21	1987	9.38	1987	6.66
1988	7.91	1988	9.32	1988	9.71	1988	7.57
1989	9.08	1989	10.87	1989	9.26	1989	9.21
1990	8.17	1990	10.01	1990	9.32	1990	8.10
1991	5.91	1991	8.46	1991	8.77	1991	5.69
1992	3.76	1992	6.25	1992	8.14	1992	3.52
1993	3.28	1993	6.00	1993	7.22	1993	3.02
1994	4.96	1994	7.15	1994	7.97	1994	4.21
1995	5.98	1995	8.83	1995	7.59	1995	5.83
1996	5.47	1996	8.27	1996	7.37	1996	5.30
1997	5.73	1997	8.44	1997	7.27	1997	5.46
1998	5.44	1998	8.35	1998	6.53	1998	5.35
1999	5.46	1999	8.00	1999	7.05	1999	4.97
2000	6.59	2000	9.23	2000	7.62	2000	6.24
2001	3.66	2001	6.91	2001	7.08	2001	3.88
2002	1.81	2002	4.67	2002	6.49	2002	1.67
2003	1.17	2003	4.12	2003	5.66	2003	1.13

Of course, the opposite is true also. When interest rates fall, the value of outstanding bonds will go up for the same reasons. So remember, when buying bonds, if interest rates are climbing, bond prices will fall, and if rates are falling, bond prices will climb. Where do you think bond prices are headed given the information in Figure 17?

Before buying his bond, Perry should have asked some "what if" questions. What if interest rates increase or decrease after buying the 8 percent General Electric bond? For example, what will the price of the bond be if rates increase or decrease 1, 2, or 3 percent? Figure 18 illustrates how rising and falling interest rates would affect the value of his 10-year bond if he decided to sell it after owning it for just five years. The first column outlines different interest-rate scenarios either up or down that could occur after purchasing his bond. The second column indicates the price Perry could sell his bond at as rates changes. You will notice that the more interest rates either increase or decrease the more impact these rate fluctuations will have on the value of his bond. Before buying a bond, it is a good idea to ask similar questions so you understand how the value of your bonds will be affected by interest-rate changes.

Figure 18

Value of a 10-year bond being sold in year five (8% coupon)	
Interest Rate Change	**Approximate Value of The Bond**
Up 1%	$961
Up 2%	$924
Up 3%	$889
Up 4%	$855
Up 5%	$824
Down 1%	$1,041
Down 2%	$1,084
Down 3%	$1,130
Down 4%	$1,178
Down 5%	$1,228

Maturities

Within each bond category, each type of bond can be classified based on when it matures: a bond can be short-term (0 to five years), intermediate-term (five to 10 years) or long-term (10 years plus). Bonds of different maturities react differently when rates go up and down. For example, if interest rates fall, the prices of long-term bonds will go up to a greater degree than short-term bonds. If rates rise, the opposite is true. Thus, there is more risk in owning long-term bonds.

If you are planning to hold your bonds to maturity, the bond's issuer guarantees that you will receive back your principal, the face value of the bond. If you are not planning to sell, the price fluctuations between now and maturity are irrelevant even though they will be reported on your brokerage statement. The price movements only become important if you are going to sell your bond before maturity.

Bond Ratings

Most bonds are rated. Bond ratings help investors determine the credit worthiness of the issuing company. Just as credit bureaus give you a credit score as an individual, bond-rating agencies give scores to companies.

Those with little outstanding debt, a solid balance sheet, and the ability to repay their debt obligations are given the highest credit ratings. To attract investors and to offset the additional risk, bonds issued by low-quality companies must offer higher yields than those issued by high-quality companies. Changes in credit ratings will also cause the value of bonds to fluctuate. If a corporation's bond rating is downgraded, the value of the bond will generally fall. A rating upgrade will often increase the bond's value. There are two main bond-rating services: Standard & Poor's and Moody's. Standard & Poor's ratings are shown in Figure 19.

Taxable and Tax-Free Bonds

All the different types of bonds that we've discussed so far are

Figure 19

Standard and Poor's Bond Ratings

Rating	Description
AAA	Bonds of the highest quality
AA	High-quality debt obligations
A	Bonds that have a strong capacity to pay interest and principal but may be susceptible to adverse effects
BBB	Bonds that have an adequate capacity to pay interest and principal but are more vulnerable to adverse economic conditions of changing circumstances
BB	Bonds of lower medium grade with few desirable investment characteristics
B	Primarily speculative bonds with great uncertainties and major risk if exposed to adverse conditions
CCC	Primarily speculative bonds with great uncertainties and major risk if exposed to adverse conditions
C	Income bonds on which no interest is being paid
D	Bonds in default

Source: Standard & Poor's Guide, June 1995

either taxable or tax-free. Taxable bonds include corporate, government (with the exception of Treasury Bonds), and international bonds. Tax-free bonds are issued by municipalities and offer interest that is not subject to federal income taxes. In some states, if you purchase a bond issued by the state, the interest is free from both state and federal taxes (double tax-free). Treasury bonds are exempt from state taxes.

To determine whether to buy taxable or tax-free bonds, compare the yields of each. To make an apples-to-apples comparison, yields must be compared after taxes are applied. Of course, tax-free bonds are not needed in a retirement account, where all interest is already tax-deferred.

James Gardner, a bond investor in the 35 percent tax bracket (state and federal combined), is considering buying a taxable bond yielding 7 percent or a tax-free bond yielding only 5 percent. Of course, there are more factors to consider than just yield, but we'll keep this example simple and stick strictly to yields.

Before applying taxes, it looks as if the taxable bond provides the greatest yield. However, the interest on the taxable bond will be taxed. James must factor in his tax rate and determine how much a taxable bond would have to yield to be equivalent to the 5 percent tax-free bond. In James' tax bracket, which bond offers the best after-tax yield? The formula in Figure 20 will provide the answer:

Figure 20

Tax Equivalent Yield

**Tax-Free Yield/(1-Investor's Tax Bracket)
= Equivalent Taxable Bond Yield**

0.05/(1-.035) = 7.70%

By inputting the tax-free yield and his tax rate, James can easily see that the tax-free bond would be the better investment. A taxable bond would have to yield almost 8 percent to be superior to the tax-free yield of 5 percent in James' high tax bracket. Based on yield alone, James would be better off owning the tax-free bond.

Bond Diversification

The many types of bonds, with their varying issuers, credit ratings, maturities, and yields all provide different rates of return from year to year. Like stocks, it is impossible to know exactly which types of bonds will be the best performing during the next 12 months. Because of this uncertainty, it is equally important to diversify your bond portfolio. Figure 21 highlights the performance of different types of bonds between 1991 and 2003. The highest returning bond each year is circled.

Figure 21

Bond Returns Compared

Year	High-Yield Bonds	Investment-Grade Bonds	U.S. Government Bonds	Municipal Bonds	Money Markets
1991	40.22%	16.18%	12.04%	14.63%	5.82%
1992	18.36%	7.22%	8.90%	6.10%	3.45%
1993	19.84%	10.00%	12.43%	8.32%	2.72%
1994	-3.68%	-3.21%	-6.04%	-4.74%	3.74%
1995	17.38%	17.12%	17.31%	16.94%	5.53%
1996	12.98%	3.43%	3.58%	2.16%	5.01%
1997	13.17%	8.79%	9.39%	9.12%	5.14%
1998	-.07%	7.87%	5.64%	7.84%	5.10%
1999	4.78%	-.98%	-4.07%	-2.66%	4.74%
2000	-9.71%	10.58%	11.10%	11.89%	5.94%
2001	-1.04%	8.22%	4.15%	6.67%	3.80%
2002	-2.41%	8.29%	9.86%	8.63%	1.32%
2003	26.36%	5.41%	1.30%	5.34%	0.62%

The returns of each asset class are represented by the following indexes: High yield bonds: Lipper High Yield Bond Funds Index, Investment Grade Bonds: Lipper Intermediate Investment Grade Funds Index, U.S. Government Bonds: Lipper General U.S. Government Funds Index, Muni Bonds: Lipper General Municipal Funds Index, Money Markets: Lipper Money Market Funds Index.

WEB BOND RESOURCES
- http://finance.yahoo.com Research bond offerings
- www.investinginbonds.com Bond education
- www.treasurydirect.gov Treasury & Savings bonds
- www.bondpage.com Research bond offerings
- www.buysellbonds.com Research bond offerings
- http://fmsbonds.com/index.html Research municipal bond offerings.

Cash

Cash equivalents are investments easily turned into cash without the risk of principal loss. This is called liquidity. Examples of cash equivalents include money market accounts, checking, savings, certificates of deposit, U.S. Treasury bills, and life insurance cash values. Cash investments can be an important component in a diversified portfolio due to their stability and consistent positive returns even during deep stock and bond market downturns. To locate the highest yielding cash investments from around the country or to compare cash investments at financial institutions in your area, visit www.bankrate.com or www.ingdirect.com.

Some cash investments make sense for retirees. If you are a retiree and living off of your investments, consider maintaining one to two years of needed annual income in cash-type investments. This is your short-term money — money that you will use immediately to supplement your income. Because you will be spending this money over the next one to two years, you should not put this money at risk in the stock or bond markets. By keeping a cash cushion in your portfolio, you can avoid having to liquidate stock and bond investments during market downturns. This added stability will help you maintain a disciplined investment strategy and keep your intermediate- and long-term money invested in the stock and bond markets. Too much cash in a portfolio, however, can hamper long-term performance and may ultimately keep you from reaching retirement goals.

Real Estate and Commodities

Adding real estate and commodities to your portfolio can further expand your diversification and reduce your portfolio's volatility. These two asset classes march to the beat of their own drums rather than following the general trends in the stock market. During recessions, when the stock market drops, real estate and commodities often do well. For example, the average real-estate mutual fund was up 27 percent in 2000, 10 percent in 2001, and 4 percent in 2002; while the average commodity fund was up 44 percent in 2000, down 31 percent in 2001, and up 27 percent in 2002. The stock market fell more than 38 percent during this three-year period. Investors owning these defensive asset classes made money in the worst period in the stock market since the mid-1970s.

Don't get too excited about these numbers; these asset classes don't always beat the stock market that handily. In 1998, for example, the stock market hit a home run beating the average real-estate and commodity fund by 55 and 73 percentage points, respectably. Investment professionals will often recommend investing 5 to 10 percent of an equity portfolio into real estate and commodities as a way to soften the blow of a bear market.

Performance of Each Asset Class

Now that you know your team Figure 22 lets you see at a glance how each asset class has performed annually for the past 14 years. The best investment of each year is circled. As you review the chart, notice that each year there are several asset classes with "zig-zag" relationships. Trying to choose the asset class that you think will perform the strongest during the upcoming year is a natural temptation. Don't fool yourself. Moving in and out of asset classes trying to find the "hot" investment is a mistake, especially when you're gambling with your retirement savings. Attempting to time the market will hurt the performance of your portfolio. Decide on an appropriate asset allocation and diversification model and then adhere to it for the long term.

Now that you know your team, you can develop a diversified portfolio that meets your risk and return objectives. As we continue our discussion of Step 2 of the investment process in the next chapter, we will examine different diversified portfolios. After reviewing these portfolios, you'll be able to determine which portfolio best suits your needs. Once you decide how to diversify your portfolio, we can then start our search to identify the best investments in each asset class.

Figure 22

Asset Class Performance 1990-2003

Year	Large Cap Growth	Large Cap Value	Mid Cap Growth	Mid Cap Value	Small Cap Growth	Small Cap Value	Int'l Stock	Corporate Bonds	U.S. Gov't Bonds	Municipal Bonds	Int'l Bonds	Cash
1990	.34%	-7.59%	-7.90%	-15.97%	-19.02%	-19.39%	-23.45%	6.48%	6.29%	7.30%	(15.29%)	7.52%
1991	46.62%	25.64%	44.07%	39.68%	(56.80%)	49.00%	12.12%	20.98%	18.68%	12.15%	16.24%	5.68%
1992	4.48%	11.14%	7.26%	21.05%	8.50%	(29.95%)	-12.17%	9.34%	8.09%	8.82%	4.77%	3.59%
1993	3.26%	16.95%	15.11%	15.93%	15.91%	22.10%	(32.57%)	13.64%	17.18%	12.28%	15.12%	3.12%
1994	1.69%	-0.80%	-1.87%	-1.65%	-3.11%	.38%	(7.78%)	-5.76%	-7.59%	-5.14%	5.99%	4.45%
1995	34.10%	(41.19%)	34.35%	34.67%	32.99%	27.33%	11.22%	27.94%	30.90%	17.46%	19.55%	5.79%
1996	(22.46%)	21.92%	14.96%	20.95%	12.76%	21.16%	6.05%	2.20%	-.83%	4.44%	4.08%	5.26%
1997	32.78%	33.26%	17.55%	32.88%	14.34%	(33.90%)	1.78%	13.46%	15.12%	9.20%	-4.26%	5.31%
1998	(42.32%)	14.94%	9.04%	-2.26%	6.92%	-6.99%	20.00%	9.16%	13.32%	6.48%	17.79%	5.02%
1999	34.73%	8.27%	(62.35%)	3.69%	52.56%	-1.41%	26.96%	-5.76%	-8.26%	-2.07%	-5.07%	4.87%
2000	-24.99%	1.09%	-15.38%	(24.91%)	-24.74%	23.21%	-14.17%	9.18%	20.28%	11.69%	-2.63%	6.32%
2001	-20.36%	-8.17%	-12.72%	7.10%	-14.31%	10.06%	-21.44%	(12.16%)	4.34%	5.08%	-3.54%	3.67%
2002	-24.98%	-17.99%	-23.71%	-12.34%	-28.9%	-13.9%	-15.94%	11.95%	16.99%	9.6%	(21.99%)	1.68%
2003	25.35%	31.68%	39.15%	48.28%	43.91%	(51.15%)	38.59%	10.45%	2.59%	5.32%	18.52%	1.05%

Returns are measured from 1990-2001, by the following indexes: Large-Cap Growth: Wilshire Large Growth Index, Large-Cap Value: Wilshire Large Value Index, Mid-Cap Growth: Wilshire Mid-Cap Growth Index, Mid-Cap Value: Wilshire Mid-Cap Value Index, Small-Cap Growth: Wilshire Small-Cap Growth Index, Small-Cap Value Index, International Stocks: Morgan Stanley EAFE Index ND, Corporate Bonds: Lehman Brothers Long-Term Corporate Bond Index, Government Bonds: Lehman Brothers Long-Term Government Bond Index, International Bonds: Salomon Brothers Non-$ World Government Bond Index, Cash: 3 Month Treasury Bill.

TWELVE

The Choice

✓ RETIREMENT DECISION #10 (continued): *How should I diversify my investment portfolio?*

Now that we have thoroughly examined and understand each asset class composing a diversified portfolio, let's select a portfolio that fits your risk tolerance and return objectives. Review the portfolios showcased in Figures 2 through 12 and choose a portfolio that suits you. As you do so, be sure to notice the performance of each portfolio during both good and bad markets.

Susan Callister, 63, chose the Balanced Growth and Income portfolio in Figure 6. She retired in December 2003 with a $650,000 nest egg. To reach her retirement goals, she determined that her target rate of return needed to be at least 9%. After reviewing each of the following portfolios, she decided that the balanced portfolio was for her.

To determine how to diversify her money into the various asset classes, she first dedicated 50 percent of her money to stocks ($325,000), 40 percent to bonds ($260,000), and 10 percent to cash ($65,000). Then, she simply applied the percentages outlined in Figure 1 to each part of her portfolio to determine how much money to invest in each asset class. For example, using the percentages in Figure 1, she took $81,250 of the stock money (25% of $325,000) and invested it in large-company U.S. growth stocks. She invested $32,500 into mid-cap growth stocks (10%) and so on. Once you pick a portfolio, simply follow Susan's lead and diversify your money using Figure 1 as a guide.

Historically, this balanced portfolio has provided investors with a 10.11% annual return (see Figure 7). Susan determined she could adhere to this investment strategy through the best and worst years. This portfolio achieved positive returns 11 out of the past 15 years. During the worst year, 2002, the portfolio lost 3.48 percent; in its best year, 1991, it gained 27.22 percent. Although there is no guarantee that these returns will repeat themselves, it is reasonable to assume that the results will be at least similar in the future.

Each of the portfolios in Figures 2 through 12 is diversified as shown in Figure 1. In addition, each portfolio was rebalanced annually (this will be discussed in detail in Chapter 13).

Buy, Hold, and Rebalance

Buying and holding a well-diversified portfolio of investments makes much more sense than trying to bounce in and out of each asset class based on your guess as to which will provide the best performance. In case you're still not convinced, let's consider the investment approaches employed by the following three investors: John Chase, Sam Rebound, and Mike Balance. Each chose a distinctly different method to build a portfolio using six investment choices—bonds, small/mid-cap stocks, large-cap value stocks, large-cap growth stocks, large-cap blend stocks, and international stocks. John and Sam attempted to guess which part of the market would deliver the best returns. Mike avoided all guesswork and simply diversified his portfolio across six market segments.

Figure 1

Stocks	
Large-Cap Growth	25%
Large-Cap Value	25%
Mid-Cap Growth	10%
Mid-Cap Value	10%
Small-Cap Growth	5%
Small-Cap Value	5%
International	20%
Total Stocks	100%

Bonds	
Long-Term Government	40%
Long-Term Corporate	45%
International	15%
Total	100%

Cash	
Cash Equivalents	100%

Figure 2

Ultra Conservative Income

Stocks	0%
Bonds	90%
Cash	10%

Portfolio Performance (1990-2004)

Average Annual Rate of Return (1990 - 2004)	9.05%
Best Year	25.66%
Worst Year	-5.50%
Number of years positive	13
Number of years negative	2

Annual Portfolio Performance

Year	Weighted Return	Growth of $100,000
1990	7.70%	$107,704
1991	17.98%	$127,072
1992	7.70%	$136,854
1993	14.06%	$156,099
1994	-3.81%	$150,149
1995	25.66%	$188,674
1996	1.67%	$191,823
1997	10.85%	$212,637
1998	11.41%	$236,896
1999	-5.50%	$223,858
2000	11.30%	$249,144
2001	6.38%	$265,030
2002	14.09%	$302,380
2003	7.77%	$325,875
2004	8.44%	$353,377

Figure 3

Conservative Income

Stocks	10%
Bonds	80%
Cash	10%

Portfolio Performance (1990-2004)

Average Annual Rate of Return (1990 - 2004)	9.26%
Best Year	25.97%
Worst Year	-3.21%
Number of years positive	13
Number of years negative	2

Annual Portfolio Performance

Year	Weighted Return	Growth of $100,000
1990	5.85%	$105,851
1991	19.46%	$126,452
1992	7.51%	$135,943
1993	14.19%	$155,235
1994	-3.21%	$150,253
1995	25.97%	$189,273
1996	3.30%	$195,521
1997	12.14%	$219,250
1998	12.10%	$245,770
1999	-2.31%	$240,098
2000	9.32%	$262,469
2001	4.49%	$274,252
2002	10.58%	$303,262
2003	10.47%	$335,000
2004	9.03%	$365,250

Figure 4

Income

Stocks	20%
Bonds	70%
Cash	10%

Portfolio Performance (1990-2004)

Average Annual Rate of Return (1990 - 2004)	9.46%
Best Year	26.28%
Worst Year	-2.61%
Number of years positive	14
Number of years negative	1

Annual Portfolio Performance

Year	Weighted Return	Growth of $100,000
1990	4.00%	$103,997
1991	20.94%	$125,778
1992	7.31%	$134,975
1993	14.32%	$154,304
1994	-2.61%	$150,280
1995	26.28%	$189,777
1996	4.93%	$199,139
1997	13.42%	$225,867
1998	12.78%	$254,739
1999	0.89%	$257,002
2000	7.34%	$275,864
2001	2.60%	$283,042
2002	7.06%	$303,034
2003	13.16%	$342,916
2004	9.62%	$375,907

Figure 5

Moderate Income

Stocks	**30%**
Bonds	**60%**
Cash	**10%**

Portfolio Performance (1990-2004)

Average Annual Rate of Return (1990 - 2004)	**9.68%**
Best Year	**26.59%**
Worst Year	**-2.01%**
Number of years positive	**14**
Number of years negative	**1**

Annual Portfolio Performance

Year	Weighted Return	Growth of $100,000
1990	2.14%	$102,144
1991	22.42%	$125,048
1992	7.12%	$133,951
1993	14.45%	$153,307
1994	-2.01%	$150,232
1995	26.59%	$190,184
1996	6.57%	$202,671
1997	14.71%	$232,477
1998	13.47%	$263,792
1999	4.08%	$274,566
2000	5.36%	$289,286
2001	0.71%	$291,354
2002	3.55%	$301,692
2003	15.86%	$349,530
2004	10.21%	$385,220

Figure 6

Income & Growth

Stocks	40%
Bonds	50%
Cash	10%

Portfolio Performance (1990-2004)

Average Annual Rate of Return (1990 - 2004)	9.90%
Best Year	26.91%
Worst Year	-1.40%
Number of years positive	13
Number of years negative	2

Annual Portfolio Performance

Year	Weighted Return	Growth of $100,000
1990	0.29%	$100,291
1991	23.90%	$124,264
1992	6.93%	$132,871
1993	14.58%	$152,243
1994	-1.40%	$150,106
1995	26.91%	$190,492
1996	8.20%	$206,109
1997	15.99%	$239,070
1998	14.16%	$272,916
1999	7.28%	$292,784
2000	3.38%	$302,690
2001	-1.17%	$299,141
2002	0.03%	$299,242
2003	18.55%	$354,757
2004	10.80%	$393,078

Figure 7

Balanced Growth & Income

Stocks	50%
Bonds	40%
Cash	10%

Portfolio Performance (1990-2004)

Average Annual Rate of Return (1990 - 2004)	10.11%
Best Year	27.22%
Worst Year	-3.48%
Number of years positive	11
Number of years negative	4

Annual Portfolio Performance

Year	Weighted Return	Growth of $100,000
1990	-1.56%	$98,437
1991	25.38%	$123,425
1992	6.73%	$131,735
1993	14.71%	$151,111
1994	-0.80%	$149,900
1995	27.22%	$190,699
1996	9.83%	$209,445
1997	17.28%	$245,632
1998	14.84%	$282,094
1999	10.48%	$311,647
2000	1.41%	$316,026
2001	-3.06%	$306,357
2002	-3.48%	$295,693
2003	21.25%	$358,520
2004	11.39%	$399,366

Figure 8

Growth & Income

Stocks	60%
Bonds	30%
Cash	10%

Portfolio Performance (1990-2004)

Average Annual Rate of Return (1990 - 2004)	10.32%
Best Year	27.53%
Worst Year	-7.00%
Number of years positive	10
Number of years negative	5

Annual Portfolio Performance

Year	Weighted Return	Growth of $100,000
1990	-3.42%	$96,584
1991	26.87%	$122,531
1992	6.54%	$130,545
1993	14.84%	$149,915
1994	-0.20%	$149,615
1995	27.53%	$190,803
1996	11.46%	$212,673
1997	18.56%	$252,153
1998	15.53%	$291,315
1999	13.67%	$331,144
2000	-0.57%	$329,247
2001	-4.95%	$312,960
2002	-7.00%	$291,066
2003	23.94%	$360,755
2004	11.48%	$403,987

Figure 9

Moderate Growth

Stocks	70%
Bonds	20%
Cash	10%

Portfolio Performance (1990-2004)

Average Annual Rate of Return (1990 - 2004)	10.53%
Best Year	28.35%
Worst Year	-10.51%
Number of years positive	11
Number of years negative	4

Annual Portfolio Performance

Year	Weighted Return	Growth of $100,000
1990	-5.27%	$94,730
1991	28.35%	$121,582
1992	6.35%	$129,299
1993	14.97%	$148,651
1994	0.40%	$149,249
1995	27.84%	$190,802
1996	13.09%	$215,786
1997	19.85%	$258,617
1998	16.22%	$300,561
1999	16.87%	$351,260
2000	-2.55%	$342,299
2001	-6.83%	$318,906
2002	-10.51%	$285,388
2003	26.64%	$361,410
2004	12.57%	$406,855

Figure 10

Growth

Stocks	80%
Bonds	10%
Cash	10%

Portfolio Performance (1990-2004)

Average Annual Rate of Return (1990 - 2004)	10.74%
Best Year	29.83%
Worst Year	-14.03%
Number of years positive	11
Number of years negative	4

Annual Portfolio Performance

Year	Weighted Return	Growth of $100,000
1990	-7.12%	$92,877
1991	29.83%	$120,578
1992	6.15%	$127,998
1993	15.10%	$147,322
1994	1.00%	$148,801
1995	28.15%	$190,693
1996	14.73%	$218,776
1997	21.13%	$265,013
1998	16.91%	$309,814
1999	20.06%	$371,976
2000	-4.53%	$355,129
2001	-8.72%	$324,157
2002	-14.03%	$278,693
2003	29.33%	$360,445
2004	13.17%	$407,897

Figure 11

Aggressive Growth

Stocks	**90%**
Bonds	**0%**
Cash	**10%**

Portfolio Performance (1990-2004)

Average Annual Rate of Return (1990 - 2004)	**10.76%**
Best Year	32.03%
Worst Year	-17.54%
Number of years positive	11
Number of years negative	4

Annual Portfolio Performance

Year	Weighted Return	Growth of $100,000
1990	-8.98%	$91,023
1991	31.31%	$119,519
1992	5.96%	$126,643
1993	15.23%	$145,926
1994	1.61%	$148,270
1995	28.47%	$190,475
1996	16.36%	$221,634
1997	22.42%	$271,324
1998	17.59%	$319,057
1999	23.26%	$393,271
2000	-6.51%	$367,680
2001	-10.61%	$328,674
2002	-17.54%	$271,025
2003	32.03%	$357,833
2004	13.76%	$407,056

Figure 12

Ultra Aggressive Growth

Stocks	100%
Bonds	0%
Cash	0%

Portfolio Performance (1990-2004)

Average Annual Rate of Return (1990 - 2004)	11.45%
Best Year	35.47%
Worst Year	-19.68%
Number of years positive	11
Number of years negative	4

Annual Portfolio Performance

Year	Weighted Return	Growth of $100,000
1990	-10.81%	$89,190
1991	34.15%	$119,652
1992	6.22%	$127,100
1993	16.57%	$146,161
1994	1.29%	$150,073
1995	30.98%	$196,572
1996	17.59%	$231,153
1997	24.32%	$287,372
1998	18.99%	$341,942
1999	25.30%	$428,465
2000	-7.93%	$394,477
2001	-12.20%	$346,371
2002	-19.68%	$278,221
2003	35.47%	$376,910
2004	15.13%	$433,919

John Chase

Like many investors, John Chase chases investment performance by paying premium prices to buy last year's winners. For each year from 1981 through 2001, John invested $10,000 in the previous year's best-performing asset class. Mutual funds from these "winning" market sectors are often in the press and on the covers of *Money* and *Smart Money* and attract record levels of new money. John's approach could be called "Invest with the Crowd." After following this strategy for 20 years and investing a total of $200,000, John's portfolio grew to $620,460 and averaged a 10.7 percent compounded annual rate of return.

Sam Rebound

Sam decided to be an investment contrarian and purchased the worst-performing investment from the previous 12 months, betting that it would rebound into profitability. On the last day of each year from December 1981 through December 2001, Sam invested $10,000 into the worst-performing investment of the previous year. Investing in these "losers" is a difficult task — after all, you don't find such investments on magazine covers — and it requires Sam to invest against the crowd. However, Sam was rewarded for his tenacity, and after 20 years, his $200,000 total investment grew to $738,804, compounding at an average rate of 12.21 percent. Sam ended up with $118,344 more than John.

Mike Balance

Mike didn't attempt to guess which part of the market was going to provide the best performance in the upcoming year based on last year's results. Nor did he try to buy last year's losers. Instead, Mike followed a simple strategy evenly spreading his annual $10,000 investment over all six different investments. After investing a total of $200,000 over 20 years, Mike's portfolio had grown to $864,868, compounding at an annual rate of 13.56 percent (see Figure 13).

Not only did Mike's portfolio outperform John's by $244,408 and Sam's by $126,064, but Mike was able to achieve this performance with less risk and volatility.

Diversifying your portfolio will help you obtain more consistent returns and dramatically decrease your overall investment risk. Understanding the ups and downs of different investment portfolios and how they perform in particular economic environments can be invaluable in helping you build a portfolio to meet your retirement goals.

Figure 13

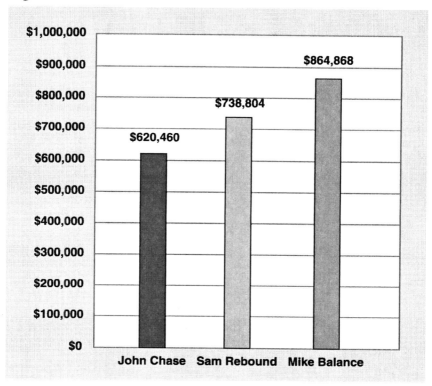

THIRTEEN

Divorce Your Stock

✓ RETIREMENT DECISION #11: *What should I do with my company's stock?*

A Modern-Day Tragedy

Linda Thompson, like many investors at retirement, did not have a complex investment portfolio. She invested her entire retirement plan in her employer's stock, a large, successful Fortune 500 company. Her bet paid off. The company stock outperformed the stock mutual funds offered in her retirement plan. In fact, she became wealthy largely due to many years of sizeable returns from her employer's stock. In 1999, for example, her $250,000 portfolio went up 58 percent and her balance climbed to $394,175. In 2000, while the stock market fumbled, her stock returned 87 percent, and her nest egg almost doubled to $743,532. She assumed she finally had enough money to retire at age 62. Based on her calculations, she was confident she could withdraw $45,000 per year from her nest egg to supplement her $12,000 of Social Security she would receive. At retirement, she rolled her company stock into her IRA.

Linda loved her company and was confident its future prospects would generate returns similar to those she'd enjoyed in the past. At retirement, however, she faced a difficult decision. Should she reduce the amount of her company's stock she held, sell all of the stock, or just continue holding it in hopes of continued off-the-charts performance? Linda was married to her company stock and emotionally couldn't divorce an investment that had rewarded her so greatly. Divorce would simply be too devastating. How could she sell a stock that was the primary reason she could retire early? Think about it, with just one more year like 1999 or 2000, she would have more than $1 million. Greed got the best of her, and she decided to continue her single-stock strategy and simply hold on.

Tragedy struck in 2001, however, and the unimaginable happened as Linda's beloved company, Enron, dropped in value by more than 99 percent. As it began its descent from $90 per share to 5 cents, she was convinced it would rebound and continued her hold-at-all-costs strategy (see Figure 1). The large nest egg that was ready and primed to support Linda for the next 30 years was worth a measly $7,435 when the dust cleared at the end of 2001.

Because she was unable to live on Social Security alone, she had to return to the workforce. To make matters worse, Linda opted to begin receiving reduced Social Security payments. Uncle Sam didn't care that Linda was a victim of the Enron mess; the Social Security rules are set in stone: Recipients between age 62 and full retirement age will have their Social Security benefit reduced by $1 for every $2 they earn over $11,280. This meant her benefit would be reduced to zero if she earned over $43,152. Not a very good scenario for someone who needs to rebuild an entire nest egg.

In hindsight you might ask, "Why didn't she sell her shares at retirement?" Usually the answer can be summarized in one word: greed. Most people want to squeeze every last drop of return from their stock before selling. No one wants to sell too soon and miss out on the next 20 percent run-up. But before you cast stones at Linda, are you certain you wouldn't have acted the same way? Let's look at Linda's line of thinking at the end of 2000.

Enron ended 2000 at $83 per share. Earlier in 2000, however, it had hit $90. Linda figured she'd just take a wait-and-see approach and see if it could climb back to $90. At $90, she told herself, she'd have almost $1 million, and she'd begin selling her shares. At the start of February 2001, the price was

Figure 1

Enron Corp.

Year	Price*	Annual Price Change
1994	$15.25	n/a
1995	$19.06	25%
1996	$21.56	13%
1997	$20.78	-4%
1998	$28.53	37%
1999	$44.38	56%
2000	$83.13	87%
2001	$0.60	-99%
2002	$0.06	-90%
2003	$0.03	-55%

* price on last trading day of each year
Source: www.bigcharts.com, (Symbol: ENRNQ)

still hovering around $80. Over the next few months, though, the stock fell to $55. No big deal, Linda thought. She had experienced volatility like this several times over many years of owning Enron and was confident it would rebound. It always had in the past. By midyear, however, Linda began to get worried. The stock dropped to the 40s, trading at nearly half of its value at the beginning of the year. She couldn't possibly sell it now; surely it would rebound, she thought, and she didn't want to miss out on it. Over the second half of 2001, the stock made a quick decent to $4 per share. Linda's retirement savings was now down to $35,776. Selling at $4 wouldn't do much for her retirement. She had missed the boat.

Linda was not the only one affected by the Enron fiasco—57 percent of assets in Enron's 401(k) program was invested in the company's stock. [1]

What Is the Maximum a Retiree Should Invest in Any One Company?

Retirement is not the time to gamble on the performance of one company, no matter how good its prospects may be. What is the maximum percentage of your portfolio that should be invested in a single stock position during retirement? At the bare minimum, you should follow the diversification laws required of mutual funds; diversified mutual funds cannot invest any more than 5 percent of their overall portfolios into any one company. Experts agree that most retirees and preretirees, who have little time to make back big losses, should generally have no more than 5 percent of their portfolio invested in any one stock.

Where would Linda be now if she had followed this simple rule? Even if she had followed an aggressive strategy and invested in a portfolio composed entirely of stocks, putting 95 percent of her money into the Vanguard S&P 500 Index Fund and left 5 percent of her money in Enron, she would have ended 2001 with $622,000 and still been in a position to reach her retirement goals; $7,435 is a far cry from $622,000.

Follow the lead of diversified mutual funds and invest no more than 5 percent of your portfolio in any one company.

What Are the Chances of Your Stock Dropping?

If you are thinking that the likelihood of an Enron situation occurring with your favorite company is impossible, consider the fate of shareholders of WorldCom, Lucent, Williams Company, and Qwest. Stock owners of these companies shared a similar fate as owners of Enron. Each of these companies seemed invincible at one time. Okay, maybe you're right, maybe the chances of encountering a monstrous Enron drop are very low. However, even the largest, most solid companies experience dramatic stock price volatility at times. During the past 10 years, 100 stocks in the S&P 500, composed of our nation's biggest companies, have dropped more than 50 percent during a three-month period. If history repeats and you own one of these "unshakable" stocks, you run a 20 percent chance of seeing a price drop in half within three months. Any way you slice it, this is far too much risk to take with money that must support for you for the next 30 to 40 years.

If a large portion of your nest egg is tied up in one or two companies, ask yourself how a 25, 50, 75, or 100 percent price drop would impinge on your retirement plan? Run your retirement analysis with these assumptions and see what the outcome is. To make up these disastrous losses, you could be forced to go back to work for a few more years, or perhaps a few more decades. If you have the lion's share of your money tied up in one company's stock, you're taking huge risks with your future.

A single stock position can make you very wealthy, indeed, if your company does well. You must acknowledge, however, that your stock can also drop abruptly and destroy years of disciplined savings and accumulation — all in a shockingly short period of time. Recognize that individual stocks can easily swing up or down by 50 percent or more in a given year. You don't have to look any further than the daily newspaper to find examples of companies that have done a nose-dive, leaving many retirees with nest eggs that will no longer see them through retirement.

Don't fool yourself into thinking that your big blue chip stock can't fall. Consider the price drops of many well-known companies in Figure 2. This chart shows how far many solid U.S. companies have fallen from their 10-year highs to their subsequent 10-year lows. It is clear to see why devoting a large portion of your retirement nest egg to just one or two stocks could be devastating. Of course, there is still

- 37 of the 291 largest U.S. stocks experienced a price drop of 50 percent or more over a three-month period at one point during the past 10 years (a 13 percent probability).

- 149 of the 793 available U.S. mid-cap stocks experienced a price drop of 50 percent or more over a three-month period at one point during the past 10 years (a 19 percent probability).

- 1,671 of the 4,337 available U.S. small-cap stocks experienced a price drop of 50 percent or more over a three-month period at one point during the past 10 years (a 39 percent probability).

- 110 of the 547 available international stocks experienced a price drop of 50 percent or more over a three-month period at one point during the past 10 years (a 20 percent probability).

- 2,061 of the 6,385 stocks listed in the Morningstar database experienced a price drop of 50 percent or more over a three-month period at one point during the past 10 years (a 32 percent probability).

potential for price drops if you diversify into a stock mutual fund, though most funds are composed of 100 or more companies. If a few are falling, chances are others will be climbing and the impact of the troubled stocks is offset.

Why So Much Company Stock?

It's easy to understand the motivation of some investors who rely heavily on the success of one stock. If the stock has performed well in the past, and as an employee of the company you can see its prospects for continued growth are good, then why not ride that train all the way to prosperity? It does happen. There are many examples of

Figure 2

Even Big Blue-Chip Companies Can Fail

Stock price drop from high to low, 1995 - 2004

Company	%
Lucent	-98%
Delta	-96%
Time Warner	-89%
Cisco Systems	-89%
Intel	-83%
Home Depot	-70%
Microsoft	-64%
General Electric	-63%
IBM	-60%
Coca-Cola	-58%
Bank of America	-57%
AIG	-56%
Procter & Gamble	-54%
Citigroup	-54%
Pfizer	-46%
ChevronTexaco	-40%
Wal-Mart Stores	-38%

Source: www.bigcharts.com, data from 1995 - 2004

companies that have brought riches to their stockholders. Nevertheless, if you can reach your retirement goals without taking the risk, then why make such a big gamble on a single stock when a steep decline could be so disastrous for you?

 $124 billion is tied up in company stock in U.S. 401(k) plans (16 percent of the total 401(k) assets).

While you are employed, your company wants you to invest heavily in its stock. If employees own company stock, they are more likely to work hard to help the company be profitable. Also, it is cost-effective for the company to provide matching contributions in company stock rather than in cash. What's good for the company, though, may not be good for you, the person who stands to be affected most adversely if the stock declines.

Knowing these risks, what are other reasons some employees have virtually all of their retirement money invested in company stock? Some of it has simply to do with loyalty. Employees want to show support for their company and reinforce their emotional ties by buying stock. As long as those ties stay strong, the stock is seldom sold. Many of these loyal employees also believe "their" company will never go through a major downturn.

Another reason for stock over concentration has to do with the way company benefit plans are set up, with incentives to purchase company stock. Many corporations, for example, match employee 401(k) contributions with company stock. Further, some employers will not allow employees to sell the stock until they reach age 55 or leave the company.

Many 401(k) plans offer company stock as one of the investment options available to plan participants. Not having a great deal of information on other investment choices leads employees to simply buy company stock as a default.

Yet another way for employees to accumulate company stock is the advent of stock options. Other companies may also offer stock purchase plans, which allow investors the ability to buy company stock at discounts as high as 20 percent. While this is usually a pretty good deal, many employees end up with these discounted shares along with the shares in their 401(k) plan and more shares given to them through matching contributions. In the end, they find themselves with too much of their retirement portfolio tied up in their company. Fortunately, at retirement you can diversify the money invested in your employer's stock in most cases without restriction.

Getting Out: Exit Strategies

If you have too much invested in one stock, it's time to develop an exit strategy. You can approach this in a couple of ways: sell all shares all at once, or sell shares over a period of time. Before doing anything, though, get a feel for where the stock is trading in comparison to where it has been trading over the past 10 years. Bigcharts.com is a good place to do this. Often looking at a company's historic stock prices reveals that the current stock price, while maybe not at an all-time high, is trading at a reasonably high price level. This will help you with your decision to sell your shares. Also, if you own a concentrated stock position in a non-retirement account, you will have to look beyond just the price and also examine the tax consequences of selling the stock.

Shares in an IRA

If you own shares in a retirement account and your stock is trading at a reasonably high price relative to its historical price and relative to the price at which your shares were purchased, don't hesitate; sell it all at once and diversify. In hindsight, this is exactly what Linda should have done with her Enron shares. At the end of 2000, Enron was trading at $83 per share. In the prior 10 years, the stock had only been priced that high for a few months earlier in 2000. Without hesitation, she should have sold all of her shares and diversified.

If you are preparing to retire and own your company's shares in a 401(k) plan, sell the shares in the plan before you transfer the money to an IRA. This will allow you to avoid transaction costs. If you sell the shares after they have been rolled into your IRA, your brokerage firm will charge you a commission to sell your shares.

What if the stock is priced a lot lower than you'd like it to be? It still may make sense to sell it. Ask yourself the following questions:

- "If I hold on to the stock, how high could it realistically go over the next 12 months?"

- "If I hold on to the stock, how low could it drop over the next 12 months?"

- "If I sold the stock and reinvested the money into diversified investments, how much appreciation is reasonable to expect?"

If, for example, you think your stock has the potential to go up 10 percent over the next 12 months, and you think the diversified investments you could purchase would also climb 10 percent, then you might as well sell and diversify. In either case, the return potential is the same. The difference is the diversified portfolio can deliver the return with much less risk. In our example, although Enron delivered some off-the-chart returns in 1999 and 2000, it would have been reasonable to conclude that it may climb another 10 percent in 2001 (10 percent being the average annual return of the stock market since 1925). However, had Linda asked herself the previous three questions, she would have sold her Enron shares and diversified.

The other alternative is to sell a portion of your holdings each year over a one- to three-year period, and with each transaction, reinvest the proceeds into a diversified portfolio. How would Linda have made out using this strategy with her Enron stock? Let's say she held 8,944 shares of Enron at the end of 1999 and assume she decided to sell one third of her stake each year for the next three years. She would have sold 2,981 shares the first year and diversified $247,795. She would have sold the next block of Enron one year later at 60 cents per share for $1,788 and the final block a year later at 3 cents for $92. These results still don't sound very appealing, but still with almost a quarter of a million dollars, Linda could salvage some kind of retirement. For most stocks, this may not be a bad approach. Enron simply showed us the worst case scenario. The key to selling over a period of time is being disciplined, for in a year's time it is easy to get caught up in the excitement that may surround your stock. Greed could set in and your diversification plan put on hold.

Shares in a Non-Retirement Account

In cases in which the stock is owned in a taxable account, selling may be a little trickier. The need for diversification is just as important, but you may have to pay capital gains taxes when you sell (see Figure 3). In most cases, it still makes sense to sell your shares as previously discussed, pay the taxes, and diversify.

Figure 3

Capital Gains Rate

Long-Term Capital Gains (holding period longer than one year)	**15%**
Long-Term Capital Gains (holding period rate for those in 15% tax bracket)	**10%**
Short-Term Capital Gains (holding period less than one year)	**Income Tax Rates**

However, if you own a huge position of stock with extremely low-basis shares, you should consider a few additional strategies before selling that can help you diversify while at the same time minimizing capital gains taxes. Following are explanations of some of these strategies.

Charitable Remainder Trusts

You can contribute your company stock to a charitable remainder trust (CRT). The trustee (whom you can appoint as yourself) can sell the stock and reinvest it in a diversified portfolio of your choice. By making a contribution to a CRT, you will receive an immediate tax credit, avoid all capital gains taxes on the prior appreciation of the stock, and obtain tax-free growth on the investments in the portfolio in the future.

As an income beneficiary, you will receive a lifetime of income from the diversified portfolio. The downside of this strategy is that you give up the right to tap into assets held in the trust. Upon death (typically the death of both you and your spouse), the assets will revert to the charity you have chosen, not to your heirs. This strategy is usually used in conjunction with a second-to-die life insurance policy, which provides for your heirs upon the deaths of both you and your spouse.

Margin or Hypothecation Loan

You can use your stock as collateral to secure a low-interest loan or to obtain margin to purchase other securities. Think of this like a home equity line; however, instead of using your home equity to obtain a loan, you are using your stock position as collateral to obtain a loan. The proceeds of the loan can be invested in a diversified portfolio of stocks and bonds, reducing the risk of being invested in just one company. For instance, if you owned $100,000 of IBM stock you could obtain a loan against it for $100,000 and use it to buy a diversified portfolio of securities. Now your overall portfolio will be composed of 50 percent diversified investments and 50 percent IBM stock. While you will be required to pay interest on the loan, you will avoid paying capital gains taxes and can reduce your portfolio risk considerably.

Exchange Funds

In an exchange fund, a group of investors deposit their low-basis stock shares into a limited partnership in exchange for a partnership interest in the fund. This is done tax-free with no capital gains taxes.

As a limited partner, you will have a partnership interest in all the stocks held in the fund and, thus, obtain immediate diversification. Because exchange funds are managed passively, meaning not a lot of buying and selling occurs, the only companies accepted into the fund are those that meet specific requirements crucial to the fund's performance. Consequently, not all stocks are accepted. If you own an obscure company, it will be more difficult or even impossible to find an exchange fund that will accept your shares. When the limited partnership interest is redeemed, usually after at least seven years, the investor will receive a diversified portfolio of stocks without having to pay capital gains taxes in the process.

While this strategy works in certain situations, investors must be able to meet strict requirements to participate, such as an initial stock deposit of at least $1 million and a net worth of $5 million.

Zero Premium Collars

There are several option strategies you can use to protect yourself from loss if your company stock nose-dives. One strategy, referred to as a zero premium collar, uses "put" and "call" options to protect an investor from losing too much if the stock turns sour. This strategy is helpful to an investor who is not interested in selling the stock due to potential tax implications but is at too much risk if the stock drops.

To initiate this strategy, an investor sells a call option on his stock and uses the income to buy a put option. The put option protects the stock position on the downside, while the call option provides a source of income to pay for the put. Protection strategies, like the "collar," are not available for all stocks.

Conclusion

If your portfolio is heavily dependent on the success of one company, it's time to seriously rethink your strategy — if that company falters, it can jeopardize your ability to reach your retirement goals. Just ask those people holding Enron stock who once thought they would be wealthy in retirement and now are resigned to working far beyond retirement age.

FOURTEEN

Ready...Set...Buy

✓ RETIREMENT DECISION #12: *What criteria should I use to identify the best investments?*

You've decided how to allocate your money among stocks, bonds, and cash (Step 1) and how to diversify your portfolio among the different segments of the stock and bond markets (Step 2). It's now time to buy the investments (Step 3). Most investors skip the first two steps and go right to Step 3. This is a big mistake. Determining which investments to purchase in each asset class is now your task at hand (see the sample portfolio in Figure 1).

You'll first need search criteria to help you screen the thousands of options available to identify the best ones for your portfolio. Think of

Figure 1

Sample Portfolio
(60% Stocks 35% Bonds 5% Cash)

Asset Class	Target Allocation %	Investment Choice
Large-Cap Growth Stocks	15%	_____
Large-Cap Value Stocks	15%	_____
Mid-Cap Growth Stocks	7.5%	_____
Mid-Cap Value Stocks	7.5%	_____
Small-Cap Growth Stocks	2.5%	_____
Small-Cap Value Stocks	2.5%	_____
International Growth	5%	_____
International Value	5%	_____
Corporate Bonds	10%	_____
Government Bonds	10%	_____
Municipal Bonds	10%	_____
International Bonds	5%	_____
Cash	5%	_____

this process as pouring thousands of investments in a big funnel to narrow your choices down to a short list of finalists representing the best of the best. You can search for and buy investments on your own or you can hire a financial advisor to do it for you.

Want A Million More?

You may ask, "What does it really matter if my investments aren't among the best?" Owning poor investments could mean having to endure unnecessary volatility, high expenses, poor or inconsistent performance, and even a reduction in retirement income. Owning better-than-average investments could put thousands or even hundreds of thousands of extra dollars in your pocket!

Let's oversimplify and assume at retirement you invested $500,000 into just one mutual fund that earned an 8 percent annual return. Your coworker Dan did a little extra legwork and found a good manager who squeezed out an extra percentage point every year and returned 9 percent annually. Big deal, you might say, what's one percentage point? Well, after 30 years, your buddy Dan is a whole lot richer than you. Your $500,000 investment grew to a little over $5 million. Not bad, until you compare that sum to Dan's kitty of $6.6 million. (That's 33 percent more than yours.) One percentage point of extra yearly return earned Dan $1.6 million. Getting an extra percentage or two could have a big impact on your retirement.

How do the investments you own stack up? Are they above-average performers? If not, you may want to make some changes.

 The average large-company U.S. value stock fund provided an average annual return of 11.41 percent for the 10 years ending 2004.[1] The top ten large-company U.S. value stock funds averaged over 15 percent.

Can You Make the Grade?

Imagine for a moment that you are a student in an investment class your company is offering. The instructor asks you to come to the front of the class and explain 1) the criteria you used to determine which investments to buy in your current investment portfolio, and 2) how you decide when it's time to sell an investment you own. Your grade on this assignment will depend on how persuasive your argument is that your strategy for identifying good investments will produce solid, above-average results. If you use a financial advisor, you can bring him or her up to the front of the class with you. (Surprisingly, many advisors themselves wouldn't do very well on this assignment.) Are you a little nervous or are you confident in the strategy you are following?

As you can guess, most investors would get an F on this assignment. What would your grade be? The following are likely the most common strategies we would hear in class: "I buy the investments with the best returns last year." "I asked a co-worker how to invest my 401(k) money." "My doctor and my brother-in-law give me hot stock tips." Your financial advisor might say, "I found an investment for my client that paid me a high commission!" Unfortunately, these approaches don't often reveal the best investments available.

How well you choose your investments has a far greater impact on your life than getting an A or F on an assignment. It literally could mean the difference of being able to retire...or not!

During the 15-year period ending in 2003, seven out of 10 U.S. stock funds reported average annual rates of return in excess of 10 percent. The top third provided returns in excess of 12 percent.[2]

Do It Yourself or Delegate?

Before we start to examine the investment selection process, you need to make a couple of decisions.

First, are you a "do-it-yourselfer" or a "delegator"? Do-it-yourselfers can use the criteria outlined in this chapter to conduct an intense hands-on search to filter out the best investments. Delegators can take the search criteria to their financial advisors and *request* that their advisor identify the best investments available for them. In either case, screening for the best investments is a must.

Second, you must decide whether you want to build your portfolio using individual stocks and bonds or outsource the day-to-day money-management responsibilities to professional money managers, such as mutual fund managers. Building and managing a large, diversified portfolio of individual stocks is difficult. I recommend that you don't attempt it. You're not equipped to do it, and most financial advisors aren't equipped to do it. The stakes are high. You want to entrust your retirement savings only to the best *money managers* available to you.

This chapter will focus on how to find the best money managers. By turning the daily management responsibilities over to professionals rather than picking stocks yourself or having your advisor do it, you will vastly improve your investment performance.

Ways to Obtain Professional Money Management

There are several ways to hire a professional money manager. In fact, you've probably already hired many managers to manage your money without even knowing it. By investing in a mutual fund, variable annuity, or variable life insurance policy, or a separately managed account (SMA) program , you are in reality hiring a money manager. If you have money in a 401(k) invested in mutual funds, you have hired several money managers. (For more detail on the different types of money management vehicles, see "Understanding Your Money Management Choices" later in this chapter.)

Hiring a good manager may seem like a daunting task, considering the fact that there are so many from which to choose. For example, there are now over 17,000 mutual funds available![3] Sound overwhelming? Be assured that with sound search criteria the process actually becomes quite easy.

 Today, there are nearly 17,000 mutual funds (all share classes) available to the public.

Once we outline the search process, we will discuss some resources you can use to help you conduct your own money manager search, view a list of funds that have already been screened, and evaluate the funds you own. Regardless of the type of financial products you choose (i.e., mutual funds, variable annuities, variable life, or SMAs), the process of evaluating money managers is the same.

Forget Short-Term Results

Finding good money managers is easy right? All we have to do is look at who's on the top-performing lists that dominate the financial media. Surely, last year's winners must be run by smart folks.

These managers may know what they're doing, but chances are they won't continue to outperform. Remember, buying last year's winners is a loser's strategy. Often, if a fund is volatile enough to top a winners list one year, it's volatile enough to lead a loser's list the next year. In a nutshell, short-term performance numbers are not effective predictors of future results.

Let's look at an extreme example by considering Joan Gibson's investment portfolio results. On Jan. 1, 2000, Joan decided to divide her $100,000 equally among the 10 top-performing funds from the previous year (1999). How did she do in 2000, 2001, and 2002? After investing for just three years, Joan's initial $100,000 investment was worth a meager $30,040, a loss of $69,960, or 70 percent. Figure 2 outlines her results.

Figure 2

Hypothetical $10,000 investment made in each fund from 2000-2002

Fund Name	1999	Total Return 2000	2001	2002	Value 12/31/2002
Amerindo Technology D	249%	-65%	-51%	-31%	$1,196
BlackRock US Opps Inst	222%	-8%	-14%	-39%	$4,962
Credit Suisse Jpn Eq A	266%	-69%	-25%	-28%	$1,681
Driehaus Intl Disc	214%	-11%	-14%	-13%	$6,619
Fidelity Japan Small Co	237%	-50%	-20%	1%	$4,136
Kinetics Internet	216%	-51%	-10%	-23%	$3,356
Nevis Fund	287%	-25%	-44%	-48%	$2,188
PBHG Tech & Commun Adv	243%	-44%	-52%	-55%	$1,212
ProFunds UltraOTC Inv	233%	-74%	-69%	-69%	$2,431
Thurlow Growth	213%	-56%	-26%	-31%	$2,259
					$30,040

Source: Morningstar Principia Pro

Although investors rarely go to the extreme of purchasing 10 funds with last year's best returns, as Joan did, you would be surprised how often people use this method to choose their investments. You have likely seen a coworker handle his or her 401(k) fund selection this way. He or she goes down the list of the 10 to 20 options available and chooses the funds with the best performance last year. Following this method of investment selection is perfect if you want to buy high and sell low, but that's a sure way to lose money. So remember, short-term returns should not be among your priority criteria for selecting a solid money manager.

Finding the Best of the Best

Studies indicate that only 25 percent of mutual funds outperform the market. The following search process will help you identify the top money managers in hopes of finding the managers that have the greatest chance of being in that 25 percent. You can also use the same criteria to analyze the investments you currently own. If you find you own some below-average, poor-performing investments, you'll want to replace them. If your advisor has recommended below-average performers, it may be time to *fire* him or her and find a new advisor (see Chapter 3). At the very least, armed with the following search criteria, you will be able to hold your advisor accountable by providing a standard by which to measure his or her investment recommendations.

Let me walk you through the process of uncovering the best and most consistent money managers, as I did for Janet Reese, a recent retiree. She accumulated $350,000 in her employer's 401(k) plan and decided to roll the money into her IRA when she retired. We settled on the asset-allocation model outlined in Figure 1 and decided to use mutual funds. We then followed a simple process to find the best mutual fund money managers for each segment of her portfolio.

We started the search by looking for a fund that invests in large-cap U.S. growth companies. We wanted to allocate $70,000 to this part of the stock market. Janet wanted to find a money manager who consistently ranked at the top of this asset category.

To locate the top funds in this category, we dumped all 17,243 mutual funds into a "funnel" to narrow them down to just a handful that are among the best and most consistent (see Figure 3). Following are the nine screens we used create a short list of top-notch managers.

Conducting a Money Manager Search

Screen 1: Asset Category

We began our investment manager search by identifying the asset category. The asset category is simply the part of the market you are searching, such as large-company growth funds or small-company value funds. A fund's category is determined by the types of companies in which it invests. Categories are outlined in Chapter 10: "Components of Diversification." For example, if we started a search looking for the best large-cap growth funds (category) we would immediately narrow the field from 17,243 funds to 1,430.

Screen 2: Manager Tenure

When you buy a fund, make sure your money manager has some experience under his or her belt. You don't want a new manager cutting teeth and learning how to invest with your money. Your retirement money is your future, and you don't want someone "practicing" with it.

Preferably the manager you choose should have at least 10 years' experience. This will ensure that he or she has been face to face with a couple of down markets and has gained experience handling adverse environments. Of the 1,430 large-company growth funds in Janet's search, only 131 of the funds have managers who have been with the fund for 10 or more years. The average mutual fund manager today has only five years of experience managing a fund.[9]

 The average mutual fund manager today has only five years of experience.

Screen 3: Performance vs. Peers (over three, five, and 10 years)

Performance vs. peers is an apples-to-apples comparison of returns for all funds in a respective investment category. It doesn't matter how a small-company stock fund compares with a fund that buys international stocks, but it does matter how it compares with all other small-company stock funds. What we want to know is how a fund ranks when stacked up against its peers during the past three, five, and 10 years. Is it above or below average? If your fund has been consistently below average, you may want to consider making a change. Often, funds that make our short list will rank in the top 10% of their asset class for all three periods. This isn't always possible but is preferable. Long-term performance comparisons will help you identify funds with the most consistent long-term returns.

Of the 131 large-company growth funds we identified for Janet with seasoned money managers, only 61 pass this three-, five-, and 10-year performance screen.

Screen 4: Performance in Bear Markets

How did the manager do when the market was falling? Checking the fund's performance versus its peers during *down* years will give you an indication of what to expect if the market heads south. If the fund ranks toward the top of its category in bear markets, the manager will likely narrow your losses during future negative years.

When you buy a fund you should also know what the worst-case scenario is. Look for the fund's worst year in the past 10 years. Could you have endured the manager's performance during the bad years? If not, don't buy the fund. For example, a fund that made the top of our list in a fund search we recently conducted had three years in which it lost money from 1993 through 2003, the worst being a return of negative 19 percent. Could you handle that?

Of the 61 large-company growth funds we identified with above average three-, five-, and 10-year performance, only 5 pass this bear market performance test.

Screen 5: Check Sales Charges and Management Expenses

Sales charges and management expenses need to be examined closely and can have a substantial impact on your performance. In a recent 10-year study, Vanguard discovered that low-cost funds produced returns from 2 to 7 percent better per year than their high-cost counterparts.[10] High built-in management expenses and sales charges can drag heavily on performance. Expenses should be, at the least, below the asset category average and preferable below 1% per year. Avoid funds with front or back-end sales charges. In Chapter 15, we will examine the costs of different financial products in detail. No-load investments could save you a lot of money. Do not purchase an investment until you've read chapter 15.

Of the 12 large-company growth funds that passed our bear market screen, only four are no-load funds. And, of these, only three have built-in expenses less than the category average. So, only three of the 1,430 large company growth funds we started out with have survived every filter to this point.

Screen 6: Alpha

Alpha is a statistical number that measures a fund's actual return to its expected return. It's a reflection of the skill of the manager. A positive alpha indicates that the fund performed better than expected based on the risk it takes. A negative alpha means the fund underperformed its expected return. If a fund has an alpha of 1 percent, it means the manager provided one percentage point more yearly return than expected. The higher the alpha, the better.

Of the three no-load large-company growth funds with below-average expenses, only two have alphas greater than 1 percent. Janet is now down to her short list.

The Short List

Once we had a short list of fund finalists, we squared them off and let them battle head to head using additional screens. This side-by-side comparison helped us identify our final choice. In addition to the criteria above, we compared the funds for performance consistency, size and style discipline, and tax efficiency.

Screen 7: Performance Consistency vs. an Index

Once the long-term returns have been examined, you will need to do a quick check of the fund's year-to-year results versus its benchmark index. An index is a group of securities chosen to represent a portion of the stock or bond markets. Each manager of a fund or separate account is given a performance hurdle. This is a rate of return the manager is expected to provide investors. The rate is determined by a stock or bond index that comprises the types of stocks or bonds the manager buys based on the portfolio's objective. For example, large-company growth managers generally use the Russell 1000 Growth Index as their performance benchmark. As the name suggests, the index is made up of 1000 large-company growth stocks.

Whether you are buying a mutual fund or a separate account, you should find out whether the manager has a record of consistently beating his or her benchmark index. At the very least, your manager should have beaten the index six of the past 10 years.

Screen 8: Size and Style Discipline

Only buy funds that have beaten their benchmark index at least six of the past ten years.

TIP

It is important to buy a fund that is true to its investment size and style discipline. This means if you buy a large-company growth fund, you can be assured it will still be a large-company growth fund in five or 10 years. If the manager begins buying small companies or international stocks or moves from growth to value stocks, it will change your overall allocation and throw your portfolio out of alignment. The manager is hired as a specialist and to manage money in only one part of the market. You should make sure your manager sticks to his or her guns.

Screen 9: Tax Efficiency and Turnover

If you are investing taxable money (as opposed to tax-deferred money in a retirement account), you should find a fund with low turnover and a high tax-efficiency rating. Low turnover means that the fund isn't overactive in its buying and selling. A 100 percent turnover rate means that every position in the portfolio is sold at least once during the year. The average stock fund has a portfolio turnover rate of 117 percent. Lower turnover rates equate to lower taxable capital-gains distributions and often lower fund expenses. Turnover is not as much an issue in a retirement account in which there are no tax consequences for buying and selling. Index funds are tax efficient and should be considered in taxable investment accounts especially if you are in a high tax bracket.

Figure 3 is a summary of the manager search at each stage using

The average stock mutual fund has turnover of 117% each year. This excessive trading within a fund can increase fund distributions and boost your tax burden.

the criteria above to identify an above-average, large-company growth mutual fund for Janet Reese.

The two funds that made our short list compared like this:

Figure 3

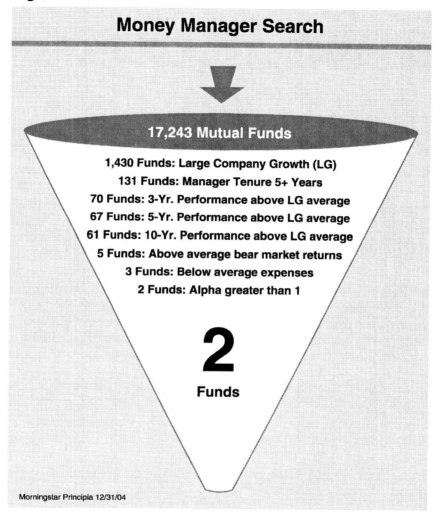

Money Manager Search

17,243 Mutual Funds

1,430 Funds: Large Company Growth (LG)
131 Funds: Manager Tenure 5+ Years
70 Funds: 3-Yr. Performance above LG average
67 Funds: 5-Yr. Performance above LG average
61 Funds: 10-Yr. Performance above LG average
5 Funds: Above average bear market returns
3 Funds: Below average expenses
2 Funds: Alpha greater than 1

2
Funds

Morningstar Principia 12/31/04

Fund No. 1:

- Beat its benchmark index five out of 10 years
- Manager with 14 years' tenure
- True to its size and style discipline
- Has a high turnover rate
- Has expenses below the category average (1.08%)

Fund No. 2:

- Beat its benchmark index four out of 10 years
- Manager with 14 years tenure
- True to its size and style discipline
- Has a turnover rate of 67%
- Has lower than the average expenses (0.98%)

After using these nine screens and comparing the funds that made our short list side by side, Janet and I made an educated decision. Fund No. 1 won the battle because of its slightly more consistent performance. We went ahead and purchased the fund in Janet's IRA.

After completing the search for the large-company growth fund, we repeated the same process for each of the other asset classes in her portfolio. Once completed, Janet and I had sifted through more than 17,000 funds and purchased nine of the best funds available.

How far would the funds you own make it through this filtering process? If the answer is "not very," then you may need to make some changes to your portfolio (and maybe to your broker if the funds are a result of poor recommendations). The Web Helps on the next page provide several resources to help you see how the funds you own stack up. If you already own funds, use the criteria listed above to check to see how they rank. Chapter 15 will discuss at what point to sell a fund when it slips from the top of the pack. Managers can fall to the bottom of their asset category in one "off" year, but be well above-average in the other nine and have fantastic track records. Don't make too much out of one bad year.

If you are working with a financial advisor, he or she can conduct for you an investment search using high tech software. Your advisor should justify his or her recommendations and show you how the investments compare with all of the options available to you. *Make sure your advisor is identifying above-average investments for your portfolio.*

Buy your mutual funds at a firm that offers a giant fund supermarket, so you can buy funds from multiple fund families and hold them all in one account. Both Fidelity Investments and Charles Schwab offer very large fund offerings.

Do Your Homework

By hiring professional money managers rather than managing a large portfolio of individual stocks and bonds on your own, you are more likely to enjoy better investment results. Using the information in this chapter, you should now be more prepared and equipped to identify the best money managers when you buy mutual funds, variable annuities or life insurance, and separately managed accounts. Identifying a money manager who can deliver better-than-average returns over the long run could put hundreds of thousands of additional dollars in your pocket. Doing your homework will pay off.

There are a handful of sites on the Internet that make mutual fund searches relatively easy. These sites can be used to see if your current funds make the grade or to identify new funds for your portfolio.

Conduct Your Own Mutual Fund Search
- Morningstar: http://www.morningstar.com
- Lipper: http://www.lipperleaders.com

Evaluate the Funds You Currently Own
- Morningstar: http://www.morningstar.com
- Lipper: http://www.lipperleaders.com

Prescreened Fund Lists by Asset Category
- Morningstar: http://www.morningstar.com. (Morningstar charges a monthly or annual fee for this service.)

The Great Debate: Passive vs. Active Investing

An index mutual fund buys and holds every stock or bond in an index in hopes of mirroring the performance of that index. Index funds are "passively managed," meaning the manager of an index fund simply follows the actions of the index. The goal of an index fund is not to beat the index but to match it.

There are different indexes that measure each asset class in the market. Most people are familiar with at least two indexes, both of which measure the performance of U.S. large-company growth and value stocks: the S&P 500 (500 stocks) and the Dow Jones Industrial Average (30 stocks). The Vanguard Index 500 Fund, for example, replicates the performance of the S&P 500 Index by owning all 500 stocks in the S&P. If you want to own just large-company growth stocks or small-company value stocks, you could purchase an index made up of just those asset classes.

Why would you settle for the performance of a boring old index? Why accept mediocrity? After all, you can buy a fund with a manager who actively buys and sells securities and whose stated goal is to earn returns better than an index's returns. You can look for a manager who has beat the index, but statistics are stacked against you finding one that can do this consistently.

Figure 4

Low-Cost Index Fund Families

Mutual Funds
    Vanguard 1-800-662-7447

Exchange-Traded Funds
    Barclays iShares 1-800-474-2737

Studies have shown that 75 percent of all fund managers are beaten by their benchmark indexes over time. By buying actively managed funds, you're essentially placing a bet that you can identify the 25 percent of money managers who can outperform their indexes. Some experts believe it is impossible to consistently identify these winning managers, no matter the level of your expertise. Oh, you might get lucky from time to time, they say, but in the long run, you won't beat the index.

 FACT 75 percent of actively managed mutual funds are outperformed by their respective market indexes.

Another advantage of index funds is expenses. Because index funds don't actively trade the securities they own, they are often much cheaper than actively managed funds. As we have seen, fees cut into returns, so a cheap index fund has a head start over an actively managed fund right out of the gate.

If you believe in index funds, then your life just became easier. No detailed fund search is necessary. Simply decide on your allocation (like the example in Figure 1) and buy the cheapest index funds available in each asset class.

Understanding Your Money Management Choices

Read the following pages if you are still unclear on the differences between mutual funds, variable life or annuity subaccounts, and separately managed accounts.

Mutual Funds

The easiest and most popular way of hiring a professional money manager is by investing in mutual funds. Mutual funds have greatly increased in popularity over the past 20 years. In 1980, only 4.6 million households in the United States owned a mutual fund. By the year 2000, that number had soared to more than 50 million. Fifteen years ago, there were only 1,180 mutual funds[4] available to investors, compared with the 17,000 *plus* available today.

 Almost half of U.S. households own a mutual fund. Of households with incomes over $100,000, 77 percent own mutual funds.[5]

In a mutual fund, investors pool their money together in a common fund and hire a professional money manager to invest and manage the money. Investors become a fractional owner of each security held by the fund regardless of the size of their investment. If the underlying stocks or bonds held in the portfolio increase in value, the value of the fund shares, or net asset value (NAV), will appreciate also. Each fund has a specific investment objective that determines the types of stocks or bonds the manager can purchase (large-company stocks, small-company stocks, etc.). It's the money manager's responsibility to search for the best securities available, usually stocks or bonds, within the fund's objective and make the day-to-day decisions about what to buy and sell. A strict buy discipline is observed to determine which securities to add to the portfolio. Once purchased, each security is monitored and eventually sold based on a sell strategy.

Most managers diversify the money in the fund by owning 100 to 200 different securities. The average stock fund owns 166 securities, and the average bond fund owns 325 securities. (See stock fund example in Figure 5). Although you are a fractional owner of all the securities in the fund, you will not see a list of these securities and the shares of each you own on your statements. Your statements will simply report the number of shares and the value of the fund, not the individual

Figure 5

Van Kampen Comstock A

Security Name	% Net Assets	Security Name	% Net Assets	Security Name	% Net Assets
Halliburton	4.34	DuPont De Nemours	1.04	Credence Systems	0.34
Sprint	4.00	ConocoPhillips	0.91	Lexmark International	0.33
Schlumberger	3.46	Unilever NV ADR	0.89	Assurant	0.32
Verizon	3.38	Kraft Foods	0.86	Scottish Power PLC	0.32
Freddie Mac	3.35	Schering-Plough	0.85	Merrill Lynch	0.32
Bristol-Myers Squibb	3.29	Jones Apparel Group	0.83	Travelers	0.31
GlaxoSmithKline	2.75	FirstEnergy	0.83	Ericsson	0.31
SBC Communications	2.41	Alcoa	0.81	SunGard Data	0.30
Dow Chemical	2.39	Ambac Financial	0.77	Rohm and Haas	0.30
Georgia-Pacific Group	2.25	Boise Cascade	0.75	IBM	0.29
Kroger	2.22	Federated Dept. Stores	0.72	CenterPoint Energy	0.29
Bank of America	2.14	Torchmark	0.71	Microsoft	0.28
Kimberly-Clark	2.03	Flextronics Intnl.	0.64	SunTrust Banks	0.24
International Paper	1.98	Hewlett-Packard	0.62	Kemet	0.20
TXU	1.82	Cognex	0.59	Andrew	0.20
Wells Fargo	1.81	Public Service Ent.	0.58	Jabil Circuit	0.19
GlobalSantaFe	1.68	Eastman Kodak	0.57	Capital One Financial	0.17
Citigroup	1.65	Burlington Northern	0.55	Renaissance Re	0.17
Transocean	1.52	Metropolitan Life	0.54	Principal Fin. Group	0.17
Walt Disney	1.48	AmerisourceBergen	0.54	Check Point Software	0.17
Pfizer	1.45	CVS	0.53	Amdocs	0.14
BP PLC ADR	1.42	Constellation Energy	0.48	Affiliated Computer	0.14
Aetna	1.31	Darden Restaurants	0.47	Exelon	0.13
Chubb	1.29	Fannie Mae	0.45	Berkshire Hathaway B	0.12
Allstate	1.28	Diamond Offshore	0.45	Novellus Systems	0.09
PNC Financial	1.22	American Electric	0.42	Goldman Sachs	0.08
McDonald's	1.22	General Motors	0.42	Cisco Systems	0.08
Altria Group	1.18	Wyeth	0.41	Intel	0.08
Total SA ADR	1.14	J.P. Morgan Chase	0.40	JDS Uniphase	0.07
Liberty Media	1.12	May Dept. Stores	0.39	Travelers	0.06
Clear Channel	1.09	Nokia ADR	0.37	Comverse Technology	0.06
Roche Holding	1.05	Merck	0.35	Nationwide	0.04

Holdings as of 2/29/2004

stock and bond positions. Therefore, it is not always apparent what you own. Professional money management and diversification are the main reasons investors choose mutual funds.

Variable Annuities

Would you like a tax-deferred mutual fund? Think of a variable annuity as a tax-deferred mutual fund account. You can buy variable annuities through brokerage firms, banks, insurance companies, and mutual fund companies. Ultimately, however, annuities are products of the insurance companies. Insurance companies administer the annuity contracts — providing tax deferral — while a mutual fund company is hired to perform the day-to-day money management. The insurance company typically hires a number of portfolio managers from different fund companies to manage individual funds (called sub-accounts) within the annuity contract.

Similar to the IRAs you own, money invested in variable annuities can't be withdrawn without penalty until you reach age 59 ½. Most contracts offer between 20 to 30 different subaccount investment choices, covering a wide spectrum of asset classes including large-company stocks, small-company stocks, international stocks, bonds, and more. Today, there are 687 variable annuities available. These annuities combined offer more than 22,000 subaccounts.

It is not a good idea to buy annuities with your IRA money, because IRA dollars are already tax-deferred. There is no sense paying an insurance company an extra fee for tax-deferral you already have. The primary attraction of variable annuities, as you can see, is tax-deferral.

 Don't buy a variable annuity with IRA money.

Variable Life Insurance

Variable life insurance combines mutual funds with life insurance. When you pay a premium to buy variable life insurance, part of your premium covers the cost of the insurance, and the balance is deposited into an investment account within the policy (cash value). Much like a variable annuity, the insurance company will generally hire 20 to 30 money managers to manage each subaccount (like mutual funds). Using these investment choices, you can develop a strategy for investing your policy's cash value. There are 332 variable life insurance policies available and more than 12,000 sub-accounts.

The nice thing about variable life insurance is that your cash value (the money you invest in stock and bond subaccounts) grows tax-deferred and can be withdrawn tax-free. A tax-free growth or income mutual fund doesn't sound too bad, does it? Unfortunately, to obtain this tax-free benefit you must buy life insurance, which comes with additional costs. If you need the insurance and can find a low-cost, no-load policy, adding an investment component to your life coverage may be worth considering.

Buying no-load mutual funds, variable annuities, and life insurance can dramatically cut your built-in investment and insurance expenses and also eliminate front- and back-end sales charges. (Read Chapter 15 before buying any of these financial products).

Separately Managed Accounts

Hiring a separate account manager (also referred to as private, independent, or institutional money manager) is another way to obtain professional money management. As with mutual funds, the market for separately managed accounts (SMAs) has also grown rapidly. In 1996, $165 billion was invested in SMAs. By the end of 1999, that number had risen to $425 billion. It is estimated that by 2006, SMAs will top $930 billion.[6]

When a separate account manager purchases a portfolio of stocks or bonds, the individual investor owns each security outright. This is different than a public mutual fund or a subaccount in a variable annuity or life policy, in which investors own a fraction of each security held by the fund and essentially share what is owned.

In the past, these private money managers managed money only for the wealthy who could meet the high $1 million or more minimum initial investment. Now, through many SMA programs, investors can invest with as little as $100,000. Portfolios in the United States are getting larger and investment minimums have fallen as assets pour into

SMAs. If you haven't yet heard about them, you will. However, even with lower minimums, it is difficult to obtain *proper diversification* without at least $1 million to invest. Hiring just two or three managers won't allow you to cover the many segments of the stock and bond markets.

Separately managed accounts are more concentrated than mutual funds. They invest in just 30 to 50 different securities. By contrast, most mutual funds invest in more than 100 securities.

Figure 6 illustrates a sample $100,000, large-cap growth portfolio managed by Rittenhouse Investment Management, Inc., the nation's second largest SMA manager.[7] Investors owning this portfolio would own only 28 stocks. Contrary to mutual funds, each statement you receive from a separate account manager will itemize each position you own, including the number of shares, share price, purchase price (cost basis), profit and loss per position, and portfolio changes from the previous month.

If you can meet the higher minimums, want more customization in your portfolio composition, and want to own securities outright rather than share them with other investors, then you should consider SMAs.

Mutual Funds Win!

In most cases, people who are looking for professional

Figure 6

Rittenhouse Investment Management
Large-Cap Growth

Portfolio Size $100,000

NAME	%
ABBOTT LABS	3.45%
AMER INTL GROUP INC	5.15%
AUTOMATIC DATA PROC	4.93%
BEST FOODS	2.13%
COCA COLA COM	4.33%
COLGATE PALMOLIVE	4.31%
WALT DISNEY COMPANY	2.95%
EMERSON ELEC CO	2.50%
FREDDIE MAE	3.44%
FANNIE MAY (USA) COM	3.83%
GENERAL ELECTRIC	5.84%
GILLETTE CO	1.77%
HEWLETT PACKARD CO	2.03%
HOME DEPOT INC	5.26%
INTEL CORP	3.60%
JOHNSON & JOHNSON	4.75%
LUCENT TECHNOLOGIES	2.31%
MEDTRONIC INC	2.36%
MERCK & CO INC	4.43%
PEPSICO INC	3.79%
PFIZER INC	5.03%
PROCTER GAMBLE	4.77%
STATE STREET CORP	2.72%
SCHERING-PLOUGH CORP.	5.08%
WAL MART STORES INC	2.02%
WALGREEN CO	2.00%
WELLS FARGO & CO NEW	2.62%
MONEY MARKET RESERVES	1.23%
TOTAL	**100%**

Source: Rittenhouse Investment Management, Sample Large Cap Growth Portfolio 2001 money management should stick with mutual funds. While the other money management options do have their place in the right situation, as you'll see in Chapter 15, good no-load funds often come with lower expenses and less restrictions. Variable annuities, for instance, are more expensive than mutual funds, often have surrender charges that last for seven or more years and in most cases shouldn't be purchased with IRA money. Variable life insurance, in addition to higher built-in investment expenses, also carries an annual premium. Investors shouldn't pay the additional insurance expenses and agree to lengthy surrender charges unless they need the insurance. And finally, while SMAs provide some customization that funds don't, the higher minimum investment requirements often make proper diversification hard to obtain. Be sure to compare all of your options before investing any money.

FIFTEEN

"No Load" Means Lower Costs

✓ RETIREMENT DECISION #13: *Should I buy load or no-load mutual funds, annuities and life insurance?*

Would you buy a blue BMW for $100,000 when you could buy a BMW of the same make, model and year for only $50,000 at another dealership? To make it even easier to decide, what if the $100,000 BMW had a condition attached requiring you to pay a penalty of up to $5,000 if you decide to sell the car during the next five years? The answer is obvious, right? Well, millions of investors are choosing the equivalent of the $100,000 BMW when they purchase mutual funds, variable annuities, or life-insurance policies that come with "loads."

Loads are sales charges. They occur when an investment or insurance product is bought or sold. The money from loads, in the form of commissions, ends up in the pockets of advisors and brokers who sell these products. Loads also go to the investment and insurance companies to help pay for distribution and marketing costs. And that's on top of the built-in expenses an investment product charges for the day-to-day management of the fund or policy. As you can see, loaded investment products can be quite expensive. Fortunately for you and me, there are thousands of mutual funds, annuities, and life-insurance products available that have no loads. You can often save thousands of dollars per year in investment and insurance expenses by using no-load products. Why pay more if you don't have to?

 According to a recent NASD survey, 78 percent of Americans can name a character on a television sitcom, but only 12 percent know the difference between a 'load' and 'no-load' fund.[1]

Let's compare the cost differences between load and no-load financial products. Thomas Rockwell during the past year changed jobs, sold some land, and decided to update his life-insurance plan. He is 55 years old and needs to make some big financial decisions. After careful consideration, he decides on the following strategy:

- Rollover the $100,000 in his former employer's 401(k) to his IRA and buy a large-company U.S. stock mutual fund.
- Take the $100,000 he received from the land sale and buy a variable annuity to build up his retirement assets.
- Buy a $1 million cash value life-insurance policy for estate-planning purposes.

After doing his homework, he's narrowed his choices to two mutual funds, two annuities, and two life-insurance policies: one carries a load; the other is no-load. He now must decide between the two. My advice to Thomas: Proceed with caution! The wrong decision will increase his expenses by more than $9,000 per year.

Mutual Funds: Load vs. No-Load

Thomas decided to roll his $100,000 401(k) balance into a U.S. stock mutual fund in an IRA. After evaluating the performance and management of many funds, he narrowed the choices to two funds with similar management, performance, and investment strategies: a load fund recommended by a commissioned advisor and a no-load fund he found on his own. Which should he choose? A quick price check will help answer the question.

First of all, with load funds there's no such thing as a *quick* price check. There's a myriad of expenses and fees, and they are complicated. In a nutshell, there are two things to look at when you're trying to figure out how much a load fund will cost you: the expense ratio and the load.

The expense ratio is straightforward. It's the amount the fund charges you annually to manage and operate the fund. The fund automatically deducts the expense ratio from your total return. If the fund returns 7 percent and its expense ratio is 2 percent, you take home a total return of 5 percent.

Loads are more complicated. Load funds are often divided into three different share classes, each with different charges and expenses, depending on how they are sold to investors. "A" shares typically carry a front-end sales charge, meaning that investors pay the charge when they buy shares. "B" shares are back-loaded; investors pay a sales charge if they sell the fund within a certain period of time. "C" shares are "level-loaded," meaning they carry a small load on the back end but have a sky-high expense ratio. In our example, Thomas is considering the B share of the load fund.

No-load funds are a bit easier to evaluate since there are no sales charges when you buy or sell them.

Figure 1

Front- & Back-End Sales Charges (Loads)

Fund Type	Front-End Sales Charge	Back-End Sales Charge
No-Load Mutual Funds	0%	0%
Load Mutual Funds Class A Shares	4-5%	0%
Load Mutual Funds Class B Shares	0%	5% in year 1 4% in year 2 3% in year 3 2% in year 4 1% in year 5 0% in year 6
Load Mutual Funds Class C Shares	0%	1% in year 1 0% in year 2

Note: This is a sample sales charge schedule. Sales charges will vary by company.

The B share load fund Thomas is considering has an expense ratio of 2.07 percent, which is average for this type of load fund.[2] On a $100,000 investment, the fund will cost him $2,070 per year in expenses. Keep in mind that these high expenses are what pays the fund manager's salary and the advisor a commission. When he invests $100,000 into a B share, the fund company will typically pay his advisor a 4% commission, or $4,000.

Also remember that the expense ratios of load funds tend to be higher than those of no-load funds. The funds' expenses are taken directly from its returns; the higher the funds' expenses, the lower your returns. John Bogle, the founder of the mutual fund company Vanguard, compared the performance of equity mutual funds over the past 10 years and found that the funds with the lowest costs outperformed their more expensive counterparts by 2 to 5 percentage points each year.[3]

The B share fund Thomas in contemplating also has a five-year back-end sales charge. If Thomas sells the fund during the first five years, he will pay a sales charge that starts at 5 percent of the balance in the first year and declines to 0 percent at the six-year mark. If he wants to make changes with his investment during the next five years, it will cost him.

By contrast, the cost of the no-load fund is just 1.07 percent.[4] That's just $1,070 annually for a $100,000 portfolio. (You could easily find even cheaper no-load funds; some no-load index funds have expense ratios as low as 0.15%.)

Which would you choose if you were Thomas: the load fund or the no-load fund?

If all other variables are equal, why would Thomas choose to pay $2,070 per year, plus a back-end sales charge, when he can pay just $1,070 (a savings of $1,000)? Multiply that difference over 10, 20, and 30 years, and he'll really see that costs do matter. We're not even taking into account the missed returns he would have earned if the money he saved with the cheaper fund was invested back into the fund.

Figure 2 outlines the annual expenses of the average mutual fund, broken down by load and no-load funds.

Figure 2

Annual Built-In Mutual Fund Expenses

Fund Type	Load Fund Class A*	Load Fund Class B	Load Fund Class C	No-Load Funds	Annual Difference NL & Load**
U.S. Equity	1.41%	2.07%	2.05%	1.07%	1.00%
U.S. Equity $100,000	$1,410	$2,070	$2,050	$1,070	$1,000
U.S. Bond	1.04%	1.76%	1.73%	0.71%	1.05%
U.S. Bond $100,000	$1,040	$1,760	$1,730	$710	$1,050

Note: Figures above represent the expense ratios for the average fund in each asset and share class.
Source: Morningstar Principia June 2003 Release. **Class B shares. *Class A shares carry upfront charges.

All mutual funds charge fees that are built in to the pricing of your shares. Because you will never receive a bill for these fees, however, most people have no idea what they are paying to have their money managed. By understanding the fees your funds are charging, you can often find ways to dramatically reduce your costs and increase your liquidity. One of the easiest ways to accomplish this is by owning no-load funds. Why pay more?

Mutual Fund Cost Calculator:
Want to find out what your mutual funds are costing you?
Log-in to www.personalfund.com and use the simple mutual fund cost calculator (registration is free).

Variable Annuities: Load vs. No-Load

After selling the land, Thomas decided to sock another $100,000 away for his retirement by purchasing a variable annuity. He's evaluated the performance and management of many annuities and narrowed his choices: the most popular load annuity or a low-cost no-load annuity. Again, as with the mutual funds, the decision is a no-brainer.

Putting $100,000 into the typical load annuity will cost Thomas about $2,440 (2.44 percent)[5] per year in insurance and fund management expenses. His agent will receive a $6,000 commission. By contrast the no-load annuity will only cost him only $720 (0.72 percent).[6] If all other variables are equal, again why would he choose to pay $1,720 more to go with the more expensive annuity? To make matters worse, the load annuity has a seven-year deferred sales charge. If he decides to move his money to an annuity at another company or surrender it during the first seven years, he will pay a surrender charge of 7 percent in year one, declining to 0 percent in year eight. In contrast, no-load annuities, like no-load mutual funds, do not tack on deferred sales charges, so his money is available without penalty.

With the choice of 687 variable annuities, there is no reason to purchase one with high expenses and surrender charges. Vanguard, Fidelity, Ameritas, and T. Rowe Price are among the most well-known companies offering no-load annuities. Like Thomas, you would be wise to consider your no-load options before buying a variable annuity. Why pay more?

Figure 3

Annual Built-In Variable Annuity Expenses

	Annuity Expense %	Annuity Expense (100K Investment)
No-Load Variable Annuity*		
Insurance Expense	0.37%	$370
Fund Expense (Average)	0.35%	$350
Total Expenses	**0.72%**	**$720**
Load Variable Annuity**		
Insurance Expense	1.52%	$1,520
Fund Expense (Average)	0.92%	$920
Total Expenses	**2.44%**	**$2,440**

*Vanguard Variable Annuity **AIG Anchor National Polaris Platnium
Source: Morningstar Principia June 2003

Life Insurance: Load vs. No-Load

No-load life insurance can also save you thousands of dollars each year. Let's assume Thomas now decides to purchase a $1 million universal life policy. His long-time agent quoted him a minimum premium of $10,032 per year. This policy has a 15-year surrender period, meaning he will incur a penalty if he withdraws any of his cash value during this time. Thomas' agent will make a commission of about 80% of the premium he'll pay in the first year, or $8,025! (Commission amounts vary company to company.) Thomas also obtained a comparable quote from a no-load life insurance company with a minimum premium of only $3,595 per year.[7] The no-load policy has no surrender charges, so his cash value is always available to him without penalty. With all assumptions being equal, why would he pay $6,437 more for the same amount of insurance and agree to restrictions when he has a need to access cash value?

Never heard of no-load life insurance? You are not alone. Insurance agents are unwilling to discuss these policies with their clients because "no-load" means "no commission." What happens to insurance when you remove the agent and strip out the commissions? Often premiums for cash value policies are slashed by 50 to 70 percent, and surrender charges are completely eliminated.

Figure 4

Life Insurance Comparison

$1 Million Universal Life (Male, Non-Smoker, Age 55)	Load Policy	No-Load Policy
Minimum 1st Year Premium	$10,032	$3,595
Cash Value (End of First Year)	$0	$910
Target Premium	$26,000	$26,000
Cash Value (End of First Year)	$7,298	$24,777

Source: Fee Planners Network 2003

Insurance companies incur expenses during the first year of a load policy of about 150% to 250% of the first-year premium payment. Because of these high costs, load premiums are high. No-load insurance costs amount to only about 28% of the first year's premium.[8] These lower expenses translate into lower premiums for you.

How long is the surrender period on your cash value policies? In order to recoup the high up-front expenses of load policies, insurance companies must charge consumers high premiums and strap on long surrender periods to policies to recover their high up-front costs. For example, if your policy has a 15-year surrender period, you will not be able to withdraw your cash value without paying a surrender charge (penalty) until the period is over. If you cancel your policy during the first few years, the surrender charge will likely equal 100%, meaning you will not receive any of your cash value.

 Investors pay more than $6 billion each year in unnecessary surrender charges.[9]

It's outrageous what investors pay each year in surrender charges ($6 billion). Some policies even carry 20-year surrender periods! Would you believe that more than 50 percent of traditional whole life policies are canceled within the first five years and more than 70 percent are canceled by the 10th year?[10] Considering your odds of canceling your policy during the first 10 years, it seems ludicrous to purchase insurance with a 10- to 20-year surrender penalty period.

With no-load life insurance, however, you won't be penalized with surrender charges if you need to make a change in your insurance strategy. Because no-load policies have no surrender charges, cash values are immediately available. Lower premiums and no-surrender charges make a pretty good case for the purchase of no-load life insurance. Ameritas Life Insurance Co., ING, Fidelity, and TIAA-CREF each offer solid no-load policies. Finally, a life insurance policy without buyer's remorse! Why pay more if you don't have to?

 Your odds of you buying a traditional life insurance policy and owning it for your lifetime are extremely low. More than 50% of traditional life insurance policies are cancelled within the first five years and 70% are cancelled within 10 years.

Buying No-Load Funds, Annuities, and Life Insurance

Before buying a no-load investment or insurance product, you must decide whether you want to do it yourself or retain the expertise of a financial advisor. If you're a "do-it-yourselfer," you can simply call the no-load companies and deal with them directly.

If you would like an investment professional to work with you face to face and help you evaluate and sift through all of the no-load products, hire a "fee-only" financial advisor. As opposed to commissioned brokers and agents, fee-only advisors do not accept commissions for recommending specific products — consequently, they can be totally objective. Fee-only advisors are compensated only by a previously agreed upon, fully-disclosed fee with you, either paid hourly, by project, or as a percentage of assets managed. Fee-only advisors can help investors:

- Compare costs of load and no-load products.
- Identify and purchase cost-effective financial products.
- Sort through all the features and benefits each product offers.
- Develop an investment strategy and financial plan.
- Manage your portfolio and financial plan on an on-going basis.

What to Do if You Own Expensive Funds, Annuities, and Life Insurance?

It's easy to make the move from load to no-load products.

First, have your investments and insurance analyzed to determine what you are paying and determine if a no-load solution could reduce your costs and increase your liquidity.

Second, check to see what you would be charged (if anything) to transfer your money from your loaded product. This is the biggest issue you'll face when making the switch from load to no-load. Beware of back-end charges and redemption fees. If these charges are substantial, you may have to wait it out until the back-end charges cease.

Third, determine if any tax consequences will result from the move to no-load. Selling your loaded mutual funds in a non-retirement account, for example, may result in a capital gain.

With mutual funds, you can directly transfer money from your load company to a no-load fund company or a discount brokerage firm. If you directly transfer an IRA, there are no taxes or penalties. With annuities and life insurance, you can transfer your cash surrender value tax-free to another annuity or life-insurance product (known as a 1035 exchange). Making the jump from load to no-load is simple, and it could save you a lot of money and increase your liquidity.

Conclusion

Remember, "load" is synonymous with "commission." Loaded financial products are sold by commissioned financial advisors. To pay your advisor a commission, companies simply increase built-in expenses. They also strap on front- and back-end sales and surrender charges that restrict your ability to sell or withdraw your money without penalty. These restrictions are intended to keep you invested, so the load companies can recoup the money they paid your advisor. No-load products, by contrast, don't pay commissions and consequently don't have to build in high internal expenses and restrictive charges.

By choosing the no-load mutual fund, annuity, and life-insurance policy in our example, Thomas would reduce his investment and insurance expenses in the first year by more than $9,000.[11] If these savings continued for 10 years, it would amount to more than $90,000. If we could account for his increased returns as a result of not having to pay these extra costs, and compound the savings over 10 years, his savings would be considerably more.

By choosing the no-load route, Thomas' commissioned advisor would miss out on about $18,000 of commissions. If, for some reason, he does choose the load products, Thomas should insist that his advisor disclose the commissions he will receive and demand service equal to this compensation.

Although cost is only one variable to consider when choosing investments and insurance, it must not be overlooked. Carefully evaluate the investment and insurance expenses you pay. By making some minor adjustments, you may save thousands of dollars.

Figure 5

No-Load Companies

Mutual Funds	Phone Number
Vanguard	1-800-662-7447
Fidelity	1-800-544-8888
American Century	1-800-345-2021
Janus	1-800-525-8983
T. Rowe Price	1-800-638-5660

Variable Annuities	Phone Number
Vanguard	1-800-523-9954
Fidelity	1-800-544-2442
TIAA/CREF	1-800-842-2733
Janus	1-800-504-4440
T. Rowe Price	1-800-460-6587

Life Insurance	Phone Number
Fidelity	1-888-343-8376
Ameritas	1-800-255-9678
TIAA/CREF	1-800-223-1200
ING (Security Life Of Denver)	1-866-464-7355
Paragon/MetLife (Group Only)	1-800-685-0124

SIXTEEN

Safer Ways to Own Stocks

Did your stock investments cause you to lose any sleep from 2000 to 2002 while the U.S. stock market suffered a 49 percent drop?[1] If so, you likely invested too aggressively. As we've discussed, a properly diversified investment portfolio could have dramatically softened the blow of this monstrous decline (see sample portfolios in Chapter 12). However, if you're still a little skittish about investing in stocks in the wake of this market plunge, diversification alone simply may not be enough for you. Many investors need the higher returns offered by stocks over the long term to reach their retirement goals, but they are scared away by the volatility and uncertainty of the equity markets.

This raises an interesting question. Is there a way to participate in the stock market while at the same time protecting investment principal? The answer may surprise you. Read on. Here are four strategies that will allow you to reap much of the gains the stock market offers without exposing your fragile nest egg to the wild west of the open market. Finally, you'll be able to get a good night's sleep.

Strategy 1: Buy Index-Linked CDs

Index-linked certificates of deposit pay interest based on the performance of the stock market, rather than a fixed interest rate with which most CD investors are familiar. Index-linked CDs are tied to major stock *indexes* like the S&P 500, NASDAQ, the Dow Jones Industrial Average, or an international stock index. However, unlike buying a stock or stock mutual fund, the investment principal is FDIC insured.

During the Bad Times

To illustrate how index-linked CDs work, let's consider the fate

266 ■ THE RETIRING BOOMER'S FINANCIAL HANDBOOK

of two separate investors, Peter Chung and Catherine Swenson, each with $100,000 to invest. In January 1999, Peter deposited $100,000 into a five-year index-linked CD tied to the S&P 500. That same month, Catherine used her $100,000 to buy an S&P 500 stock index mutual fund.

How did each investor fair from 1999 to 2003, a period marked by the *largest losses* in the stock market since the mid-1970s? Peter got his principal back at maturity without losing a cent; Catherine was left with $97,000. The difference in ending values doesn't seem too dramatic. However, at one point in August 2002, Catherine's mutual fund balance dropped to a low of $69,500. Think of the difference in stress and anxiety Peter and Catherine must have been feeling during this time. While Catherine was losing sleep, Peter knew that he would at least get his principal back at maturity regardless of what happened in the stock market. Imagine the peace of mind this guarantee may have provided from 2000 to 2002.

Like many investors, Catherine was wondering at her low point if she would ever recover her $30,500 loss, and she was tempted to sell her fund and give up entirely on investing in stocks. Though she nearly recovered her original investment by patiently holding on and riding out the stormy markets, many investors fared much worse. Thousands of people simply could not handle the continued stress of a plummeting stock market and incurred big losses as they sold their stock positions to get out of the market. Unlike Catherine, these impatient investors weren't invested when the stock market quickly rebounded in 2003 and will consequently spend years trying to recapture their losses.

During the Good Times

The results are dramatically opposite during times when the market is strong. For example, if Peter had invested his $100,000 into an S&P 500 CD in January 1995, he would have received $224,956 at maturity in January 2000. This doesn't sound too bad, unless you compare it to what Catherine would have earned. Catherine's investment into an S&P 500 *mutual fund* over the same period would have provided $93,418 more, finishing at $318,374 (dividends reinvested). So what was the difference? The answer is caps, calls, and participation rates.

So, What's the Catch?

The trade-off for principal protection is restrictions. Index-linked CDs often have caps, limited participation rates, and call provisions that can limit upside potential.

Caps limit the maximum gain you can receive. An investment into an index-linked CD with a 100 percent cap, for example, would limit your gain to 100 percent. A $100,000 investment in a CD with a 100 percent cap would return a maximum of $100,000, plus the $100,000 principal, even if the market went up 200 percent during the CD's term.

Participation rates are another way returns are curbed. Some index-linked CDs will allow investors to participate in only 80 percent to 90 percent of the stock market index increase. Call provisions give the bank the option of redeeming the CD prematurely to avoid having to pay huge sums of interest in the event of a big stock market run-up.

In addition to these drawbacks, money invested in index-linked CDs is normally tied up for at least five years, and any early withdrawals by investors are penalized. Also, index-linked CDs are tied to the absolute performance of a stock index and don't take into account dividends, which can compound growth if reinvested in a mutual fund.

Even with all the restrictions, index-linked CDs still make sense for investors looking for stock market participation and peace of mind.

Where to Buy?

Banks issue index-linked CDs. They are FDIC insured up to $100,000 per institution per account type (individual, joint, IRA, etc.). To obtain FDIC insurance for portfolios over $100,000, investors can purchase CDs from multiple banks. If you plan to manage a large portfolio of index-linked CDs, use a single brokerage account to buy and hold CDs from multiple banks.

If you like the idea of being ultra-safe even if it means having to endure some restrictions and limited access to your money, index-linked CDs may be the perfect investment for you. You could buy a diversified portfolio of CDs and essentially guarantee your entire equity portfolio. Add to that a portfolio of insured municipal bonds or U.S. Treasury bonds and a money market account or traditional certificate of deposit, and you

Figure 1

Sample Principal Protection Portfolio

Stocks
1. S&P 500 Index Linked CD
2. Dow Jones Ind. Index Linked CD
3. Nasdaq Index Linked CD
4. Nikki Index Linked CD

Bonds
5. U.S Treasury Bond
6. Insured Municipal Bond

Cash
7. Money Market Interest Account
8. Traditional Certificate of Deposit

could participate in the stock, bond, and cash markets without risking principal at all. See the sample principal protection portfolio in Figure 1.

Strategy 2: Zeros & Stocks

Keith and Rose Young retired in 2001 with a savings of $100,000. They needed this sum to grow at a fairly good rate during their retirement but were afraid to invest money in stocks. Investing in stocks had always caused them too much anxiety. It stressed them out to think about their life savings being exposed to the illogical ups and downs of the market, and they vowed not to live their retirement in a panic. So they decided to employ the "zero strategy." As you will see, using an instrument called U.S. Treasury zero coupon bonds, Keith and Rose, were able to participate in the stock market without risking their $100,000 savings.

The Zero Strategy

Here's how the zero strategy works. First, because Keith and Rose wanted to protect their $100,000 foremost, they purchased a 10-year zero coupon bond yielding 5 percent from the U.S. Treasury for $61,391. In return, the Treasury promised to give them $100,000 in 10 years. Zero coupon bonds are purchased at a discount ($61,391 in our example), pay no interest during the life of the bond, and mature at face value ($100,000 in our example). The difference between the purchase price and the face value represents the investment return on the bond. Because the zero coupon bond will mature at $100,000, Keith and Rose have guaranteed their initial principal if they hold on to the bond until maturity in 2011. Knowing they'll receive $100,000 at maturity gives them the peace of mind to place the rest of their money in more volatile investments.

Next, they invested the remaining $38,609 in a diversified portfolio of stock mutual funds. They are hoping their stock funds will produce a 10 percent average annual return over the next 10 years. If this occurs, note their results in 2011. The original $61,391 they invested in the zero coupon bond will mature at $100,000, and their $38,609 stock fund investments will be worth $100,141, giving them an ending balance of $200,141 and a 7 percent annual return. Not bad. If everything goes as planned, Keith and Rose will double their investment in 10 years without risking their initial principal.

Worst-Case Scenario

If Keith and Rose's stock portfolio produces a 8 percent annual return, they would end up with $219,913. A 6 percent annual stock return will bring their total to $183,353.

In the unlikely event that, after 10 years, their stock funds are only worth half their original amount ($19,304), they would end the 10-year period with a total of $119,304 (2 percent annual return). A 2 percent return isn't too exciting in this extreme scenario, but it's not disastrous. Remember, their objective would still be met—they would not lose any of their original principal. They are willing to trade big returns in the stock market for modest returns and no principal risk.

Another benefit of this strategy is its liquidity. If something unforeseen occurs and they need cash quickly, they can sell their zero coupon bond and stock mutual funds at the going rate at any time without penalty.

Adopting the Zero Strategy for Your Situation

If you, like Keith and Rose Young, are willing to accept modest returns to avoid risking principal and have the patience to stay the course for a long period of time, the zero coupon bond strategy may work for you. To employ the zero strategy, you must first determine what percentage of your portfolio you would need to invest in a zero coupon bond to insure your portfolio principal. The answer depends on the yield on your zero coupon bond and the years until the bond matures. Figure 2 shows that if you obtain a zero coupon bond yielding 5 percent and want to protect your portfolio over a 10-year period, you would need to invest

Figure 2

Amount to Invest in a Zero Coupon Bond at 5% to Insure Principal

Current Yield	Years to Maturity	Percentage of Portfolio in Zero	Amount of $100,000 Portfolio to Invest in Zero Coupon Bond
5%	15	48%	$48,000
5%	14	51%	$51,000
5%	13	53%	$53,000
5%	12	56%	$56,000
5%	11	58%	$58,000
5%	10	61%	$61,000
5%	9	64%	$64,000
5%	8	68%	$68,000

Figure 3

Amount to Invest in a Zero Coupon Bond at 7% to Insure Principal

Current Yield	Years to Maturity	Percentage of Portfolio in Zero	Amount of $100,000 Portfolio to Invest in Zero Coupon Bond
7%	15	24%	$23,939
7%	14	26%	$26,333
7%	13	29%	$28,966
7%	12	32%	$31,863
7%	11	35%	$35,049
7%	10	39%	$38,554
7%	9	42%	$42,409
7%	8	47%	$46,651

61 percent of your portfolio into the bond. Figure 3 shows you the same results for a 7 percent zero coupon bond.

You might ask yourself, "How good is the bond's guarantee?" That depends on the strength of the bond's issuer. If the U.S. Treasury issues the zero, then it's backed by the full faith and credit of the U.S. government. This is the strongest guarantee in the world today.

So, if you, like the Youngs, are willing to accept modest returns to avoid risking your principal, and you have the patience, the zero strategy may work for you.

Strategy 3: Equity-Indexed Annuities

Another way to participate in stock market gains without risking principal is through an insurance-company instrument called an equity-indexed annuity. An equity-indexed annuity is a hybrid of a fixed annuity and a variable annuity. Fixed annuities pay low interest rates but guarantee principal, and variable annuities offer participation in the returns of the stock market but no guarantee. Equity-indexed annuities fall in between. They offer a minimum guaranteed interest rate combined with an interest rate linked to market index. Like our first two strategies, you'll need to accept some trade-offs to employ this strategy.

The Story of Edward and Van

Edward Baxter's experience investing in equity-indexed annuities provides a helpful example of how they work. In 1998, he invested $250,000 into an annuity pegged to the S&P 500 with a 10 percent annual cap. With a 10 percent cap, Edward couldn't make more than 10 percent per year, even when the market returned more than 10 percent. However, when the stock market dropped as it did from 2000-2002, his account value didn't fall. He finished 2004 with a balance of $366,025. Let's examine his year-to-year experience (Figure 4).

For comparison, Edward's brother Van invested $250,000 in the Vanguard 500 Index Fund at the same time. At the end of 2004, Van had $344,884. However, Van's Vanguard fund took him on a roller-coaster ride. It dropped from a high of $389,162 at the end of 1999 to $242,366 at the end of 2002[3], a 37.72 percent plunge!

Edward's annuity, while capped on the upside, provided him tremendous peace of mind during the 2000-2002 bear market. For him, the equity-indexed annuity proved to be a good investment choice during this period of time.

The Trade-Off

For comparison, let's look at another period of time, like the bull market years from 1995 through 1999. Suppose in 1995 Edward and Van invested their respective $250,000 into the same index annuity and

Figure 4

Index vs. Index Annuity 1998-2004

Year	S&P 500 Return	S&P Fund Year-End Balance	EIA Return	EIA Yr-End Balance
1998	29%	$321,509	10%	$275,000
1999	21%	$389,162	10%	$302,500
2000	-9%	$353,420	0%	$302,500
2001	-12%	$311,293	0%	$302,500
2002	-22%	$242,366	0%	$302,500
2003	29%	$311,468	10%	$332,750
2004	11%	$344,884	10%	$366,025

* Vanguard 500 Index Fund

Vanguard 500 Index Fund. Van's investment in the Vanguard fund would have finished this bullish five years with a massive $875,188 balance. Edward's annuity would have performed well but much less dramatically (see Figure 5). His original $250,000 would have ended the period at $402,628, a whopping $472,560 less than Van's investment. During big bull markets, Edward traded huge returns for peace of mind.

Figure 5

Index vs. Index Annuity 1995-1999

Year	S&P 500 Return	S&P Fund Year-End Balance	EIA Return	EIA Yr-End Balance
1995	37%	$343,355	10%	$275,000
1996	23%	$422,213	10%	$302,500
1997	33%	$562,227	10%	$332,750
1998	29%	$723,043	10%	$366,025
1999	21%	$875,188	10%	$402,628

* Vanguard 500 Index Fund

Beware of Commissions and Complexities

Equity-indexed annuities are only available from insurance companies. Beware that insurance agents have tremendous incentive to push investors into equity-indexed annuities whether they are a good fit for them or not. Some annuities pay commissions as much as 12 percent. This means Edward's $250,000 investment would have generated a $30,000 commission for his agent. That's a lot of money considering there are no further investment decisions to make once the initial paperwork is completed and the contract is issued.

Another trade-off is the complexity of equity-indexed annuities. Buying them can be difficult and confusing. Virtually every major insurance company offers them with dramatically different features. The differences between annuity policies make shopping for them a time-consuming process.

When shopping for an equity-indexed annuity, I strongly urge you to use the checklist below.

1. Index: Determine which stock index you would like your returns to be tied to: S&P 500, NASDAQ, Dow, or Russell 2000.

2. Participation Rate: Seek out an annuity with a 100 percent guaranteed participation rate for the life of the contract. A contract with a 90 percent participation rate, for example, will provide investors with only a 9 percent return if the market goes up 10 percent.

3. Cap Rate: Look for a contract with a high cap rate. The highest caps are generally 10 to 11 percent. If a contract has a 100 percent participation rate up to a 10 percent cap, investors will make a maximum of 10 percent even if the market went up 20 percent.

4. Surrender Charges: Surrender charges range from five to 15 years. Only consider annuities with five- to six-year surrender charges. Agents make more commissions on an annuity with a long surrender period, so they may push people in this direction. Some annuities have surrender charges that last for as many as 15 years. Do not buy a contract

with a term this long. The surrender charge is essentially a penalty charged to investors who cash out of the policy early. For example, let's say you buy a contract carrying a 10-year surrender charge. You will pay a 10 percent penalty for surrendering the contract in the first year, 9 percent in the second year, 8 percent in the third year, and so on until the 10th year. So find an annuity with a short surrender charge period. If you want to change your investment plan, you don't want to have to wait 10 to 15 years to do so. Also, ask how much commission is being paid to your agent.

5. Minimum Guarantee: This feature guarantees a minimum annual interest to be credited to the policy. Guarantees generally range from 0 to 3.5 percent.

6. Interest Crediting Method: Insurance companies use three methods to determine how much interest equity-index annuities are credited: point-to-point, annual reset, and high water mark. Point-to-point annuities are straightforward and simply take the difference between the starting and ending value of the underlying index during the term of the annuity to calculate the interest to be credited. Annual reset annuities credit interest based on the change in the index annually (the disadvantage being that participation rates may change annually). High water mark annuities look at different points during the term of the contract, and they credit interest between the starting point and high point of the index (the disadvantage being typically lower participation rates).

7. Asset Fees (Spreads): Some contracts charge investors an annual fee. Look for an equity index annuity with no spreads.

8. Bonus: To attract clients, some insurance companies offer an upfront bonus to investors when they buy the contract. Essentially, the insurance company will pay you for buying the annuity. This might amount to an additional 3 to 10 percent credited to your contract value. Some contracts pay this upfront while others spread it out, paying it over the life of the contract. Beware: The bigger the bonus, the longer you will be locked into surrender charges. Think about it: If they

pay you a big sum upfront, they need to make sure you stay invested in the contract for the long term so they can recoup the bonus they pay you. In my opinion, a short surrender charge period is more important than a bonus. Too many people lock into long surrender charge periods only to change their plan midstream and are forced to pay large penalties for early withdrawals. This is a mistake.

It is helpful to visit a Web site like www.annuityadvantage.com or ask your agent for a report comparing the hundreds of annuities from different insurance companies side by side. Currently, there are more than 165 equity-index annuities available, two-thirds of which are tied to the performance of the S&P 500.

With all these trade-offs, make sure you understand the features of the equity-index annuity you choose. Because you are going to own your annuity for a long time, you don't want to be surprised five years down the road and find out the features and guarantees were not what you thought.

Strategy 4: Use Variable Annuities with Principal Protection Riders

Insurance companies are continually adding features to their variable annuity contracts to make them more attractive. A little-known feature called a "living benefit" can be added to a variable annuity to provide another way of protecting your portfolio.

What's a variable annuity? Think of it as a tax-deferred mutual fund account. You can buy variable annuities through brokerage firms, banks, insurance companies, and mutual fund companies. Ultimately, however, they are products of insurance companies that administer the annuity contract — providing tax deferral — while a mutual fund company is hired to perform the day-to-day money management. The insurance company typically hires a number of portfolio managers from different fund companies to manage individual funds (called subaccounts) within the annuity contract. Most contracts offer between 20 to 30 different investment choices, covering a wide spectrum of asset classes, including large-company stocks, small-company stocks, international stocks, bonds, and more.

Living Benefit

When you invest your money into some variable annuities, you can opt to have a living benefit rider added to the contract. Here's how the living benefit works. Regardless of the performance of the investments you choose, you are guaranteed that your principal will grow at a rate, usually 5 to 6 percent per year, which varies by contract. While you can cash in on this guarantee typically any time after the seventh year many investors falsely believe this means they can take a complete withdrawal and walk away. It's a little trickier than that.

For example, Ruth White invested $100,000 into a variable annuity with a 6 percent living benefit in 1996. She invested the entire amount into an aggressive stock subaccount. The subaccount performed well initially, and her investment grew to $175,000 by 1999. Between 2000 and 2002, however, Ruth's portfolio balance dropped to just $75,000. Under most circumstances, an investor like Ruth would have been deeply concerned. But because of her annuity's living benefit feature, however, Ruth had two options to handle this loss: 1) Ride out the market downturn in hopes of a future rebound, or 2) Exercise her living benefit option.

Ruth elected to exercise her living benefit option. She got her original investment of $100,000, plus a 6 percent annual rate of return for the previous seven years. This gave Ruth an additional $50,363, making the living benefit value $150,363. The living benefit option allowed Ruth to *annuitize* this $150,363. Ruth liked the fact that she could start receiving payments from the annuity that would provide her with income for life. It was much like receiving a traditional corporate pension payout. (Payments are based on age, life expectancy, and an interest-rate assumption.)

Ruth had many annuity payout options from which to choose. She chose the life-only annuity option and is receiving $13,000 per year for the rest of her life.

So, even though the living benefit does not exactly guarantee your principal investment, it does guarantee the stream of income that your principal can provide. This makes good sense. The reason you have a retirement portfolio is not to admire the dollars it contains but to provide you with income. Why not guarantee your future income?

The Downside

This strategy does have a downside, however. Once you annuitize, you cannot touch your principal from that time forward. Ruth can make no additional withdrawals from the $150,363 portfolio, except for the $13,000 that is being paid out annually. Keep in mind, however, that annuitization is optional and typically would be used only if the markets performed very poorly for a long period of time.

Although this principal protection feature seems somewhat restrictive, it does make sense for two main reasons. First, if the markets perform as they have historically and provide good, solid returns, you will probably never annuitize your contract and exercise the living benefit option. However, having this option provides peace of mind during times of market turmoil and will help you stay invested. You can be confident that no matter what happens in the market, your future retirement income will not be at risk if there is a severe market downturn. Second, the annuity provides tax deferral, which can help your money grow more rapidly.

Know Their Features

You should be familiar with other annuity features available whenever purchasing variable annuity contracts. Again, the features offered by each annuity contract will vary. Here are some examples:

- Many variable annuities will pay you a bonus when you invest. In some cases, this can amount to 4 to 6 percent of the amount you initially deposit. If you invest $100,000, the annuity company will add an extra $4,000 to $6,000 to your account.

- Variable annuities provide a death benefit. Many guarantee a benefit that is equal either to your initial investment or to the highest annual market value of the annuity, whichever is greater. This feature protects the portfolio for your heirs in the event of a market drop.

- Some contracts provide an additional payout at death to cover taxes that may be owed from portfolio gains.

- At one time, virtually all annuities had to be held for five to seven years before they could be liquidated without surrender charges. Now, many contracts offer zero to one-year holding periods, providing tax deferral with liquidity.

- Many variable annuities offer special introductory rates of return if you choose to dollar-cost average money from a fixed account into the variable accounts over a six- to 12-month period. In many cases, these fixed accounts yield 7 to 9 percent.

Before You Buy

Before you buy a variable annuity, consider the following important factors. First, the money cannot be withdrawn before age 59 ½ without a 10 percent IRS early withdrawal penalty, much like the penalties that kick in when you withdraw money early from an IRA. Second, while variable annuities offer additional features, they also carry additional expenses. In addition to the cost of the underlying mutual fund management (usually about 1 percent annually), there is an additional insurance company fees. These fees typically range between 1 to 1.5 percent. Furthermore, if you purchase an annuity and opt for the living benefit, you may pay an additional 0.25 to 0.5 percent per year for this additional rider. You will not see any of these expenses because they are all built into the price of each subaccount. Using no-load annuities can often reduce the built-in expenses you will pay (review Chapter 15 on no-load investing before buying an annuity).

Therefore, when you purchase an annuity, an important consideration is whether or not the additional benefits are worth the extra expense. Regarding the living benefit feature, if it gives you the peace of mind to stay invested in stocks for the long run instead of pulling your money out of the market, then it is definitely worth the extra cost.

Conclusion

These four strategies are certainly not for everyone. But as we've seen, it is possible to participate in the gains of the stock market while protecting your principal. Each strategy is worth considering if the volatility of the stock market is too much for you. Most retirees need some exposure to the stock market to keep their retirement portfolio growing. Being too conservative could keep you from attaining your goals. So if you need peace of mind to stay in the stock market, consider what we've detailed in this chapter.

But remember, if an investment product seems too good to be true, it probably is. Be informed. Each of the above strategies has considerable trade-offs that you must weigh before investing. Only you can decide what your peace of mind is worth.

SEVENTEEN

A Mission Statement for Your Money

✓ RETIREMENT DECISION #14: *How will I manage my portfolio on an ongoing basis?*

Have you ever found yourself in the same position as Calvin Morton? At retirement, a few years ago, Calvin invested $350,000 into several stock and bond mutual funds. He grew increasingly frustrated with the performance of his portfolio after listening to friends tout their investment successes. He decided it was time to make some changes. He diligently read the most popular investment magazines and surfed financial Websites for several months looking for investment ideas. At last, he found an article, "The 10 Best Funds." It highlighted ten funds that beat the pants off his diversified portfolio over the past year. He sold each of his funds and bought the top five funds listed in the magazine article, all of which happened to be small-company growth stock funds. Mistake? Probably. The funds he purchased racked up big numbers during the previous year, but lacked long-term performance consistency, had high expenses, and were invested entirely in just one part of the stock market. By adjusting his portfolio, Calvin reduced his diversification and increased his level of risk, two things he shouldn't be doing during retirement.

Although Calvin started out with a well-balanced diversified portfolio, greed set in and his strategy was quickly abandoned and forgotten. You, like Calvin, may have already found that the first three steps of the investment process are easy; the hard part is sticking to your investment strategy over time. Adhering to an investment discipline is extremely difficult without a predetermined set of written rules to govern your future investment decisions.

Calvin would likely have made better decisions if he had prepared a mission statement for his money, a statement answering the following questions:

- What is your target investment return?
- How will you diversify your portfolio?
- What amount of risk is acceptable?
- How are you going to measure performance?
- When will you sell an investment?
- What criteria will you use to choose new investments?

Mission Statement for Your Money: Investment Policy Statement

Now that you have determined your asset allocation (Step 1) and diversification mix (Step 2), and you have selected the best investments available (Step 3), it's time to formalize your investment strategy by developing a written mission statement for your money. This mission statement is more commonly called an investment policy statement. Your investment policy statement will establish a clear set of rules that you will use to govern your future investment decisions and will be an integral part of Step 4: Ongoing Portfolio Management. This will take the guesswork out of your future decisions and help you discipline your own actions. This step is imperative; in fact, if you fully understood its importance, you wouldn't invest a penny without first developing a mission statement for your money.

The purpose of an investment policy statement is to:

1. Establish a clear understanding of your investment objectives.
2. Outline your investment time horizon.
3. State income needs.
4. Establish reasonable risk and return expectations.
5. Outline a portfolio framework and structure, including permissible ranges of exposure into different asset classes.
6. Outline the investment philosophy to which you are adhering (buy and hold, rebalancing, etc.).
7. State the selection process used to identify your investments and the types of investments that will be used in the portfolio.
8. Establish a sell discipline and determine at what point you will sell.
9. Provide an outline of duties and responsibilities of your financial advisor, if you're working with one.

Investment Policy Statements Made Simple

An investment policy statement does not have to be extravagant like those used by money managers to govern the investment decisions of 401(k)s, pensions, and endowment funds. The important thing is that it is in writing, so you can refer back to it when you review your portfolio or get a little anxious about the direction your portfolio is taking at the moment. By going through this process, you'll eliminate the guesswork of investing.

To make this easy, I have created a fill-in-the-blank investment policy statement for you to use or copy as you develop your own investment policy:

My Investment Policy Statement

Name_____

Date_____

Age_____

OBJECTIVE
My investment objective is to_____

_____.

TIME HORIZON
My investment time horizon is _____(years).

INCOME NEEDS & TAXES
I will need to withdraw $_____ from my portfolio each year.

The money I am investing is _____ (taxable/non-taxable/both).

TARGET RETURN AND ASSET
My target average rate of return is _____. This was determined when I developed my financial plan.

To obtain this rate of return, I am investing _____% of my portfolio in stocks, _____% in bonds, and _____% in cash.

RISK

To set my risk and return expectations, I am using historical data to measure risk.

Long-Term: 1926-2002 A portfolio allocated similar to mine from 1926 to 2002 averaged _____% per year. The worst year this portfolio experienced was _____%, while the best years it produced a _____ return (see Figure 7 in Chapter 9).

Short-Term 1990 – 2003 A portfolio allocated similar to mine from 1990 to 2004 averaged _____% per year. The worst year this portfolio experienced was a return of _____%, while the best year it produced a _____ return. My model portfolio experienced _____ (how many) positive years and _____ negative years from 1990 through 2004 (see Figures 2-12 in Chapter 12).

I can accept this amount of risk in the future _____ (initial).
I understand that using past performance to determine my risk and return requirements will give me a rough idea of what to expect from the mix of investments I have chosen. However, I do realize that there is no guarantee of these results repeating.

DIVERSIFICATION

I am adhering to the following diversification strategy:

Stocks

Large-Cap Growth	_____%
Large-Cap Value	_____%
Mid-Cap Growth	_____%
Mid-Cap Value	_____%
Small-Cap Growth	_____%
Small-Cap Value	_____%
International Growth & Value	_____%

Bonds

Government Bonds	_____%

Corporate Bonds	_____%
Municipal Bonds	_____%
International Bonds	_____%
Cash	
Money Market/CDs/T-Bills, etc.	_____%
Other	_____%
Total:	_____%

INVESTMENT SELECTION

I will identify the best investments for my portfolio by screening the investments I buy and applying the following criteria:

_____

_____

_____

_____

_____

_____

_____

(For example, you might state, "*I will start with the whole universe of mutual funds within a specific asset class. I will narrow my search by looking for funds that have above-average performance for the past three, five, and 10 years versus their peers. I will only buy funds with managers who have more than 10 years' experience managing money. I will only buy funds that have beaten their respective benchmark index for at least six out of the past 10 years. I will buy funds with managers who have been true to their size (i.e. large-cap,) and style (growth/value) objectives. Whenever possible, I will buy no-load funds with expense ratios below 1 percent. I will review my investments every six months and will sell only if there is a manager change or if the fund is no longer meeting my performance criteria. Of course, I will evaluate each possible sell on a case-by-case basis and take taxes into consideration.*")

TYPES OF SECURITIES

I will purchase _____ (individual stocks, stock mutual funds, or separately managed stock accounts) for my stock portfolio.

I will purchase _____ (individual bonds, bond mutual funds, or separately managed bond accounts) for my bond portfolio.

I will purchase _____ (certificates of deposits, money market mutual funds, treasury bills or other) for my cash portfolio.

I will follow a "buy and hold" investment strategy.

I will rebalance my portfolio _____ (quarterly, semiannually or annually). (See Chapter 18).

FINANCIAL ADVISOR EXPECTATIONS

I am working with an investment advisor. He/she has agreed to meet with me every _____ months to review my financial plan and investment portfolio. My financial advisor is charging me _____% each year to manage my portfolio. (Note: If you are buying loaded funds and don't know what fees you are being charged, refer to Chapter 15 to see how to determine what your built-in fees are and Chapter 3, Figure 2, to calculate how much money your advisor and his/her firm will be making on your investment. In dollars, I am paying my advisor (and his/her firm) $_____ per year. I expect my financial advisor to provide advice and service equal to what I am paying in fees; if not I will fire him/her. We have outlined this in a contract signed on_____ (date).

Signature _____ Date _____

If Calvin had an investment policy statement in place before he evaluated his portfolio, do you think he would have acted so impulsively? I believe he would have handled the pressure much better. First, he would not have compared his investments to those of his friends who have different investment objectives than his own. He would have instead compared his performance to the performance expectations outlined in his investment policy statement. If a few of his investments were in fact underperforming, he would have followed his plan of attack for identifying new investments to take their place. Ultimately, he would have done much better.

It is not important whether you type up a formal statement, scribble some notes on a yellow pad, or fill in the blanks in the above sample investment policy statement. The important thing is that you establish a clear set of rules in writing to govern your investment decisions. By having prepared your mission statement ahead of time, you will avoid making impulsive decisions when your portfolio goes through difficult times. When you set your objectives in advance, it becomes easy to stick to them. It is easy to adhere to an investment strategy if you've done your homework ahead of time and know what to expect from your portfolio.

EIGHTEEN

Routine Checkups

✓ RETIREMENT DECISION #14 (continued): *How will I manage my portfolio on an ongoing basis?*

Congratulations! By following the steps outlined in the previous nine chapters, you are light years ahead of most investors. You have properly allocated your money, diversified it, and purchased good, consistent investments using the help of professional money managers. Surprisingly, however, the first three steps are the easiest in the investment process. Would you believe that the real work begins after you purchase your investments?

It's not easy to adhere to a disciplined investment strategy. You should review your investment portfolio twice a year and update your overall financial plan once a year. Following the steps outlined in this chapter will help you regularly evaluate and make adjustments to your portfolio to keep it on track to meet your goals.

If you want to make money investing, you should buy good investments with the intent of holding them for the long term, while making only occasional adjustments. That may sound easy, but it's not. Compared to the hyper-trading habits of many investors, making only minor, infrequent changes may feel like you're doing nothing to increase your wealth. Buying and holding good investments requires a tremendous amount of self discipline. For example, if a portion of your portfolio is underperforming, your natural instincts will tell you to take immediate action and make changes. The more it lags, the more changes you'll want to make. This is where your self discipline needs to kick in. The investment decisions you make at these points will greatly determine your investment success or failure.

Taking too much action too often leads to poor investment results. However, by avoiding excessive adjustments to your portfolio and keeping your eye focused on long-term investment results, you're far more likely to enjoy success. Remember, it is not important how your portfolio performs during a one-month stretch or even over a single year, but rather how it does during the next five, 10, 15, and 20 years.

Although this sounds like a buy-and-hold strategy for investing, I'm not suggesting that you invest your money and then completely forget about it. You should monitor your portfolio every six months and make adjustments when necessary. Most of the time, you will be better off simply being patient with the investments you own. However, as you will learn in this chapter, there are times when you'll have valid reasons to sell investments and replace them with others.

Investors who remain patient with their investments and stay disciplined through the markets' ups and downs will be rewarded for their ability to stay the course.

Portfolio Reviews

Every six months, you should review your investment portfolio. There is no reason to do this more frequently if you have hired good professional money managers and are properly diversified. It's your money managers' job to watch your individual stocks and bonds daily, so there is absolutely no reason to spend hours each day on the Internet looking at your money. Constant monitoring will only increase the temptation to start tinkering.

The purpose of a semiannual review is not to change your asset allocation or dramatically alter your investments, but rather to give your portfolio a routine checkup and do whatever fine tuning is needed. Often semiannual reviews can be completed in just 10 to 15 minutes.

If you are working with a financial advisor, request that he or she review your portfolio with you at least every six months. Don't be afraid to ask for a review if your advisor hasn't taken the initiative to set up a schedule for review meetings. Semiannual reviews can often be conducted informally over the phone, particularly if nothing alarming is occurring in the market. Financial advisors have tools that make such reviews an easy task.

Your investment checkup will help you determine if your portfolio is performing within the parameters you established in your investment policy statement (Chapter 17). Conducted properly, a review will bring to the surface any problems that exist in the portfolio. Start by evaluating your portfolio as a whole before breaking it down into its individual pieces. Once a problem is identified, changes can be made. However, as a general rule, if you can make a case for keeping an investment, you should probably do so. If you can't, then you should sell it and seek a better alternative.

There are a number of questions you should ask when conducting a portfolio review. Use these questions when you meet with your advisor or conduct your own portfolio review. Your answers to these questions will determine if your portfolio is meeting expectations or if modifications should be made. Use the questions below as a checklist for conducting your reviews:

Portfolio Allocation
- Is my portfolio out of alignment? Does it need to be rebalanced?
- Will there be tax consequences and other costs if I rebalance?

  Note: Your target stock, bond, and cash allocations need to be adjusted only every three to five years if your investment objectives change. You should never alter your allocation due to short-term market gyrations.

Overall Portfolio Performance
- Is my portfolio meeting performance and risk expectations as outlined in my investment policy statement?

Individual Investments
- Are my money managers meeting performance expectations?
- How are they performing versus their peers and benchmarks over the short and long term?
- Has any size or style drift occurred with any of my funds?
- Have there been any money manager changes?

- Are any of the managers causing unwanted tax consequences due to excessive trading? (This question is not applicable for money in retirement accounts.)

Let's take a closer look at each of these questions and why you need to get good answers to each of them.

Is My Portfolio Out of Alignment?

Your portfolio allocation — how your money is divided among different asset classes — will change over time as a result of individual investments growing at different rates of return. Rebalancing is the process of realigning the portfolio back to its original allocation targets. By rebalancing your portfolio annually, it will grow more consistently, maintain the level of risk you initially outlined as acceptable, and often enhance your portfolio returns.

To better understand the need for rebalancing, let's assume you invested in an aggressive diversified portfolio consisting of 80 percent stocks, 15 percent bonds, and 5 percent cash beginning in 1990 (see Figure 1). Left unchecked and never rebalanced, this portfolio was dramatically out of alignment by 1999 (see Figure 2). As you can see, the portfolio shifted from 80 percent stocks in 1990 to 90 percent stocks by the end of 1999. This increase in the amount invested in stocks put your money more at risk of the ups and downs of the stock market. In addition, the portfolio shifted heavily to growth stocks. This portfolio by 1999 was sitting at 51 percent large-, mid-, and small-cap growth stocks, up from the 35 percent in 1990. This shift to stocks (and specifically growth stocks) occurred in many investors' portfolios before 1999.

Once you start banking heavily on one sector of the market, one style of investing, or one asset class, you run the increased risk of experiencing heavy losses if your over weighted investments under perform. And for growth stocks, that's exactly what occurred in 2000. Growth stocks took a beating in 2000 and continued to get hammered in 2001 and 2002. In 2000, large-growth stocks fell 25 percent, while large-value stocks rose 1 percent; mid-cap growth stocks dropped 15 percent, while their mid-value competitors jumped 25 percent; and small-growth stocks dropped 25 percent, while small-cap value stocks gained 23 percent.

Figure 1

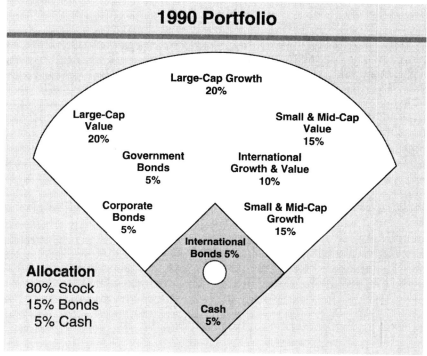

1990 Portfolio

Large-Cap Growth
20%

Large-Cap
Value
20%

Small & Mid-Cap
Value
15%

Government
Bonds
5%

International
Growth & Value
10%

Corporate
Bonds
5%

Small & Mid-Cap
Growth
15%

International
Bonds 5%

Allocation
80% Stock
15% Bonds
5% Cash

Cash
5%

Figure 2

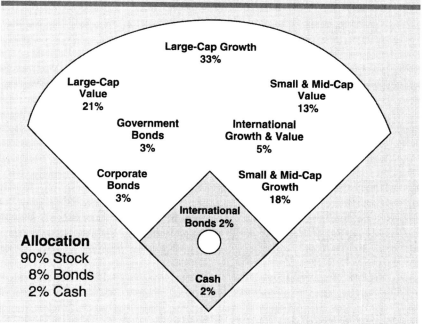

1999 Portfolio

Large-Cap Growth
33%

Large-Cap
Value
21%

Small & Mid-Cap
Value
13%

Government
Bonds
3%

International
Growth & Value
5%

Corporate
Bonds
3%

Small & Mid-Cap
Growth
18%

International
Bonds 2%

Allocation
90% Stock
8% Bonds
2% Cash

Cash
2%

Would you really have wanted to be that overexposed to growth stocks during the 2000-2002 recession? In hindsight, the answer is no. Annual rebalancing will protect you from the possibility of becoming overexposed to one or two asset classes or investment styles.

Rebalancing is difficult because it requires you to do the opposite of what you think you should do: sell some of your winning investments and buy more of your losing investments. This will go against your natural instincts. Who is excited to sell a recent winner to buy a recent loser? By following this course of action, however, you will be forcing yourself to *sell* some of your investments *high* that have recently done well and *buy low* as you add underperforming asset classes to your portfolio. This disciplined process of selling high and buying low to rebalance will help you enhance your investment returns.

Rebalancing also allows you to control your portfolio risk and sustain growth at a more consistent rate. If your portfolio consists of stocks and bonds and is not checked regularly, stocks, because of their higher expected growth, will likely outperform bonds causing your stock weighting to become a larger piece of your portfolio, while your bond weighting shrinks. This imbalance will make your portfolio more aggressive than you initially planned and put you in a riskier position. By rebalancing your portfolio, risk is controlled.

Will I Face Tax Consequences and Other Costs If I Rebalance?

Once you make the decision to rebalance, there are two additional factors to consider. First, will there be any tax consequences? If so, do your rebalancing in a retirement account where taxes can be avoided. Second, will there be any cost to rebalance? In many cases, you may be required to pay a small transaction fee to move from one fund to another.

Is My Portfolio Meeting Performance and Risk Expectations as Outlined in My Investment Policy Statement?

During your semiannual portfolio evaluation, take another look at your investment policy statement. It will outline realistic short- and long-term expectations and acceptable levels of risk and volatility. Is your overall portfolio meeting the performance and risk expectations as outlined in your investment policy statement?

For example, your portfolio may be built to provide annual returns between –10 percent and 20 percent annually, with a target long-term average of 10 percent. If your portfolio drops 8 percent or gains 18 percent, you're operating within the range of your expectations. If in a given year the portfolio drops 25 percent, however, you may want to take a closer look. Some of your money managers may be investing too aggressively or dramatically underperforming their benchmarks. Further examination of each manager is recommended if this occurs.

Are My Money Managers Meeting Performance Expectations?

To answer this question, you need the correct performance yardstick. For example, you can't compare the performance of a small-company stock mutual fund to the Dow Jones Industrial Average or the S&P 500 (both large-company stock indicators). It's an apples-to-oranges comparison. The correct performance yardstick for small-company stock funds is the performance of other small-company stock funds or a small-company index.

Now let's suppose your money manager, who once had performance numbers in the top of an investment category, slides below average for a year or two. What should you do? This is likely to happen to even the best managers at one time or another. Yes, it's frustrating to see a fund slip from among the best in its category to below average, but your best course of action is still to stay put. A quick study of any of today's top mutual funds will reveal that they don't stay at the very top of their respective categories year in and year out. This would be virtually impossible. Money managers' investment styles will naturally go in and out of favor with the market, outperforming in some years and underperforming in others.

When extended poor performance occurs, put the money manager on trial and see if you can build a case for continued ownership; if not, make a change. Below are several items to consider as you attempt to make a case for your investment.

How Are My Managers Performing Versus Their Peers and Benchmarks over the Short and Long Term?

Short-Term Performance

Let's suppose you owned a small-cap value stock fund that was up 10 percent in 1999. You can't help but notice that the S&P 500 climbed 21 percent for the same period. It would be easy to get down on your small-cap value fund, wouldn't it?

Actually, this comparison doesn't provide you with enough information to make a decision with your investment. Remember, it doesn't really matter how your small-cap value fund did against the S&P 500. A far more useful and accurate comparison would be to match your fund's performance versus all of the other small-cap value funds. In this example, you would find that the average small-cap value fund posted only a 5 percent return in 1999. If your fund provided you with a 10 percent return, then you should be quite pleased. This performance would have placed your fund in the top 25 percent of all small-cap value funds in 1999.[1] As a general rule, if your fund posts performance numbers that are above the average when compared with its respective category, then you should hold on to it.

The same comparison can be made against a market index. An index measures a representative group of stocks to provide information about how certain sectors of the market are performing. Each money manager uses an index as a benchmark to evaluate their performance. For example, our small-cap value fund provided a 10 percent return in 1999 while the Russell 2000 Value Index posted a –1.5 percent return. This is another indication that your fund did a nice job.

Long-Term Performance

Let's change the scenario and assume that your fund isn't doing well and its performance is below the average of its peer group and respective tracking index. What do you do then? The smart thing is to turn to its performance over longer time periods, such as three, five, and 10 years. By looking at the long-term numbers, you can see how your fund did through complete business cycles. Although future performance will not be identical to past years, studying historical returns should provide an indication of the fund's potential.

For example, what would you do with the Weitz Partners Value fund if you owned it when you conducted your 2001 annual review? You may be concerned because, for the previous 12 months, 74 percent of the mid-cap value funds had better one-year performance numbers than the Weitz Partners Value fund. In addition, the fund posted a -0.86 percent return in 2001, while its respective index, the Russell Mid-Cap Value Index, was up 2.34 percent.[2] In 2001, Weitz Partners Value fund underperformed its peer group, mid-cap value stocks funds, and its respective index. Research tells us that before 2001, the fund was considered one of the best-performing mid-cap value funds available; in 2001, it was one of the worst. Should it be held or sold? Further examination is required.

Figure 3

Weitz Partners Value Fund

	Performance	% Rank Vs. Category	+/- Index
One Year	-0.86%	74	-3.20%
Three Year	13.57%	27	6.76%
Five Year	21.61%	3	10.15%
Ten Year	18.93%	1	4.52%
Fifteen Year	16.42%	1	2.95%

Source: Morningstar Principia Pro, December 31, 2001

How did the fund perform over the longer term? The performance column in Figure 3 outlines the average annual returns for the fund for various periods of time through Dec. 31, 2001. Although performance was poor in the short term, Weitz Partners Value Fund was one of the leading mid-cap value funds for longer time periods. Its rank was in the top 3 percent of its category for the five-, 10-, and 15-year periods. It has also consistently outperformed the Russell Mid-Cap Value index.[3]

What should we do with this fund? Watch it more closely in upcoming reviews to see if the manager can turn the performance around. Hold it for now; it's been a good, solid long-term fund but check it in your next review.

If a manager has done a good job over the long term but just recently stumbled, you should hold on. Every manager is going to have a rough year occasionally. Flag the fund, however, and watch its performance for another year. If the fund continues to under perform, it will be a sell candidate next year. This was the fate of the Weitz Value Partners Fund. Its performance remained below average in subsequent reviews and was sold.

Manager Tenure and Performance Figures

When reviewing long-term performance numbers, remember to check the length of time the manager has been handling the portfolio. If the term is, say, just two or three years, then the five- and 10-year performance numbers are irrelevant because they were achieved by a different manager. In the case of Weitz Partners Value Fund, the manager, Wallace R. Weitz, has been managing the fund since 1983.

Has Any Size or Style Drift Occurred with Any of My Funds?

Is your fund manager staying true to the fund's size and style objectives? If not, it often means the manager is chasing returns and not adhering to the fund's stated investment discipline.

This frequently happened in 1999. Value managers, after enduring several years of poor performance relative to growth managers, began buying growth stocks to get in on the action. Growth stocks were leading the market at the time. Unfortunately for their shareholders, when value stocks came back into favor in 2000, many value funds didn't do as well as they should have because of this shift in strategy. Many of their portfolios were overloaded with technology growth stocks, and this hurt performance in 2000.

If you have developed a well-diversified portfolio, a manager who suddenly changes the fund's size or style objectives could dramatically throw your portfolio diversification out of balance. For example, if you had allocated your portfolio as outlined in the Target Allocation column in Figure 4, what effect would it have on your portfolio if your large-cap value manager began buying growth-oriented stocks and your small-cap value fund began buying mid-cap value stocks? Your allocation would entirely change and your portfolio would no longer be covering all of the desired bases (see the last column in Figure 4).

Figure 4

Sample Aggressive Growth Portfolio

Investment Category	Target Allocation	Portfolio Allocation After Style Drift
Large-Cap Growth Stocks	22.5%	35.0%
Large-Cap Value Stocks	22.5%	10.0%
Mid-Cap Growth Stocks	12.5%	12.5%
Mid-Cap Value Stocks	12.5%	15.5%
Small-Cap Growth Stocks	5.0%	5.0%
Small-Cap Value Stocks	5.0%	2.0%
International Growth Stocks	10.0%	10.0%
International Value Stocks	10.0%	10.0%
Bonds	0.0%	0.0%
Total	100.0%	100.0%

The portfolio in the previous example is no longer as diversified, as it should be. If this style drift had occurred sometime in 1999, this portfolio would have suffered much worse than it should have in 2000 and 2001 when growth stocks fell out of favor.

How do you avoid this problem? During each review, check your fund's size and investment style to make sure the manager is handling your money as you intended. If the manager is not adhering to his or her size and style mandates, consider another fund.

Have There Been Any Money Manager Changes?

What do you do if one of your fund managers leaves a fund? This is often a signal to sell but don't do so hastily without diligently collecting and reviewing all of the essential information.

Find out how successful the newly hired money manager was in his or her previous fund management experience. If the manager has successfully handled a similar fund, you may want to hold tight and take a "wait-and-see" approach. Give the manager some time to prove him- or herself before deciding to sell the fund. However, if the manager does not have much management experience or has not managed successfully in the past, consider selling the fund immediately. In many cases, the new fund manager will dramatically alter the portfolio and management discipline. This is typically not a good thing for investors.

Are Any of My Managers Causing Unwanted Tax Consequences Due to Excessive Trading?

If you are investing in a non-retirement account, taxes are most likely a concern. Although you should have a rough idea of what taxes to expect from a fund before you purchase it, it is still a good idea to check the fund during reviews to see that its turnover rate hasn't ramped up recently. Increasing turnover rates in funds drive up the chances you will get hit with higher-than-expected capital gains distributions.

If no manager changes have taken place, your managers are staying true to their size and style mandates, the funds are performing in line with their respective indexes, and the overall portfolio performance is within expectations, there is no reason to make any adjustments.

Selling a Fund

If you do sell a fund, don't repeat the big mistake made by so many investors — taking your proceeds and reinvesting them in a fund from whichever asset class has recently enjoyed the most success during the past 12 months! This is a classic way to sell low and buy high. Replace a large-growth fund, for example, with a better large-growth fund. By approaching changes this way, you will be able to maintain your asset allocation and diversification targets.

Morningstar.com is an excellent source when conducting a portfolio review. In addition, Morningstar offers other services that will help you monitor your portfolio, including e-mail bulletins to alert you to any fund-manager changes, performance problems, style drift, and much more.

Most financial advisors have computer programs that allow them to save your investment criteria on their systems when you initially invest. They can call them up easily for you during each semiannual review.

Remember, reviewing your portfolio is important, but don't confuse regular reviewing with excessive trading. The latter will do little to aid your success as an investor.

Adhere to Your Strategy

If you have followed the first three steps for developing a successful investment strategy as outlined in the past nine chapters, you have properly allocated your money, diversified it, and purchased good investments using the help of professional money managers. As was noted at the beginning of this chapter, however, the first three steps are actually the easiest in the investment process. The real work begins after you purchase your investments. By following the guidelines outlined in this chapter on how to best manage your portfolio, you will greatly increase you chances of adhering to a solid investment strategy and obtaining good long-term returns.

INSURANCE AND RETIREMENT

—Health Insurance
—Long-Term Care Insurance
—Life Insurance

NINETEEN

Heart Surgery Isn't Cheap

✓ RETIREMENT DECISION #15: *How will I cover my medical expenses during retirement?*

Walter Sheller, a seasoned attorney at a small firm, and his wife, Margaret, a nurse, retired at age 61 with a nest egg of $500,000. They had planned carefully for a retirement filled with golf, grandkids, and travel. Shortly after retiring, they applied for individual health insurance policies. Some health conditions surfaced during Walter's medical examination, and he was denied coverage. Without health insurance, and not eligible for Medicare until age 65, Walter was forced to use some of the money he and Margaret had accumulated in their retirement nest egg to cover his medical expenses. Although Walter's medical problems took a toll on their savings, the couple estimated that their nest egg was more than sufficient to maintain their lifestyle and to cover the costs of doctors' visits and medicine until Walter turned 65 and qualified for Medicare. At least that was the plan.

Their plan, if you can call it that, backfired. At age 63, Walter suffered a severe heart attack, which required open-heart surgery. In the year after his heart attack, Walter racked up huge medical expenses. To cover the costs of ambulance rides, hospital stays, doctors' visits, and medications, the couple was required to spend more than $250,000 of their retirement nest egg.

Walter's heart attack certainly affected his quality of life, but it also damaged his and Margaret's retirement plans. It wiped out any hope they had of spending carefree days on the beach or at the country club. The disappearance of half their savings so early in retirement will substantially reduce the amount they can withdraw from their nest egg each year without running the risk of completely depleting their assets. They now must learn to live on much less retirement income than they had planned. Even a large nest egg can be destroyed by serious and expensive medical treatments.

What could Walter have done differently? He could have researched and evaluated his health options before retiring. He could have made sure he qualified for health insurance before giving up his coverage at work. Had he done his homework and applied for coverage before leaving his company, he actually may have decided to continue working just to maintain coverage.

Think about your health and your money. Do you have a health condition that would exclude you from obtaining coverage? Could a major medical expense destroy the nest egg you've worked so long to accumulate? Even if you've never been sick a day in your life, illness can set in quickly. Figure 1 lists the 15 most costly medical conditions. The total medical cost for any one of these conditions can easily run between $25,000 and $50,000 per year. As you age, the chance of needing an expensive medical procedure increases. Because health costs are soaring and aging increases your risk of suffering from a serious health problem, insurance coverage is a necessity whether it means buying your own policy or continuing to work to maintain coverage.

Figure 1

The 15 Most Costly Medical Conditions

1 Heart Disease
2 Cancer
3 Trauma
4 Mental disorders
5 Pulmonary conditions
6 Diabetes
7 Hypertension
8 Stroke
9 Osteoarthritis
10 Pneumonia
11 Back problems
12 Endocrine disorders
13 Skin disorders
14 Kidney disease
15 Infectious disease
16 All Other Causes

Source: 2000 Medical Expenditure Panel Survey

Most retirees receive health insurance from either Medicare, private insurance, or a continuation of their employer-provided coverage (see Figure 2). This chapter will discuss these health insurance options and how understanding them will help protect your nest egg and ensure that you are able to make the most of your retirement years.

Figure 2

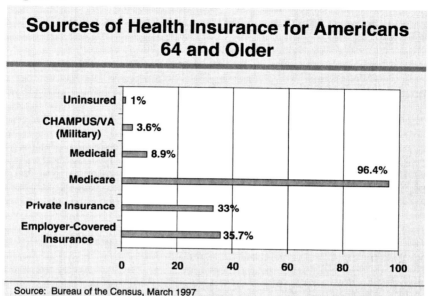

Source: Bureau of the Census, March 1997

  One of every three retirees is covered by private health insurance.

Private Insurance

If you're planning on early retirement, you have some major health insurance decisions ahead of you. Medicare coverage doesn't kick in until age 65. That means most people retiring early will need private insurance, and it's a tough market out there for people between the ages of 50 and 64. This age group is largely unprotected by government programs and is most likely to be denied coverage or be hit with high insurance premiums that are hard to swallow. If you have serious health problems, you may want to continue working just to keep your coverage.

  The average cost of coverage from ages 62 to 64 ranges between $4,000 and $8,000 per year.

For people ages 62 to 64, private health insurance costs between $300 and $700 per month (see Figure 3). If you are planning to retire before age 65, start evaluating your health insurance options as soon as possible. To see what your coverage will cost, visit one of the Websites at the end of this section to obtain an instant online health insurance quote, or contact a local health insurance agent.

Figure 3

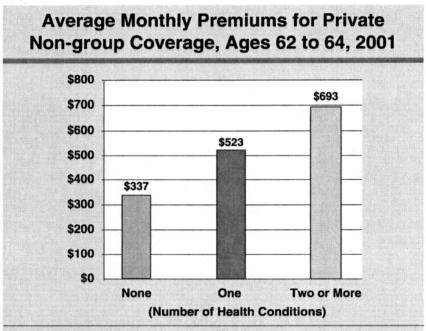

Average Monthly Premiums for Private Non-group Coverage, Ages 62 to 64, 2001

Source: Urban Institute tabulations from the 1998 Health and Retirement Study and Survey of Private Insurers, 2001

If you have preexisting conditions, it will be much more difficult or impossible to obtain private coverage. An insurance company could reject you for coverage completely or cover you for everything except your preexisting condition, even though that's usually the very reason you need the insurance. If you have a group policy, you're in a better position. Federal law forbids all group health plans from denying coverage due to preexisting conditions.[1]

Purchase a high-deductible policy to contain your premium costs.

Strategies for Keeping Premiums Down

You can keep your premium costs down by purchasing a comprehensive medical policy (major medical) with a high deductible. This will mean you'll cover a sizable portion of the routine medical costs out of your own pocket, like doctor visits and prescriptions. Purchasing a high-deductible policy could save you $4,000 to $5,000 in premiums each year. Figure 4 compares the same policy at different deductibles. The policy with a $500 deductible is 142% more expensive than the policy with a $5,000 deductible.

Another way to cut health insurance costs is to purchase catastrophic health coverage (limited coverage). As the name implies, catastrophic coverage generally covers only serious medical problems. Hospital stays and surgeries are usually covered, while doctors' visits and prescription drugs are not. The policy will be used only in the event that catastrophe strikes and major medical expenses are incurred.

Figure 4

Premium Comparison
60-Year-Old Couple

Deductible	Premium
$500	$7,236
$1,000	$5,820
$2,500	$4,068
$5,000	$2,988

Note: 80/20 coverage, $5,000 max out of pocket

Health Savings Accounts

If you are going to buy a high-deductible health insurance plan, you may as well buy one that will provide you with some tax advantages, too. Through the new Health Savings Account (HSA), you will receive a tax deduction for money you spend on health care.

To qualify for the tax deduction, you must purchase a *qualified* high-deductible health-insurance policy. Annual deductibles must be between $1,000 and $5,000 for an individual and $2,000 and $10,000 for a family. Opening an HSA is similar to opening an IRA. You simply deposit money into an HSA at a financial institution of your choice. The money you contribute to your HSA is tax deductible up to the HSA contribution limits. You can contribute up to $2,600 for individual coverage and $5,150 for family coverage. Individuals over age 55 can also contribute an additional $500 each year. From your HSA, you pay your medical expenses.

If you are not yet 65, consider purchasing a high-deductible health-insurance policy and open a Health Savings Account to cover your medical expenses on a pre-tax basis.

Any money you don't use this year can be used in subsequent years or be invested. HSA money not used to cover medical expenses, grows tax-deferred and can be withdrawn after age 65 without penalty and used as an additional source of retirement income.

Private health insurance is expensive, but when you consider that it protects your well being and your nest egg, it's worth every penny. If you retire before age 65, you must consider your health insurance needs and your available insurance options. If you don't have insurance, you will be jeopardizing the assets you've built over years of hard work. A serious illness can deplete your resources in the blink of an eye.

Shopping for a Health Insurance Policy

Consumer Reports suggests you ask the following 10 questions before buying a policy:

1. What kind of network and products do you offer?
2. What's the maximum lifetime benefit I can receive?
3. Do I have to take a health exam or submit lab tests to apply for this insurance?
4. How long is your "look back" period for preexisting conditions?
5. Do you figure your rates by attained age or entry age?
6. How much did your rates rise last year nationally? How often do you raise rates? Annually? Bi-annually?
7. Will my rates go up if I file lots of claims? Can I be singled out for a rate increase for any reason?
8. Do you have any services that help me manage my health-care needs?
9. Can you cancel this policy for any reason except non-payment, fraud, or a moving out of the area served by this policy?
10. What is your company rated by *Standard and Poor's* and *A.M. Best*?

Source: "Shopping for Your Own Policy," www.consumerreports.org

SHOPPING FOR HEALTH INSURANCE
• www.insure.com
• www.ehealthinsurance.com

Continued Employee Coverage: Group Health Insurance

In the cost-cutting corporate world, fewer and fewer companies provide free or low-cost health insurance to their retirees. For most, employer-provided health insurance terminates when they retire. You are fortunate if you have continued employer coverage. If you don't, there are legal requirements that prevent employers from completely eliminating health coverage for a period of time after an employee is off the payroll.

Group health insurance provides 36 percent of retirees with coverage.

Under COBRA, which stands for Consolidated Omnibus Budget Reconciliation Act of 1985, employers with 20 or more employees are required to provide continued health insurance coverage to former workers for up to 18 months (29 months if the worker is disabled). COBRA only guarantees you access to coverage, however; it doesn't help pay your premiums. Under COBRA, your employer will not subsidize your monthly premiums and you will be responsible for paying the entire amount, plus an administrative fee of up to 2 percent.

The cost for continued group coverage could range from zero to $500 per month.

Thomas Caldwell, 59, a recent retiree, was shocked by how expensive his COBRA premium was. While he had been working his employer paid the bulk of his insurance premiums, and Thomas was only required to pay $100 per month for his group health-insurance coverage. When he retired and enrolled in COBRA, the same coverage cost more than $800 per month—a jump of more than 700 percent. Because COBRA coverage must be identical to the coverage he had while working, he was unable to choose a less expensive plan to save money, although his employer did allow him to drop certain "non-core" benefits like dental and vision care.[2]

Although COBRA's costs may seem substantial (see Figure 5), it may be your best route if you can't obtain less-expensive private health insurance. COBRA can also buy you some time while you are searching for a private health-insurance plan.

To initiate COBRA, you and your employer must follow proper procedures. If you don't, you could forfeit your coverage rights. First, the employer must notify the health-plan administrator within 30 days of your "qualifying event" (job termination, reduced hours of employment, or eligibility for Medicare). Once notified, the health-plan administrator has 14 days to alert you and your family members of your right to

Figure 5

Sample Cobra Premiums	
Single	$342
Enrollee + Child	$677
Enrollee + Spouse	$683
Family	$1,060

elect COBRA coverage. The IRS is tough on this point. If the plan administrator fails to act, he or she can be held personally liable for this breach of duty.

You, your spouse, and your children have 60 days to decide whether or not to buy COBRA insurance. The 60-day clock starts running on the date your eligibility notification is sent to you or the date you lost your health coverage, whichever is later. As long as you pay the premium, your COBRA coverage will be retroactive to the date you lost your benefits.

If you elect COBRA, you have 45 days to pay your first premium. The first premium is likely to be high because it covers the period retroactive to the date your employer ended your coverage. Successive payments are due according to health-plan requirements, but COBRA rules allow for a 30-day grace period after each payment due date.[3]

If you have questions about COBRA or self-insured employer plans (both governed by the U.S. Department of Labor), contact the regional or district office of the Pension and Welfare Benefits Administration of the U.S. Department of Labor www.dol.gov.

Not every company discontinues its insurance for employees who retire. Some firms will not only continue to offer coverage, but will subsidize all or part of the premiums. Be sure to check with your company's personnel department regarding its policy on health coverage. The number of companies that are generous in this respect will continue to diminish as health-care costs continue to soar.

 96.4 percent of all retirees obtain coverage from Medicare. For those with private coverage or a continued group plan, Medicare becomes a secondary coverage.

Medicare

Medicare provides more than 40 million Americans with basic health coverage. For many people, Medicare is their only source of health insurance during retirement. Because this program is such an integral part of retirement health-care planning for so many, it's important that we cover it here in detail.

Eligibility for Medicare is similar to that of Social Security. You or your spouse must have worked 40 quarters (10 years) in Medicare-covered employment to receive Medicare coverage. Additionally, you must be 65 years old and a citizen or permanent resident of the United States. The Social Security Administration recommends applying for Medicare benefits when you turn 65, whether or not you begin collecting Social Security at that time. Contact the Social Security Administration toll-free at 1-800-772-1213 or visit www.ssa.gov if you have questions about your eligibility or want to apply for Medicare.

Medicare consists of two parts: Part A and Part B. Medicare Part A helps pay for inpatient hospital care, skilled nursing facilities, hospice care, and some home health care. Part B helps pay for doctors' services, outpatient hospital care, and some other medical services such as blood work, medical equipment, lab tests, and physical and occupational therapy. Part B may also cover preventive services such as mammograms and flu shots.

Medicare Part A: Hospital Insurance

For most retirees, no premiums are required for Medicare Part A because premiums were taken from your paycheck each month while employed. Even if you or your spouse did not work the required 40 quarters of Medicare-covered employment, you may still be eligible, but you will be required to pay a monthly premium. In 2004, the premium was $343 per month if you worked less than 30 quarters and $189 per month for those with 30 to 39 quarters.

Although the majority of people do not have to pay a premium, there are still expenses involved. For every benefit period, a $876 deductible must be met (2004 rates). Also, if you stay over 60 days in the hospital, you will have to pay up to the following co-insurance rates:

- $219 per day, between the 61st and 90th day in the hospital.
- $438 per day, between the 91st and 150th day in the hospital.
- Up to $109.50 per day between the 21st and 100th day of each benefit period, for a skilled nursing facility.

Medicare Part B: Medical Insurance

Medicare Part B helps pay for doctors' services and outpatient hospital care. Part B, however, will not pay for routine physical exams, eyeglasses, custodial care, dental care, dentures, routine foot care, hearing aids, orthopedic shoes, or cosmetic surgery. It does not cover most prescription drugs or any health care you receive while traveling outside the United States.[4]

Part B coverage requires a premium of $66.60 per month (2004 rates). If you did not sign up for Part B at age 65 when you first became eligible, the premium may go up 10 percent for each year you wait. You will have to pay this extra amount for the rest of your life. Also, as in Part A, you are required to pay a deductible. However, the deductible is significantly less, amounting to only $100 per year.

For those eligible, Medicare Part A (hospital insurance) is free, while Medicare Part B (medical insurance) costs $66.60 per month (2004).

Applying for Benefits

If you receive Social Security benefits before age 65, you will be automatically enrolled in both Medicare Part A and Part B, effective the month you turn 65. Your Medicare card will be mailed to you about three months before your 65th birthday. The enrollment package contains information on how to "un-enroll" yourself from Part B coverage if you don't want it.

If you decide to delay receiving Social Security benefits until age 65 or later, you will not be automatically enrolled in Medicare. However, you should still apply for Medicare three months before you turn 65, so your coverage start date will not be delayed.

You can apply using any one of the following three options:

- Visit your local Social Security office.
- Call Social Security at 1-800-772-1213.
- Apply online at www.ssa.gov.

You may want to delay signing up for Medicare Part B if you are receiving medical coverage through either your or your spouse's employer. There's no need to pay that $66.60 per month if you already have adequate coverage.

The Social Security Administration advises that you should sign up for Medicare Part A even if you keep working past age 65. The Part A coverage carries no premium costs and may help pay some of your health costs not covered through your employer or union group health plan.

Also remember, if you plan to join a Medicare managed care plan or a Medicare private fee-for-service plan (more on this later in this chapter), you will need to be a Medicare Part B participant.

If you didn't sign up for Medicare Part B when you were first eligible because you were still enrolled in a group plan, you can sign up for Medicare Part B during a "special enrollment period," thus avoiding the 10 percent penalty for late enrollees. Special enrollment allows you to sign up within eight months of when your employer health plan coverage ends, or when your employment ends, whichever comes first.

Filling in the Gaps of Medicare Coverage

Medicare enrollees must use a doctor, specialist, or hospital that accepts Medicare. Medicare pays the fee charged for each visit or service after you have met the annual deductible and paid the monthly Part B premium of $66.60. To pay for medical costs not covered by Medicare, you can:

- Keep or obtain employer or union health coverage.
- Buy a Medigap policy (a private Medicare supplemental insurance).
- Join one of the other Medicare health plans.

Medigap

You might think that Medicare doesn't provide you with the sufficient coverage you desire. Who could blame you? With a whole array of services not covered by Medicare, you could still be looking at a substantial sum of out-of-pocket health costs if you wind up needing one of these uncovered services.

Medigap plans are private health insurance policies that cover some of the costs and services basic Medicare does not cover, such as prescription drugs. You can obtain Medigap coverage without having to submit medical evidence to prove that you are healthy if you do so within six months of obtaining Medicare Part B coverage. This means an insurance company cannot deny you coverage during this period or require you pay higher premiums. After this six-month window, you may be denied coverage if you have certain medical conditions. Although some groups may offer you a Medigap policy if you have medical problems, you will still pay a higher premium for the coverage.

Sign up for Medigap coverage within six months of obtaining Medicare Part B.

In 1992, Congress mandated that Medigap plans be categorized into 10 types (lettered A through J) to make it easier for consumers to shop for coverage and avoid scams.[5] The 10 plans differ in areas such as deductibles, coverage for eyeglasses, prescription drugs, or medical care received while in foreign countries. Insurance companies must sell A plans, which offer basic benefits, but not all firms offer the full range of Medigap plans, and some plans might not be available at all in your state.

Another type of Medigap coverage is the Medicare SELECT policy. These policies use specified hospitals and doctors, except in emergencies, and generally cost less as a result.

Premiums can vary by hundreds of dollars, so it pays to shop around. You can use the Medicare Personal Plan Finder at www.medicare.gov (located in Search Tools) to see Medicare health insurance options in your area and compare plans.

Insurance companies may charge a fixed level premium for all participants, based on your age at time of purchase. Other companies charge a variable premium based on how old you are each time you renew the policy, which means that your premiums will increase as you get older. It is necessary to shop around.

Other Medicare Health Plans

Medicare offers two other health-plan choices within the program: the Medicare Managed-Care Plan, sometimes called an HMO, and the Medicare Private Fee-For-Service Plan. Even if you choose one of these options, you must still pay the Medicare Part B premium. However, you will receive all of the Medicare Part A and Part B covered services. For both types of plan, Medicare pays a set amount of money each month to a private insurance company. Study your options carefully and choose the one that best fits your personal circumstances.

 MEDICARE QUESTIONS?
Visit www.medicare.gov

Medicaid

Medicaid helps pay medical costs for people with low incomes. Because state governments, rather than the federal government, administer these programs, benefits can vary depending on the state in which you live. Medicaid can help pay for nursing home care and outpatient prescription drugs not covered by Medicare. Some states also have programs that help subsidize Medicare's premium, deductibles, and co-insurance.

The Inflation of Health-Care Costs

With the pace of rising health-care costs increasing, all people nearing retirement must give considerable thought to their health insurance plans. If you retire early, be sure you qualify for some type of health insurance to bridge the gap between your retirement and age 65. Even when Medicare kicks in, you may decide you need additional coverage. With the post-war baby boomers beginning to reach retirement age, the projected population of Americans over 65 is expected to reach 60 million in 2005. That's an increase of 25 million in just four years (see Figure 6). Retiring baby boomers are going to put an enormous strain on the Medicare program. It's unlikely Medicare will continue operating without reducing benefits, increasing retirees' out-of-pocket costs, or cutting payments to doctors and hospitals. By the time you retire, or sometime during your retirement, Medicare's health-plan options will likely be more limited and more expensive than they are now. You can count on it.

Already, health-care insurance is too expensive for 15 to 17 percent

Figure 6

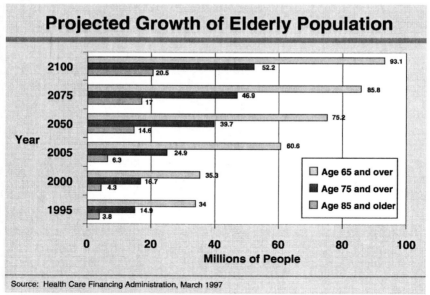

Projected Growth of Elderly Population

Source: Health Care Financing Administration, March 1997

of Americans, who live without coverage.[6] The Health Care Financing Administration predicts that the amount of money America spends on health care will double every 10 years (see Figure 7). Health costs will continue increasing rapidly for individuals, employers, and the government.

Figure 7

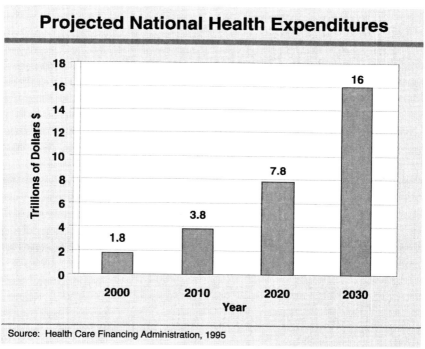

Source: Health Care Financing Administration, 1995

There is no way to protect yourself from rising health-care expenses. It's not all doom and gloom, however. You're not powerless. You can fight back. My first suggestions: Stay active, eat healthy, and eliminate stress. A healthy body and mind can better fight off sickness and disease. Second, plan properly. Make sure you're covered. As you age, you are more susceptible to disease, and if you get sick, it will be expensive to treat. Retirement is not the time to roll the dice, as Walter did in the beginning of this chapter, and risk all that you have saved. Before you retire, you must examine all of your health insurance options for retirement and obtain the coverage that best protects your nest egg. Don't let health-care costs ruin the retirement you've worked so hard your entire life to achieve.

TWENTY

Toileting and Retirement

✓ RETIREMENT DECISION #16: *Should I purchase long-term care insurance?*

"Toileting" is not a term you'd expect to find in a retirement-planning book like this. However, it is a term that describes what many retirees, their families, and care givers must face every day. The definition of toileting is "getting to and from, and on and off the toilet and performing associated personal hygiene."[1] As you age and your health deteriorates, you may need help with many of the things you take for granted today. If you do need assistance performing the basic activities of everyday living, who is going to provide it for you? Not being prepared for this possibility carries some devastating consequences, such as prematurely depleting your assets, receiving substandard long-term care, or becoming a burden to your family.

 44 percent of those reaching 65 will enter a nursing home.[2]

How interested do you think your children would be in applying for the following job listed in your local paper?

> Home Health-Care Aide: Home health-care aide needed to provide 24-hour, seven-day-a-week care for a poor, 85-year-old bedridden patient suffering from Alzheimer's disease. The elderly patient requires room and board and must move in with you and your family. The patient requires constant supervision and will need a baby-sitter when you leave your home. Must be able to administer eight to 10 medications

daily and make frequent trips to the doctor's office. Applicant should enjoy cooking and cleaning and be proficient at toileting. Diaper changing skills are also a plus. The job will likely last one to two years but may last 10 or more. This is a volunteer position. No experience necessary.

Now ask your children how they would feel about accepting this health-care aide position if you were the patient needing the care. Would you like to heap this burden upon your children and their families? If you don't want to take the risk of becoming a burden to your family, you need to do some planning. You can either purchase a long-term-care insurance policy or acquire sufficient assets to provide for both you and your spouse if you should enter a nursing home during retirement.

Becoming a Burden to Your Family

The above scenario is one Howard and Karen Everett know all too well. Three years ago, while visiting Karen's 84-year-old parents, Glenn and Shirley Kramer, they discovered that the Kramers were no longer able to take care of themselves. For example, Karen noticed that her parents weren't washing their clothes regularly, and when they did wash them, they did it by hand because they couldn't remember how to use the washer and dryer. Karen also noticed that her parents left the stove on frequently and were eating spoiled food. Cleanliness was becoming an issue.

It looked as if Shirley and Glenn had forgotten how to live. It was clear that Glenn was beginning to exhibit some early signs of dementia, and Shirley was diagnosed soon after with Alzheimer's disease. Allowing them continue to live alone would be dangerous. They clearly needed help.

 By the year 2005, 9 million Americans over age 65 will require long-term care. By 2020, this number is expected to soar to 12 million.[3]

Because of her parents' limited assets and lack of planning, Karen believed that she and Howard had only two options: First, they could place her parents in a nursing home and let Medicaid pick up the bill, or second, they could move Glenn and Shirley into their own home and take on the daunting task of 24-hour care.

They started to explore nursing-home options and visited several inexpensive homes. Unfortunately, the facilities were run down, often smelled bad, lacked cleanliness, and were understaffed. The Everetts concluded that their parents deserved better and immediately made arrangements to move them into their own home. Little did they know what they were getting themselves into.

Most of us wouldn't have the stomach and stamina required to take care of one elderly parent, let alone two. Watching up close as both parents completely lost their dignity and were reduced to the equivalent of one-year-olds took its toll emotionally and physically. Would you like your children to do for you what Karen and Howard did for their parents? Consider for a moment their daily routine.

Karen worked around the clock: cooking, cleaning, bathing, toileting, dressing, feeding, blowing noses, administering medicines, clipping toe nails, changing bed sheets when wet or soiled, cleaning up when accidents occurred due to incontinence, changing diapers, answering the same questions over and over, and helping them find their beds when they wandered the house at night. Around-the-clock care was utterly exhausting.

Although less costly than a nursing home facility, home care carries its own financial drain. Adult diapers and specialty dietary items are not cheap. Utility costs also increased since neither parent could sleep with the lights off. Home maintenance costs rose due to accidents like the basement flooding when Shirley left the water running in the bathroom. Also, many modifications were made to the home to assist with deteriorating physical health.

 One out of four families provides care to an elderly relative.[5]

The Everetts' lifestyle changed completely. Three years ago, with their kids grown, they were looking forward to winding down Howard's career by traveling and enjoying their increased freedom. This is not exactly what happened. All travel was completely out of the question.

In fact, it was difficult just to go to the store. Somebody always had to be home. This meant that the Everetts rarely, if ever, went out together, or even visited other relatives. If they did leave the house, they had to find a baby-sitter. Their married and college-age children helped out when they could but weren't always excited about having to change Grandma's diaper.

Besides not being able to leave the house, Karen and Howard found that they couldn't have friends over, either. Shirley had difficulty getting dressed by herself, but she had mastered the skill of taking her clothes off (and often did) making stark-naked appearances at the least expected times. Most dinner guests would prefer not to see an 84-year-old in her birthday suit. Their only social outings, it seemed, were occasional visits with support groups to cope with the pressures of taking care of elderly parents.

The worst component, however, was the realization that their *relationship* with their parents had changed. Adoration grew into aversion, and respect decayed to resentment. While they still love their parents and will continue to provide the needed care, they privately wished their parents would have been more wise by preparing for this stage of life.

So what advice would the Everetts give you? "Buy long-term-care insurance. You will maintain your relationship with your children and grandchildren, and they won't have to experience with you the loss of your dignity." The Everetts felt so strongly about this that they bought themselves a long-term-care policy.

Most people put the burden of long-term care on their families. While about 12.8 million Americans require long-term care, only 2.4 million live in nursing homes.[6]

Leaving Your Spouse with Nothing

Let's fast forward to the day you reach age 80 and assume you enter a nursing home and stay for five years before dying. Let's also assume your spouse is healthier and younger than you. Could the assets you've accumulated cover the additional expense of a nursing home stay? A nursing-home stay could double your annual retirement expenses. Of course, in addition to covering the cost of a nursing home, your spouse, who will likely continue to live in your family home, will still need money to meet the expenses of everyday life. And who knows, your spouse may need a continued stream of income for another 20 years.

If your assets aren't sufficient to cover the costs incurred by your going to a nursing-home and also the continued cost of retirement for your spouse, then you are a candidate for long-term-care insurance. If your nursing-home stay completely drains your nest egg, your spouse could be literally left with nothing but your home and a monthly Social Security check. No one wants to be forced to live on Social Security alone.

$500,000 to Spare or $0 and Destitute

David Sanders, a 62-year-old office manager, plans to retire this year and begin enjoying the good life with his wife, Mary, age 60. According to his retirement calculations, he has accumulated enough money to enjoy a $50,000 annual retirement income (after taxes and inflation). In fact, using modest rates of return, his projections show that 30 years from now they will still have a nest egg of more than $500,000. A modern day success story right? Well, maybe. (See Chapter 1 on how to estimate how much money you'll need in retirement.)

One thing David did not plan on is the possibility that some of their assets may be needed to cover long-term-care expenses. What would happen if either David or Mary require nursing-home care sometime during retirement? Could their nest egg withstand the additional expense? To answer this question, David needs to take a few extra steps in his retirement calculations.

What if at age 70, David enters a nursing home that costs $60,000 per year and stays for five years before he dies? Of course, $60,000 per year will have to be withdrawn from the Sanders' nest egg for five years to take care of David in the nursing home, while Mary will continue to need $50,000 of income each year to cover the originally planned retirement expenses. The additional nursing-home expense will more than double the amount they must withdraw from their investments during these years. Should this occur, their investment assets would be completely depleted by the time Mary is age 80. She would have to live out her remaining life on Social Security alone.

If David does not require this nursing-home care until he reaches 75 or 80, their assets would last a little longer. Mary would run out of assets at age 81 and 83, respectively (See Figure 1). Needless to say, an extended long-term-care stay by David would leave Mary penniless.

Figure 1

Retirement Nest Egg With and Without Long-Term Care Expenses

Retirement: David and Mary Sanders
Starting Portfolio: $1,025,000

David's Age	Mary's Age	No Long-Term Care Is Needed	Long-Term Care Needed At age 70	Long-Term Care Needed At Age 75	Long-Term Care Needed At Age 80
62	60	$1,042,491	$1,042,491	$1,042,491	$1,042,491
63	61	$1,060,012	$1,060,012	$1,060,012	$1,060,012
64	62	$1,082,612	$1,082,612	$1,082,612	$1,082,612
65	63	$1,105,618	$1,105,618	$1,105,618	$1,105,618
66	64	$1,129,060	$1,129,060	$1,129,060	$1,129,060
67	65	$1,152,971	$1,152,971	$1,152,971	$1,152,971
68	66	$1,177,391	$1,177,391	$1,177,391	$1,177,391
69	67	$1,202,364	$1,202,364	$1,202,364	$1,202,364
70	68	$1,217,542	$1,133,272	$1,217,542	$1,217,542
71	69	$1,231,423	$1,024,867	$1,231,423	$1,231,423
72	70	$1,243,825	$892,821	$1,243,825	$1,243,825
73	71	$1,254,547	$743,768	$1,254,547	$1,254,547
74	72	$1,263,369	$576,230	$1,263,369	$1,263,369
75	73	$1,269,211	$526,485	$1,131,343	$1,269,211
76	74	$1,264,833	$470,116	$973,931	$1,264,833
77	75	$1,256,907	$406,560	$796,524	$1,256,907
78	76	$1,245,083	$335,212	$597,391	$1,245,083
79	77	$1,228,983	$255,421	$374,667	$1,228,983
80	78	$1,208,198	$166,487	$294,080	$1,040,461
81	79	$1,182,289	$67,658	$204,183	$828,363
82	80	$1,150,781	$0	$104,208	$590,655
83	81	$1,113,162	$0	$0	$325,146
84	82	$1,068,881	$0	$0	$29,475
85	83	$1,017,346	$0	$0	$0
86	84	$957,919	$0	$0	$0
87	85	$901,900	$0	$0	$0
88	86	$838,053	$0	$0	$0
89	87	$765,709	$0	$0	$0
90	88	$684,148	$0	$0	$0
91	89	$592,595	$0	$0	$0
92	90	$490,219	$0	$0	$0

The Sanders have two basic options: accept the risk of depleting their assets and do nothing in hopes that neither one of them requires care *or* purchase a long-term-care insurance policy to cover the cost of long-term-care expenses should they arise. What would you do? Have you considered long-term care expenses in your retirement projections?

FACT More than half of married couples with one partner requiring long-term care become impoverished within one year.[7]

Playing the Odds

What are the chances you could be afflicted with a chronic illness or disability that would leave you unable to care for yourself for an extended period of time during retirement? The answer might surprise you.

The vast majority of Americans (72 percent) don't believe they will ever enter a nursing home or need any long-term-care services.[8] If you're age 65, you have a 44 percent chance of entering a nursing home.[9] Over one-half (55 percent) of those who enter nursing homes stay for more than one year, while one out of five (21 percent) remain for five years or longer.[10] Those odds, of course, increase with age (see Figure 2).

Figure 2

Source: Statistical Abstract of the United States, 1992

Women, because they live longer than men, have a 50 percent greater likelihood of needing long-term care at some point.[11] In 1997, there were 1.3 million people in nursing homes; three-fourths of them were women.

The High Cost of Aging

Long-term care is not just a health issue, but also a financial concern that can throw a wrench into your retirement planning. Currently the average cost for a one-year stay in a nursing home is $56,000 ($153 per day); assisted living facilities average $22,476 per year ($62

Figure 3

Average Daily Nursing Home Cost

State	Cost	State	Cost
Alabama	$127	Montana	$124
Alaska	$321	Nebraska	$134
Arizona	$131	Nevada	$129
Arkansas	$99	New Hampshire	$173
California	$147	New Jersey	$209
Colorado	$130	New Mexico	$126
Connecticut	$274	New York	$269
Delaware	$142	North Carolina	$135
DC	$193	North Dakota	$156
Florida	$137	Ohio	$151
Georgia	$122	Oklahoma	$97
Hawaii	$173	Oregon	$122
Idaho	$135	Pennsylvania	$179
Illinois	$160	Rhode Island	$170
Indiana	$123	South Carolina	$125
Iowa	$103	South Dakota	$112
Kansas	$109	Tennessee	$114
Kentucky	$124	Texas	$102
Louisiana	$89	Utah	$112
Maine	$164	Vermont	$186
Maryland	$158	Virginia	$184
Massachusetts	$220	Washington	$169
Michigan	$139	West Virginia	$154
Minnesota	$137	Wisconsin	$165
Mississippi	$100	Wyoming	$113
Missouri	$110		

Source: MetLife Market Survey of Nursing Home and Home Care Costs, April 2002 per day), and part-time home health care can run $12,000 to $16,000 per year ($33 to $44 per day).[12]

Today, the average nursing home stay is 2 ½ years[13] (see Figure 4) at a total cost of $140,000. The same stay will cost roughly $370,000 in 20 years assuming nursing-home costs continue to rise 5 percent per year.[14] What will it cost for a 2 ½-year stay when you turn age 80? You can see the impact these costs can have on reaching your retirement goals. Large long-term-care expenses could deplete your assets prematurely.

Figure 4

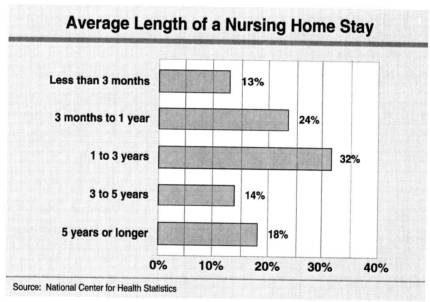

Average Length of a Nursing Home Stay

Source: National Center for Health Statistics

Who Pays for Long-term Care?

Long-term care leads to poverty for a disturbing number of retired Americans. Of those receiving long-term care, 37 percent pay for it out of pocket. Within a year of admission, more than 90 percent of these private-pay residents are impoverished.[15] Medicare and health insurance coverage typically pay little for long-term-care nursing home facilities. Medicaid, a government welfare program, will pay but only after you have depleted all other financial resources. The government currently pays about 57 percent of all nursing-home costs.

According to these statistics, if you don't own a long-term-care policy, the odds are very high that a lengthy nursing home stay will completely eat away your assets and leave you dependent upon Medicaid. Although long-term-care coverage is affordable, only 3 percent of nursing home costs are funded this way. Figure 5 summarizes who gets stuck with the long-term-care bill.

Figure 5

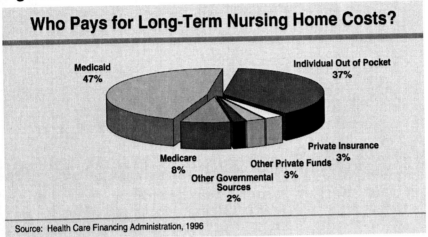

Who Pays for Long-Term Nursing Home Costs?

Medicaid 47%

Individual Out of Pocket 37%

Medicare 8%

Other Governmental Sources 2%

Other Private Funds 3%

Private Insurance 3%

Source: Health Care Financing Administration, 1996

Cost of Coverage

Long-term-care coverage, like life insurance, is cheaper if you purchase it when you are younger and healthier. A policy purchased at age 65 will generally cost twice as much as a policy bought when you're 55. For example, a 55-year-old can plan on paying a premium between $500 and $1,000 per year for four years of coverage. That same policy would cost a 65-year-old between $1,000 and $2,000. Those in their late 70's may be required to pay as much as $3,000 to $8,000 for similar coverage, depending on the policy's features. Premiums will almost double for coverage purchased for a married couple.

Buying coverage when you are younger will reduce your premiums, though you will likely pay them for a longer period of time. To obtain a quick, free quote to get an idea of how much a long-term care policy will cost, spend five minutes at http://www.ltcq.net or http://www.insure.com.

Who Should Purchase Long-Term Health-Care Coverage?

Long-term-care insurance is not for everyone but very essential for some. Figure 6 will help you decide if you should buy a long-term-care policy.

Figure 6

LTC is for you if:	LTC is not as important for you if:
You would like to insure your independence and not become a burden to your family.	You have health conditions making the cost of LTC coverage too expensive compared to the benefit you may receive.
Your family has a history of ailments requiring long-term care (e.g. alzheimer's, diabetes, strokes).	You are likely to cancel the policy because your fixed income won t keep up with increasing premium payments
You have sufficient money to pay premiums every year until death.	Your only source of income is a Social Security benefit or Supplemental Security Income (SSI).
You want to preserve assets for family members.	
Having to pay for long-term care for one spouse would seriously hamper your ability to accomplish your retirement plan.	Buying a LTC policy stretches your budget to the point of having to forego other financial needs (e.g. paying for utilities, buying food or medicine.)
You are in good health and qualify for lower premiums.	You're self-insured due to the size of your financial portfolio.
You are between 45 and 60 and can lock in lower premiums for life.	You are 79+ (although you may need coverage, premiums may be too high.)

How Much Coverage Do You Need?

You can purchase coverage that will provide a daily benefit of anywhere from $50 to $400. To determine how much long-term coverage you need, first decide how much long-term care you can afford to cover out of your own pocket. For example, if the average nursing home cost is $150 per day in your area (see Figure 3), and you can afford to pay $50 per day, then you would need a policy to cover the $100 difference. You should plan on needing this benefit for at least 2 ½ years, which is the average nursing home stay.

Estimating what you can pay out of pocket can be a difficult process. You must attempt to predict your future financial status and the future cost of long-term care. The best method for doing this is to revisit the retirement section of your financial plan and enter some additional hypothetical situations (see Chapter 1). For example, how would it affect your retirement assets if you or your spouse entered a nursing home at age 75, 80, or 85, and you had to pay $56,000 per year, adjusted for inflation? Would this eat up all of your assets? Would the spouse living outside the nursing home have enough money to meet living expenses? Your retirement plan can help you answer all these questions. Be more exact in your planning by contacting nursing homes in your area and base your estimates on local costs (see Figure 3).

Nursing Home, Assisted Living, and Home Health Care

Nursing home coverage is just one of several types of long-term care. Most policies also include coverage for assisted living facilities and home health care. Figure 7 lists the different types of long-term care and their definitions.

Assisted living is the step between living in your own home and living in a nursing home. If your health won't allow you to continue living at home, but you don't require round-the-clock nursing-home care, an assisted living facility will suit you nicely. The goal of assisted living is to help you continue living as independently as possible. Assisted living facilities provide the privacy and feel of living in your own apartment, condominium, or small home. However, assistance is available to help you with the basic activities of daily living. Assisted living facilities average $30,288 per year.

 70 percent of seniors reaching age 65 will need home health care.[16]

No one wants to leave his or her home any sooner than necessary, even when health conditions begin to deteriorate. The best way to ensure you can remain in your home as long as possible is to hire a home health-care agency to provide you with the level of help you need. Non-skilled help, which can assist with dressing, bathing, preparing meals, and other household duties, can cost $1,000 per month. Skilled help provided by a physical therapist or health-care professional can cost much more. Home health-care averages about $16 to $20 per hour.[17]

Figure 7

Types of Long-Term Care

Type of Care	Definition
Nursing Home Care	Nursing homes serve as permanent residences for people who are too frail or sick to live at home or as a temporary facility during a recovering period.
Home Health Care	Home health care ranges greatly in its definition and can cover a broad range of needs both temporary and permanent. Often times people require only minimal assistance: a couple of hours each day or a visit in the morning and the evening. Some clients require only a couple of brief visits per week, while others need someone available around the clock because of either physical or mental disabilities. Home health care and homemaker services can also cover needs ranging from help with meals and home maintenance to supervision as well as medication administration.
Assisted Living Facility	The assistance you need may not require the round-the-clock, skilled health care a nursing home provides, yet your needs cannot be met living by yourself. These facilities provide meals, social activities, and even on-call assistance with bathing and dressing. The goal of assisted living is to help people continue living as independently as possible.
Adult Day Care	A planned program that includes a variety of health, social and supportive services in a safe, protective environment during daytime hours. It is a community-based service designed to the needs of each individual.
Respite Care	Short term, temporary care provided to people with disabilities in order to provide families a break from the daily routine of care-giving.

What Is Not Covered by Long-Term-Care Insurance?

If you purchase a policy, make sure you understand exactly what is covered and what is not. Long-term-care policies do not cover a number of items, and the exclusions in each policy differ. Treatment that was under way or recommended before obtaining long-term coverage is usually not covered (preexisting conditions). In addition, the following ailments are often excluded:

- Mental disorders (other than Alzheimer's disease or other dementia)
- Nervous disorders
- Alcoholism
- Drug abuse
- Care necessitated by an act of war
- Intentional self-inflicted injury

Shopping for Coverage: Focus on the Benefits

The most serious blunder people make when purchasing a long-term-care policy is that they focus on the premium more than the benefits they may need. Here are some benefits to focus on:

Coverage Amount

Long-term-care policies generally pay benefits on a daily, weekly, or monthly basis. Check the costs of nursing homes in your area to determine the amount of coverage you need. For example, if nursing homes in your area run $150 per day, you can buy a policy that will pay $150 per day, $1,050 per week, or $4,500 per month. Usually, assisted living and home health-care benefits will be paid as a percentage of the nursing-home coverage amounts.

Inflation

Many people save a lot of money on premiums by purchasing a policy that doesn't adjust for inflation. They'll save money in the short run, but it's not likely that their policy will provide them with nearly enough benefits if they enter a nursing home. If nursing-home costs continue to increase at 5 percent per year, a nursing home that costs $150 per day today could cost $400 per day in 20 years. If costs continue to soar at this pace, wouldn't it be wise to add a feature to your policy that adjusts your benefits by 5 percent per year to combat this inflation?

 The cost of long-term care is increasing at a rate of 5 percent per year.[18]

Choosing a policy that adjusts for inflation will increase your premium. For example, one plan that pays a $150-per-day benefit for four years of nursing home coverage would cost a 65-year-old about $1,500 annually without an inflation feature. With 5 percent compound inflation protection, the same policy would cost $2,700 yearly. However, the additional cost is worth it if it protects you and your spouse from bankrupting your life savings.

Elimination Periods

An "elimination period" represents the number of days you must be in a nursing home before your policy kicks in and begins paying benefits. Most policies offer a range between zero and 100 days. Not surprisingly, the longer the elimination period you select, the lower your premium will be. You can determine your optimum elimination period by looking again at your retirement plan to estimate whether or not your investment resources are sufficient. If you have plenty of assets, you may want to opt for a policy with a longer elimination period.

 Most people put the burden of long-term care on their families. While about 12.8 million Americans require long-term care, only 2.4 million live in nursing homes.[6]

How Long Will Benefits Be Paid?

Most policies provide a maximum dollar amount, or ceiling, on the number of covered days. Often, benefits will last two to six years or a lifetime. In addition, some policies have various limits for different types of coverage — nursing homes, assisted living facilities, home health care, etc.

When Will the Policy Pay?

Most policies will begin paying benefits when you need substantial assistance with at least two of six activities of daily living. These activities include bathing, continence, dressing, eating, toileting, and transferring (moving in or out of bed or a wheelchair). Incidentally, the ability to bath is typically the first daily living skill to go.

 More than half of married couples with one partner requiring long-term care become impoverished within one year.[7]

Getting a Quote

When you begin shopping for a long-term-care policy, you may want to follow the example of Alan Rucker, a recently retired 62-year-old. To get the ball rolling, Alan requested premium quotes from three top-rated companies using the following key parameters:

- Coverage for both Alan and his wife, Margaret, age 60, who both enjoy excellent health
- Three-year benefit period
- $100 per day of coverage
- 90-day elimination period
- 5 percent compound inflation protection
- Nursing home, assisted living, and home health-care coverage

For this coverage, premiums ranged from $2,100 to $2,400 per year. Alan then used the following questionnaire to compare the policies and narrow his choices down to the policy that best fits his needs.[19]

Long-Term-Care Questionnaire

1.   What services are covered?
   A) Nursing home care
   B) Home health care
   C) Assisted living facility
   D) Adult day care

E) Alternate care
F) Respite care
G) Other

2. How much does the policy pay, per day, for nursing home care? For home health care? For an assisted living facility? For adult day care? For alternate care? For respite care? Other?

3. How long will benefits last in a nursing home? At home? In an assisted living facility? Other?

4. Does the policy have a maximum lifetime benefit? If so, what is it for nursing home care? For home health care? For an assisted living facility? Other?

5. How long must I wait before preexisting conditions are covered?

6. How many days must I wait before benefits begin for nursing home care? For home health care? For an assisted living facility? Other?

7. Are Alzheimer's disease and other organic, mental, and nervous disorders covered?

8. Does the policy require an assessment of activities of daily living? An assessment of cognitive impairment? Physician certification of need? A prior hospital stay for nursing home care? Home health care?

9. Is the policy guaranteed renewable?

10. What is the age range for enrollment?

11. Is there a waiver-of-premium provision for nursing-home care? For home health care?

12. How long must I be confined before premiums are waived?

13. Does the policy have a non-forfeiture provision? (This feature returns part of your premium if you cancel or lapse your policy.)

14. Does the policy offer an inflation adjustment feature? If so, what is the rate of increase? How often is it applied? For how long? Is there an additional cost?

15. What does the policy cost per year?

A) With the inflation feature?

B) Without inflation feature?

16. Is there a 30-day free look?

17. What is the insurance company rated?

18. Is the policy tax qualified or non-tax qualified?

19. Has the insurance company ever raised its long-term-care insurance rates?

 Avoid long-term-care insurance that is built into a life-insurance policy. At retirement with your debts paid off and your children independent, you likely have very little need for life insurance. Don't pay for life insurance you do not need.

Is Long-Term-Care Coverage Worth the Cost?

The answer depends, of course, on whether you wind up needing long-term care. Let's assume you purchase a policy at age 65 to cover the average cost of a five-year stay in a nursing home. The premium is $2,500 per year. Let's also assume your policy has an inflation feature, so your benefits will increase as long-term-care costs escalate.

At age 80, you incur a chronic illness that requires your admission into a nursing home for the average stay of 2 ½ years. Was this a good investment? For 15 years, you paid $2,500 per year in premiums for a total of $37,500. The total cost of your 2 ½-year nursing home stay, adjusted for inflation, is $183,500. By having the coverage in place, you avoid having to withdraw $183,500 from your investment accounts to pay for your stay. The ability to keep this money invested may prove vital if your spouse is using it as a source of retirement income.

In this scenario, buying a long-term-care policy was a very wise investment decision. If you never used the coverage, you would have spent $37,500 on a policy you didn't need. But would it be worth the risk of financial ruin to bet that you and your spouse will never require long-term care? Looked at in that light, $37,500 may seem like a small sum for peace of mind.

Conclusion

Understandably, "toileting" is not a term most people want to think about when they're dreaming about their happy retirement. It's not enjoyable to consider a future where you might need others to care for you, either in your own home, in an assisted living facility, or in a nursing home. But by thinking about it now and planning for its eventuality, you'll save your spouse and children the burden of caring for you later on. By taking the simple steps outlined in this chapter, you'll have enough money to cover your long-term-care needs, leaving your spouse a healthy nest egg. After all, no one wants their kids to be forced to take the job of home health-care aid.

RESOURCES
Long-Term-Care Insurance Quotes:
- www.longtermcarequote.com
- www.ltciquote.com
- www.insure.com
- www.ltcinsurance.com

Insurance Companies Financial Ratings
- www.ambest.com
- www.bankwatch.com
- www.moodys.com
- www.standardandpoors.com
- www.weissratings.com (Each company rating costs $14.99.)

Please! No More Life Insurance Premiums

✓ RETIREMENT DECISION #17: *Should I cancel my life insurance since I no longer need the coverage?*

Reid and Sylvia Jeppson, age 60 and 59, have decided to retire in three months. For the past 15 years, Reid has been paying $1,500 per year on a $150,000 life insurance policy. He is tired of paying premiums and would like to avoid this expense during retirement. He purchased the insurance coverage for two main reasons: to pay off the remaining $100,000 balance owed on the couple's home and to provide Sylvia with income upon his death. The policy was to supplement the insurance his employer provided him.

Since the time he purchased the life insurance, however, his situation has changed dramatically. First, the Jeppsons now own their home free and clear and carry no other debt. And second, their retirement nest egg is large enough to provide them both with a comfortable income for the next 35 years. Sylvia would not need any of the $150,000 insurance to maintain her standard of living upon Reid's death. With no debt and no need to replace income, does Reid really need this policy? Why should he pay a $1,500 premium each year for coverage that is not needed? What should he do with his policy?

Many retirees find themselves in a position similar to that of Reid and Sylvia. They want to eliminate unneeded expenditures. Does it make sense to continue paying premiums on a policy that is not needed? Probably not, in most cases, but let's answer the following questions, and look at your options.

1. Why did I purchase life insurance?

First, ask yourself *why* you purchased your life insurance coverage in the first place? Most people purchase coverage for the following reasons: to replace income to a surviving spouse and family, to pay off debts, to cover college education expenses, and for large estates, to pay estate taxes.

Look at Alex Jackson, a married 35-year-old with several young children and a large mortgage. He absolutely needs life insurance coverage. If Alex died, income for his family would be lost. Life insurance can provide his wife, Janice, with a lump sum of money that she can use to support the family. If Alex wants to make sure the home and other debts are paid off and also be ensured the children will have the opportunity to obtain college educations, this too could be built into the amount of coverage needed. In Alex's situation, to cover all of these needs, he would need to buy a $2 million policy.

But if you, unlike Alex, are retired, you no longer need to replace income to support a surviving spouse upon your death. Whatever income you were planning to use to support both of you and your spouse during retirement will continue to support one of you if the other dies. If you have no debt, then you don't need life insurance to pay off debt upon death. If your kids are grown and through college, there is no need for life insurance to ensure that there is money available to accomplish this.

2. Do I still need coverage?

Next, update your financial plan and ask yourself an important question: "If I die right now, would my spouse be left with enough money to support him or her throughout the remaining years of his or her life?" Both the retirement and life insurance segments of a financial plan should address this question for you. If you determine coverage is no longer needed, read "Canceling Coverage" (Option 1 or 2) to help you decide what to do next. If your analysis indicates that you still need coverage, continue making premium payments or "pay-up" your policy (Option 3).

3. Canceling Coverage

If you determine that you no longer need coverage and want to stop paying premiums, you have several options.

This is really easy if you own a term life insurance policy; just stop paying your premiums and cancel the policy.

If you own a cash value policy (whole life, universal life, or variable life) you have several choices and more things to consider. These policies are a little trickier because of the cash value (the savings component within the policy). Insurance companies often impose penalties for withdrawing cash value, so before considering any of the options below, call your insurance company and ask if there will be any surrender charges if you surrender your policy. Most cash value policies penalize people who take policy withdrawals within the first 10 to 15 years of owning a policy. These penalties or surrender charges may be as much as 100 percent of the cash value balance in year one and not decline to zero until the 10th or 15th year! Incurring big surrender charges for making changes to your insurance strategy may be reason to keep paying on the policy.

Option 1: Send Me Cash

Your first option is to simply cancel the coverage and ask that a check be sent to you for the balance of your cash value. Be careful, however; this can have severe tax ramifications. If the policy's cash value is greater than the total premiums you've paid over the life of the policy, then you will pay taxes on the difference. For example, Reid and Sylvia have paid a total of $22,500 in premiums and have $40,000 of cash value. Because their cash value is higher than the premiums they've paid, they will be required to pay income taxes on the difference, or $17,500. This is treated as ordinary income.

Option 2: Tax-Free Exchange

If your goal is to eliminate the premium and also to keep the money invested on a tax-deferred basis, your best bet is to move the cash value via a "1035 tax-free exchange" from your life insurance policy directly to an annuity (fixed or variable). Your annuity carrier can provide you with the forms necessary to accomplish this. Once the money is in the annuity, you can stop making premium payments and cancel your policy. Reid and Sylvia decided to do this and moved their $40,000 cash value to a no-load variable annuity. They used the money to buy mutual funds (called subaccounts in a variable annuity).

TIP　If you transfer your cash value to an annuity, be sure to purchase a no-load annuity and keep your investment and insurance expenses low (see Chapter 15).

Option 3: Pay It Up

Another way of eliminating unwanted premiums is to "pay up" your policy. In simple terms, this means using the cash value you've accumulated to make the premium payments each year for you. Although you are still paying a premium, it's not coming directly out of your pocket. Consider this option if you decide to keep your coverage but want to stop writing checks to pay premium payments. Call your insurance company and ask how long the premiums could be paid from your cash value before the cash value would run completely out and the policy lapses. If your cash value is large enough, there may be enough money to the pay the premiums for the rest of your life. If you own an expensive policy that carries a commission, you may want to consider transferring your cash value via a 1035 exchange to a similar, but cheaper, no-load life insurance policy. Your cash value can then be stretched further to "pay up" the policy. With lower premium costs, your cash value may cover premiums for many more years. If you go this route, don't cancel your old policy until your health has been reviewed and the new policy is issued. If you have health problems, this strategy of moving to another policy likely won't work.

Do the Math

Do you think Reid and Sylvia made a good investment decision by moving the cash value of their life insurance policy to an annuity? Of course, it depends entirely on when Reid will die. Let's do the math.

If the Jeppsons would have kept the policy, and Reid died this year, Sylvia would receive the $150,000 tax-free. But because they canceled their life insurance and moved their $40,000 cash value into a variable annuity, Sylvia will receive the market value of the annuity. If no growth occurs in such a short span of time, Sylvia will simply receive $40,000. If we knew Reid was going to die this year, the best investment would have been to keep the life insurance policy and receive the full $150,000.

How many years will it take before the annuity is a better investment than the life insurance? Or, in other words, how long will it take for the $40,000 in the annuity (after-tax) to be equal to $150,000 of life insurance proceeds that would have been paid out to Sylvia at Reid's death?

At 8 percent interest, the answer is 20 years, or when Reid is 80 years old. This is the breakeven point, assuming the Jeppson's policy is paid up and no more premiums remain. If Reid lives past age 80, the annuity will yield him more money; if he dies sooner than 80, the insurance policy would have been the better investment. (See Figure 1.)

If Reid dies in 25 years at age 85, the annuity will be worth $227,516 after-tax (8 percent growth) as opposed to the life insurance death benefit at $150,000, thus yielding Sylvia $77,515 more. On the other hand, if Reid dies after just 15 years, Sylvia would receive $150,000 from the insurance policy and only $100,790 from the annuity resulting in the insurance paying $49,210 more than the annuity.

The breakeven point drops to 16 years if the Jeppsons can earn 10 percent on their annuity. Further, if Reid has to continue making premium payments throughout retirement, the breakeven drops to 18 years at 8 percent and 15 years at 10 percent.

Again, whether or not the Jeppsons made a good investment decision to drop their coverage and move their cash value to an annuity depends entirely on how long Reid lives. Reid and Sylvia are betting, by using this strategy, that Reid will live past age 80 and that they will maintain an 8 percent growth rate on their annuity throughout retirement.

If Reid had any life-shortening health conditions or a family history of such conditions, obviously it wouldn't make sense to cancel the policy.

Other Considerations

There is more to making the decision to drop your policy than just the math, however. There are many legitimate reasons to keep your coverage and continue making premium payments during retirement.

First, you may own life insurance so you can maximize your company pension plan (see Chapter 7). This insurance strategy allows you to choose the pension payout option with the highest payment, *single life with no survivor benefits,* and still provide for your spouse upon your death.

Also, some retirees may actually use cash value via a tax-free policy loan to supplement their retirement income. In addition, you may need life insurance for estate-planning purposes, especially if your over-

Figure 1

Amount Paid At Reid's Death

Age	Life Insurance Payout (Tax-Free)	Annuity Payout (After-Tax)*	And The Winner Is . . .
60	$150,000	$38,025	Life Insurance
61	$150,000	$40,617	Life Insurance
62	$150,000	$43,416	Life Insurance
63	$150,000	$46,440	Life Insurance
64	$150,000	$49,705	Life Insurance
65	$150,000	$53,231	Life Insurance
66	$150,000	$57,040	Life Insurance
67	$150,000	$61,153	Life Insurance
68	$150,000	$65,595	Life Insurance
69	$150,000	$70,393	Life Insurance
70	$150,000	$75,574	Life Insurance
71	$150,000	$81,170	Life Insurance
72	$150,000	$87,214	Life Insurance
73	$150,000	$93,741	Life Insurance
74	$150,000	$100,790	Life Insurance
75	$150,000	$108,403	Life Insurance
76	$150,000	$116,626	Life Insurance
77	$150,000	$125,506	Life Insurance
78	$150,000	$135,096	Life Insurance
79	$150,000	$145,454	Life Insurance
80	$150,000	$156,640	Annuity
81	$150,000	$168,721	Annuity
82	$150,000	$181,769	Annuity
83	$150,000	$195,860	Annuity
84	$150,000	$211,079	Annuity
85	$150,000	$227,516	Annuity
86	$150,000	$245,267	Annuity
87	$150,000	$264,438	Annuity
88	$150,000	$285,143	Annuity
89	$150,000	$307,505	Annuity
90	$150,000	$331,655	Annuity
91	$150,000	$357,737	Annuity
92	$150,000	$385,906	Annuity
93	$150,000	$416,329	Annuity
94	$150,000	$449,185	Annuity
95	$150,000	$484,670	Annuity
96	$150,000	$522,994	Annuity
97	$150,000	$564,383	Annuity
98	$150,000	$609,084	Annuity
99	$150,000	$657,361	Annuity
100	$150,000	$709,499	Annuity

* assumes a tax rate of 25% and an 8% rate of return

all estate is worth more than $3 million (in 2004). Life insurance can provide liquid assets to pay estate taxes upon your death.

The decision to cancel a policy can largely be made by answering one question, "Why do I own this coverage?" If your answer is, "To replace income or pay off debt when I no longer have an income or debt to repay," then canceling your policy may make sense for you.

Don't be too quick to act, and be sure to carefully evaluate each option before making any decisions. Whether you decide to keep your policy, cash it out, or exchange it there is likely a strategy that will help you reduce your retirement expenses by eliminating future premium payments.

OTHER RETIREMENT
CONSIDERATIONS

—MORTGAGES
—ESTATE PLANNING

TWENTY-TWO

To Pay or Not to Pay?

✓ RETIREMENT DECISION #18: *Should I pay off my mortgage at retirement?*

Monty Van Wagner, like many Americans, had the admirable goal of paying off his mortgage by the time he hit retirement at age 65. Unfortunately, things didn't go as he planned. He reached retirement with a $100,000 outstanding mortgage and seven more years of $1,500 monthly payments. Now at the tail end of his mortgage, he is faced with a difficult question. Should he use some of his $400,000 retirement nest-egg money to pay off the mortgage, or should he keep the money invested and continue making mortgage payments?

 In 2001, 32 percent of retirees ages 65 to 74 carried a home mortgage, up from 26 percent in 1998.
Federal Reserve Board's Survey of Consumer Finances

Like many decisions retirees must make at retirement, the answer largely boils down to risk and return. Which do you think is the greatest priority at this stage in life – higher investment returns *or* peace of mind. Let's look at both sides of the equation and help Monty make a decision.

 The average mortgage debt for retirees ages 65 to 74 is $44,000.
Federal Reserve Board's Survey of Consumer Finances

Simple Math Says, "Don't Pay It Off"

Many financial professionals look at paying off a mortgage strictly from a financial perspective, a "just do the math" approach. This conventional wisdom suggests that if you believe you can obtain investment returns greater than the interest rate you are paying on your mortgage, you shouldn't pay off the mortgage. In Monty's case, he has a 6 percent mortgage. If he believes his nest egg will earn 8 percent, logic suggests it would be advantageous for him to stay invested rather than paying off his mortgage. Let's do the math.

With a $100,000 mortgage balance, he will pay almost $6,000 in interest this year. If he keeps his $100,000 invested and it returns 8 percent this year, he will make $8,000 and pocket the $2,000 difference. If the growth of his investments continues at that rate for the remaining seven years of his mortgage, he will accumulate an additional $18,000 by not paying off the mortgage. That's $18,000 worth of profits he would have left on the table if he had taken a $100,000 withdrawal from his portfolio to pay off the mortgage.

Of course, the deal is sweetened if he can still itemize his mortgage interest when he files his taxes. Itemizing his mortgage interest will give him a $6,000 tax deduction, which will save him $1,800 in taxes. When the tax savings are added into the calculation, Monty's after-tax mortgage interest rate is only 4.2 percent (see formula below).

After-tax cost of debt: Mortgage interest rate multiplied by (1- tax bracket) = after-tax interest rate. Example: 0.06 x (1-0.30) = 4.2%

Although there is no guarantee, it is reasonable to expect even a conservative investment portfolio will achieve a rate of return that is higher over time than the interest rate most homeowners are paying on their mortgages. For example, since 1926 a moderate income and growth portfolio made up of 40 percent stocks, 50 percent bonds, and 10 percent cash has *averaged* 8 percent annually.

Although you still must make a mortgage payment, choosing not to pay off your mortgage will put more money in your pocket, if you experience good long-term rates of return on your investment money. However, beware! During years when your investments don't perform as expected, you will actually be worse off by using this strategy. For instance, if your portfolio loses 10 percent in a given year, then you're faced with a double whammy: investment losses and paying mortgage interest. If your investments experience a period of multiple years with losses, you could actually end up with negative compounding on your money. Ultimately, the investment markets will determine whether or not the *don't-pay-it-off* approach is effective.

 77 percent of those over age 65 are homeowners of which 84 percent own their homes free and clear. Source: Fannie Mae

Peace of Mind

On the other hand, people who pay off their mortgage and rid themselves of the burden of a monthly mortgage payment can live on much less income and are often better equipped to survive economic storms. This means peace of mind. In Monty's case, by paying off his $100,000 mortgage, he would eliminate his mortgage payments and reduce his annual expenditures by $18,000. Essentially, he would be guaranteed to make a 6 percent return by getting rid of the mortgage (not having to pay 6 percent interest on his mortgage is essentially the same as making 6 percent). A guaranteed 6 percent return sounds pretty good in periods when the stock and bond markets are declining in value.

In addition, Monty would own his home and save having to pay $26,000 of interest over the next seven years. No matter what the financial markets do during his retirement, he would have the security of knowing that his home is paid for and he has a place to live. If the economy encounters serious problems during his retirement, Monty can always tighten his belt and survive, a luxury he may not have if his investments are down and he must make a large mortgage payment each month.

Owning your home free and clear might boost your sense of security. To many, this financial security takes precedence over making a little extra return when comparing the two options.

Where's Your Money Stashed?

Monty must consider the tax implications of withdrawing money from his various investment accounts before deciding to pay off his mortgage. If Monty has all of his money invested in tax-deferred retirement accounts, any money he withdraws will be taxed as income. Taking a large withdrawal will put him in a higher tax bracket. If he taps into a taxable account that has experienced a lot of growth, he'll have to pay capital-gains taxes. Let's take a closer look at Monty's situation.

Monty is fortunate enough to have a taxable brokerage account with a $150,000 balance and an IRA with $250,000—giving him more than enough money to pay off his $100,000 mortgage balance. But which money should he use to pay it off? His decision will boil down to the tax consequences of each choice. Let's look at his IRA first, then his taxable brokerage account.

As you know, an IRA withdrawal will trigger state and federal income taxes and penalties for those not yet 59 ½. Monty will not face an early withdrawal penalty, but any money he takes out of his IRA will be added to his taxable income for the year. A $100,000 withdrawal would propel him into the 25 percent federal tax bracket and a 5 percent state tax bracket. That's a 30 percent combined tax rate. To cover these taxes and still have enough money to pay off his $100,000 mortgage, he would need to take a $142,857 withdrawal from his IRA. And if that weren't bad enough, the IRA distribution would boost his income over the $44,000 threshold (for joint filers), causing 85 percent of his Social Security income to be taxed also. Does it make sense for Monty to deplete his IRA by more than 50 percent and pay all of this extra tax just to avoid $26,000 of mortgage interest? The answer is "No." It's apparent that if he dipped into his retirement funds to pay off his mortgage, the effects on his retirement would prove devastating. He would likely run out of assets prematurely.

What about his taxable account? If Monty decides to use the money in his taxable brokerage account to pay off his mortgage, he would have to sell some investments first before taking the $100,000 withdrawal. He would need to be careful here. Selling investments that have appreciated a lot will trigger capital-gains taxes. To combat the taxman, Monty should look to sell investments where the tax consequences would be the smallest. Monty was smart when he assembled his portfolio in his taxable account. He purchased tax-friendly investments, such as municipal-bond mutual funds and tax-managed mutual funds. Although many of his investments have increased in value, he could offset most of those gains by selling his losers. Monty found that he could take $100,000 out of his taxable portfolio and pay hardly any capital-gains taxes.

It's Time to be Conservative

Monty has determined that he will need $36,000 each year during retirement after paying taxes and mortgage payments to meet his spending needs. His pension and Social Security will provide him with $28,500 of after-tax income. Without a mortgage, he will only need to withdraw $7,500 from his investment portfolio to meet his annual spending needs. On the other hand, with a mortgage he would have to pull out an extra $18,000 each year for the next seven years to make mortgage payments.

Monty needs to ask himself this question: "If the economy turns sour and my investments are losing money, do I want to be in a position where I have to sell investments at lows to meet my $1,500-a-month mortgage obligation?" His answer is no. Therefore, paying off the mortgage now will eliminate the monthly burden and not put him in position where he is forced to sell investments when they are down in value.

"But wait a minute," you might say. "If Monty pays off his mortgage, isn't he giving up the last great tax break Uncle Sam offers?" Being able to deduct mortgage interest is often cited as a reason to keep paying on a mortgage. Of course this tax deduction will be lost when Monty pays off his mortgage. Is this a big deal? For many retirees, and in Monty's case, it's not. He does not have enough tax deductions to *itemize* and will instead claim the standard deduction when he files his taxes ($9,700 in 2004 for married filing jointly). Consequently, he wouldn't receive a tax deduction at all for the $6,000 of mortgage interest he would pay this year if he chooses not to pay off his mortgage.

At this stage in his life, Monty decides that peace of mind is more important to him than a little extra investment return. Plus, Monty has the resources in a taxable account that will allow him to pay off his mortgage with minimal tax consequences. Monty decides it's time to settle his mortgage debt. It's better to be safe than sorry.

Don't pay off your mortgage if...

If the bulk of your money is in a retirement plan and you are comfortable with investment volatility, you may want to consider maintaining your mortgage and keeping your money invested. As we've discussed, withdrawing money from retirement accounts to pay off your mortgage is not often a good idea due to the tax hit you'll absorb. If you are successful in investing and obtain a rate of return greater than your mortgage interest rate, you will end up with more money than you would if you pay off your home.

Pay off your mortgage if...

Conservative retirees who have non-retirement money available and who are uncomfortable with risk should consider paying off their mortgages. If you fall into this group, your portfolio is likely to be invested more conservatively, making it less likely that the returns will be much greater than the interest you'll pay on your mortgage. Paying off your home certainly has an emotional appeal, too. Many people, particularly those nearing retirement, absolutely hate the idea of debt looming over them, and they want to stop having to make burdensome monthly payments. Once the debt is eliminated and your monthly payments stop, you will be better able to handle tough, unforeseen financial times, if they should arise, such as job loss, poor economic conditions, and periods of lackluster investment performance.

Other Ways to Get Rid of Your Mortgage

From Monty's example, we can see that there are advantages to using a taxable account to pay off a mortgage. There are major draw-backs to taking large distributions from a tax-deferred retirement account to do the job. However, what if that's all you own? What if, for peace of mind, you want to retire your mortgage but all of your savings are in retirement accounts? Is there a way to use your IRA or 401(k) without getting hammered by taxes? Absolutely. I have three solutions.

First, you don't have to pay off your mortgage all at once. Rather than pulling the entire amount out of your retirement account all at once, you could take out $10,000 or $20,000 chunks each year until you pay down your mortgage. This strategy shouldn't dramatically affect your income tax bracket or taxation of your Social Security. Still, be cautious so that you don't deplete your retirement savings too quickly.

Second, you could refinance your mortgage to a shorter term. This will, of course, increase your monthly payments, but it will also get you closer to being "free and clear" from debt and save you a lot of interest in the process. For example, a $100,000 30-year mortgage at 6.5 percent requires a monthly payment of $632. The interest alone over the 30 years would equal $127,542, making the total outlay for a $100,000 loan $227,542. In contrast, a shorter 15-year $100,000 mortgage at 6.5% requires a slightly higher $871 monthly payment, but the total interest paid over the life of the mortgage would equal only $56,798 for a total outlay of $156,798. The 15-year mortgage is $70,744 cheaper than the 30-year.

Third, you could simply begin making half a payment every two weeks rather than a whole payment once per month. With this strategy, instead of making the standard 12 payments per year, you would make 26 half payments. This translates into making one extra monthly payment every year, which would also reduce your total interest. For example, a traditional 30-year $100,000 mortgage at 7 percent requires a regular monthly payment of $665.30. Over the course of 30 years, the total interest paid would equal $139,508. By making just one extra monthly payment per year, the total interest would drop substantially to $105,033, and the home would be paid off six years earlier. For a fee, your mortgage company will set up a biweekly payment plan. You can obtain the same result for free by simply saving up an extra payment and sending it in each year.

The Hard Realities

You, like many retirees, may have to face some hard realities. If your mortgage payment is too large and you are forced to withdraw too much from your portfolio to meet expenses, you may run the risk of running out of money prematurely during retirement. If, after completing a retirement analysis, you find this is the case, you need to seriously consider cutting your expenses. Often the easiest way is to downsize. Trading down to a smaller home or condo will not only lower your mortgage payments, but it will also lower many other costs associated with living in a larger home. It's never easy to move, especially from a home you planned to live in throughout retirement; however, moving is much better than running out of money before you run out of life.

A Last Resort: Reverse Mortgage

Most retirement projection calculators assume you will stay in your home throughout retirement and never use your home equity to supplement your living expenses. This, of course, is the ideal but is not always possible. If worse comes to worst, you can obtain a reverse mortgage and pull money out of your home to supplement your income. If your retirement projections show you running out of money prematurely, add in the equity in your home as an additional source of income during retirement.

Reverse mortgages allow homeowners age 62 and over to borrow money against the value of their home. As long as you don't move, the loan doesn't have to be repaid until after death.

With a reverse mortgage, you can take out a lump sum or choose to have fixed monthly payments sent to you for the rest of your life. The amount you can borrow depends on several factors including your age, the value of your home, and where you live (see Figure 1). To determine how much you can borrow and to examine your options, simply plug your home value into the reverse mortgage calculator at www.reversemortgage.org. For example, if you are age 85 and own a $250,000 home, you could pull out a lump sum of $174,367 or begin receiving monthly payments of $1,469 for life through a reverse mortgage.

Figure 1

Reverse Mortgage
Home Value $250,000 (FHA/HUD)

Payout	Age 65	Age 70	Age 75	Age 80	Age 85
Lump Sum	$132,821	$142,429	$152,839	$1,63,624	$174,367
Monthly Income	$758	$854	$984	$1,171	$1,469

Source: www.reversemortgage.org

Reverse mortgages are fairly expensive. Origination fees and insurance premiums can run from $4,000 to $7,000 for a $150,000 loan. Paying these upfront costs doesn't make much sense if you plan to move during the next few years. Your home is likely one of your largest assets and can be your safety net if it looks like you are going to deplete your nest egg too soon.

Conclusion

Choosing to pay off your mortgage or to keep your money invested is a decision that should be incorporated into your planning as you assemble your retirement strategy. Once again, some professional advice and a retirement analysis are needed to truly examine the viability of each option. Plugging multiple scenarios into a retirement calculator (including both paying off your mortgage and continuing to make mortgage payments) will help you view the hard facts before making your decision.

Remember, the goal at retirement is no longer to obtain off-the-chart returns; the goal is to meet your retirement objectives with as little risk as possible. Don't take more risk than is necessary and get caught short changing your retirement. It's time to be conservative.

9 out of 10 people age 55 and older are planning to stay in their home during retirement. Source: AARP, "Fixing to Stay" Survey 2000

TWENTY-THREE

You Can't Take It With You

 RETIREMENT DECISION #19: *What strategies should I use to ensure that my estate passes to my heirs and not to Uncle Sam?*

Just two years after retirement, Wade and Cheryl McGrath were injured in a car accident and died. Their estate was valued at $1.3 million. They had intended to update their estate plan but never got around to it; going to see an attorney just seemed too costly and too painful for them. Besides, who wants to talk about death? As it turned out, their 10-year-old will was contested in probate court as their four children squabbled over the estate. The probate, which oversees the distribution of one's estate to heirs, resulted in a two-year delay and cost the estate 5 percent, or $65,000, in fees. An additional $210,000 was due for income taxes. The McGraths sure hadn't planned on such as mess. They hadn't planned...period.

Could these expenses and delays have been avoided? The answer is, unequivocally, "Yes!" In fact, there are many things they could have done without ever seeing an attorney. They could have avoided probate by just implementing some simple strategies.

Don't follow the McGraths' lead and let your good intentions slip away. Retirement is a good time to update your estate plan; double check the titling of your assets and the beneficiaries you've named. To help

Figure 1

McGrath's Estate	
IRA (Wade)	$600,000
Home (jointly owned)	$400,000
Brokerage Account (jointly owned)	$200,000
Bank Account (jointly owned)	$100,000
Total	**$1,300,000**

you with your planning, let's examine some of the strategies the McGraths could have adopted.

First, if you are married you should know that estate taxes are due upon the death of the second spouse, not the first. Probate, too, with a little planning, can also be avoided until the second death. Estate taxes, whether you are married or not, only apply to estates that are larger than $1.5 million (2005).

There are many mechanisms for transferring your assets to your heirs. The question is which are the most efficient and cost-effective.

Joint Tenants

Setting up accounts titled as "joint tenants with rights of survivor- ship" is the most common estate-planning strategy. Very simply put, if one joint owner dies the assets pass to the other joint owner. There are no probate proceedings required. The McGraths did take this step. They had titled their $400,000 home, a $200,000 brokerage account, and a $100,000 bank account as "Wade and Cheryl McGrath, joint tenants with rights of survivorship" (JTWROS). Had Cheryl not died in the car accident, all of these assets would have transferred directly to her with- out going through probate. Joint tenancy alone works well as long as both joint tenants don't pass away at the same time.

Wills

Many people have the misconception that by having a will their assets will somehow pass to their heirs without probate court proceedings. This is simply not true. In fact, it is kind of a funny notion. A will is largely nothing more than a list of instructions to a probate judge about how to divide up an estate among heirs. Passing assets through the use of a will actually guarantees probate. Probate costs will usually run be- tween 3 and 7 percent of the value of an estate.

It is important to note that any assets with a beneficiary desig- nated avoid these proceedings, and beneficiary designations trump wills. For example, if your will says "My wife gets everything I own at my death," but your IRA or life insurance policy lists your ex-wife as the beneficiary, then guess who gets the money? You got it, your ex-wife. Remembering this little gem of knowledge about beneficiaries can save you and your heirs a lot of confusion, time, and money.

If you have a will, make sure it is up to date and is drafted properly! If it is more than a few years old or your life situation has changed, you should have it updated. If there are legal holes in your will, you are leaving it open to being contested. While I am sure you have perfect kids who would never fight over your money, it has been known to happen.

If you don't have a will, guess what? Your state, with the help of your state legislature, has been so kind as to draft one for you. So if you don't have a will, you in reality do have a will. It may just not be a will that is in line with your express desires. Most state wills pass assets to "next of kin." If you are in your retirement, the distribution of your assets would generally start with your children, then your parents, then your siblings, in that order. If your desires are the same as those outlined in the will the state has drawn up for you, you can save the money you set aside to pay an attorney to draft you a will. However, this is seldom the case.

The McGraths' will was outdated, having been drafted over 10 years ago when they lived in another state. Their will referenced assets they no longer owned and made bequests the children felt didn't reflect their parents' intentions at their death. Consequently, the will was challenged; the children hired attorneys, and the battle over their parents' assets began.

POD/TOD

In which type of accounts can you name beneficiaries? Many people believe this can only be done with retirement accounts like IRAs, 401(k)s, and annuities; this is not the case. You can, and likely should, name beneficiaries for many of your non-retirement accounts. For instance, you can establish Pay-on-Death (POD) instructions on all of your bank accounts. POD simply provides the bank with instructions regarding whom you would like to receive the bank assets when you die. For example, the McGraths had $100,000 in a joint bank checking and savings account at their local bank. Had they spent an extra couple of minutes in the bank one day signing a POD form, this $100,000 could have passed directly to their four children in whatever proportions they decided upon, with no probate proceedings. Upon Wade and Cheryl's deaths, the bank would have read the POD instructions and paid the money directly to their children without argument.

The McGraths also had $200,000 invested in stocks and bonds in a joint brokerage account. Once again, had they filled out another simple, one-page form, this money could have also passed to their heirs without probate. You can name beneficiaries to your brokerage accounts by completing a form to provide Transfer-On-Death (TOD) instructions. Ask your brokerage firm or mutual fund company to provide you with a TOD form.

Stretch IRA

At retirement, Wade had rolled his 401(k) money into an IRA. At his death, the account was worth $600,000. Unfortunately, Wade made a big mistake when setting up his IRA account. He listed Cheryl as the primary beneficiary but didn't name any secondary beneficiaries. Had Cheryl not died at the same time as Wade, she could have taken Wade's IRA money and transferred it into her IRA and avoided all taxes and penalties in the process. With no secondary beneficiaries listed, the IRA money was paid to the McGraths' estate and divided up via probate proceedings.

Remember, most IRA money has never been taxed. Uncle Sam allowed Wade to accumulate this money before taxes and didn't tax the investment earnings each year. As you can imagine, Uncle Sam is eager to tax this money. The $600,000 was assumed to be income paid to Wade in the year of his death. A $600,000 income put Wade in the highest federal income tax bracket (35 percent) and created a $210,000 income tax bill. If he had lived in a state with a state income tax, this would have been levied at the highest state tax rate, too. In addition, since this money went through probate, probate costs were also levied against this account. The huge tax bill and probate expenses could have been totally avoided.

Wade should have named his children as secondary beneficiaries on his IRA account. The children would then have had the option to stretch the taxes owed on this IRA over their lifetimes. This is how it works. Let's assume Wade's son Chris, age 35, was named as a 25 percent secondary beneficiary. At the death of his parents, he could take his 25 percent in one of two ways:

1. Take the $150,000 in cash now or over the next five years, and pay the income taxes.
2. Transfer the money into a beneficiary IRA (also called an inherited IRA) in his name. Moving the money to his own IRA would allow the money to continue to grow on a tax-deferred basis and avoid having to pay a big income tax bill at his parents' final tax rates.

Even in this second option, Uncle Sam wants to get his hands on this money and will require that Chris begin taking withdrawals so the money can be taxed. But Uncle Sam will allow Chris to pay income taxes on this money over his life expectancy of another 48 years, according to IRS tables, rather than all at once. That means the income taxes will be imposed at Chris's tax rate of 15 percent, rather than his parents' final tax rate of 35 percent, and Chris will only have to pay a little in taxes each year. Because Chris is expected to live another 48 years, he will need to withdraw enough to pay taxes on 1/48th of the balance this year, 1/47th next year, 1/46th the next and so on. This equates to only a little over 2 percent annually or about $3,000. This would have been a nice gift for Wade to give his son; $150,000 growing tax-deferred until Chris's retirement could easily be worth more than $1 million when he reaches age 65, even after taking withdrawals each and every year.

So the big question is this. Would you like to give your children the option of transferring your IRA to an IRA in their name, pay income taxes at their tax brackets over their own lifetimes, and allow them to create their own retirement nest egg?

If Mr. McGrath had the chance to do it all over again, he would have made sure to list secondary beneficiaries to his IRA. You should do the same.

Living Trusts

With the strategies we've discussed so far, the McGraths could have kept their bank account, brokerage account, and IRA account out of probate and had an iron-clad will in place to distribute the only asset left, their $400,000 home. The probate for the home and some personal property alone would be fairly quick and easy and would require very little expense. Furthermore, the McGraths could have taken things even a step further by having their attorney set up a living trust.

Living trusts serve two purposes. First, they can keep your assets out of probate court, and second, they can reduce your estate-tax bill. What would have happened if, years earlier, Wade and Cheryl had drawn up The McGrath Family Living Trust, named themselves as trustees, and named their children as beneficiaries? They could have placed their home in the trust and as trustees would have continued to control the home and any other trust property just as they did as joint owners. In their case, a trust would have acted like a beneficiary designation for their home. Upon their death, the home would have been transferred to the beneficiaries named in the trust. This strategy would have allowed the home to change hands without probate.

You may be wondering why we haven't talked about the McGraths having to pay estate taxes? While $469,800 of estate taxes were levied against the McGraths' estate (see estate-tax rates in Figure 2), Uncle Sam has given everybody a tax credit to use toward paying these estate taxes. The tax credit, called the unified credit, which is a maximum of $555,800 in 2005, covers all of the taxes owed on an estate valued up to $1.5 million (see Figure 3). Because the McGrath's estate was valued at $1.3 million, their unified credit ($555,800) satisfied their entire estate-tax bill ($469,800).

Figure 2

Federal Estate Tax Rates

Estate Size	Tax Rate
$10,000	18%
$20,000	20%
$40,000	22%
$60,000	24%
$80,000	26%
$100,000	28%
$150,000	30%
$250,000	32%
$500,000	34%
$750,000	37%
$1,000,000	39%
$1,250,000	41%
$1,500,000	43%
$2,000,000	45%
$2,000,000+	47%

(2005)

What if the McGrath's estate was valued at $2.3 million instead of $1.3 million? Would you believe an estate this size would put them in a 47% estate-tax bracket (see Figure 2)? Their estate-tax bill would be a monstrous $921,800.

Figure 3

Estate Tax

Year	Unified Tax Credit	Exemption Equivalent
2000	$220,550	$675,000
2001	$220,550	$675,000
2002	$345,800	$1,000,000
2003	$345,800	$1,000,000
2004	$555,800	$1,500,000
2005	$555,800	$1,500,000
2006	$780,800	$2,000,000
2007	$780,800	$2,000,000
2008	$780,800	$2,000,000
2009	$1,455,800	$3,500,000

However, they could apply *one* of their unified credits of $555,800 toward this tax bill. They would be left owing $366,000 in estate taxes. This is where a living trust would come to the rescue.

While everyone has a unified credit, not everyone can use their credit without doing some additional planning and having their assets titled properly. A trust with a unified credit provision (AB Trust) takes care of this. With a trust, both Wade's and Cheryl's credits could be used. If they have two unified tax credits totaling $1.1 million and an estate tax bill of $921,800, how much will they have to pay in taxes? You're right, zero. In this scenario a trust could have saved their estate $366,000 in taxes. Not a bad savings considering most trusts only cost $500 to $5,000 to create.

Other Estate Planning Documents

While you're getting your estate plan updated, be sure to have the following documents created as well:

- Durable Health Care Power of Attorney: This document gives someone you designate the right to make health decisions in your behalf at the point you are no longer able to make them yourself.
- Springing Power of Attorney: This document gives the legal

right to manage your affairs in the event that you no longer can. Whomever you designate as power of attorney can sign in your behalf as if it were you signing.

- <u>Living Will</u>: This document states your desire to be allowed to die if terminally ill and incapable to make such decisions on your own.

There are some additional strategies you may want to explore if you have a large estate, such as family limited partnerships (FLP), family limited liability companies (LLC), irrevocable life insurance trusts (ILIT), and charitable trusts (CRT).

Estate-Planning Costs

TIP

Go to the attorney's office prepared with a list of your assets, how each asset is owned, values and beneficiaries, and knowing how you would like your estate divided. Not having to answer these questions while on the clock at the attorneys office will save you money in attorney's fees.

What will it cost to develop a sound estate planning strategy? Figure 4 outlines the estimated costs of various estate-planning strategies.

Most attorneys will charge an hourly fee to prepare your estate-planning documents. This hourly fee could range from $100 an hour to $500 an hour. To keep your costs as low as possible, go to your attorney's office prepared. Prepare a list of all of your assets, including who owns the asset, the value of the asset, beneficiaries named, and where it is held. Also, prepare a list of your family members and their dates of birth. Give some thought as to whom you want your assets transferred. If you do this beforehand, it will reduce the hours you'll be charged. If your attorney is doing your estate planning for a flat fee, obviously this isn't as crucial.

Figure 4

Estate Planning Costs

Strategy	Costs
Joint Tenancy with Rights of Survivorship	$0
Transfer on Death (TOD)	$0
Pay on Death (POD)	$0
Simple Will	$300 - $1,000
Living Trust	$500 - $5,000

Estate planning is one aspect of financial planning that most often gets pushed to the back burner. Because there are many steps you can take without the additional expense and time associated with seeing an attorney, there is no excuse not to get your strategy in motion. It literally only takes minutes and costs nothing to establish beneficiaries on your IRA, annuity and life insurance, and to establish POD and TOD instructions on your bank and brokerage accounts. There are plenty of people who have put off their estate planning for years and ultimately leave a mess for their heirs to clean up. Don't be one of them. You can't take it with you but you can, with just a little planning, make sure your heirs, not Uncle Sam and the probate court, get your estate.

WEBSITES:

Find an estate-planning attorney in your area:

• www.lawinfo.com

• www.legalmatch.com

Do-it-yourself estate-planning documents:

• www.legalforms.com

• www.uslegalforms.com

RETIREMENT PLAN
DISTRIBUTIONS

—TAKING A CASH DISTRIBUTION
FROM YOUR 401(k)
—TAKING A STOCK DISTRIBUTION
FROM YOUR 401(k)

TWENTY-FOUR

Cash It, Roll It, Leave It, Roth It, Annuitize It, Stock It!

✓ RETIREMENT DECISION #20: *Which retirement plan distribution option should I choose?*

In 2003, Bruce Richardson, an engineer, retired at age 59. One of the first decisions he faced was what to do with the $625,000 in his 401(k) plan? Without fully understanding his distribution choices, Bruce quickly took the advice of fellow employees, who suggested he just "roll it to an IRA." Unfortunately for Bruce, like many retirees, his quick decision will end up costing him thousands of dollars in unnecessary taxes during retirement. At first glance it looks as if he made the right choice. However, because the bulk of his 401(k) money is invested in company stock there is a better option. As you will see, had he spent just a little time comparing and evaluating his choices, he would be in a much better position to handle his 30-year retirement.

 401(k) plan assets have soared to more than $1.9 trillion[1]

How are you going to take distributions from your 401(k) at retirement? Your answer to this question will have a serious impact on whether your retirement plan is a success or failure. In this chapter, we'll discuss your six distribution options. The information in this chapter and Chapter 25 will prepare you to make the right distribution decision and avoid costly mistakes. You'll understand how to get the most out of the money you have worked so hard to accumulate during your working years.

 Three out of four people have retirement savings plans through their employers. [2]

Each distribution option has its own set of advantages and disadvantages. There's not one option that's best for all retirees. Your choice of distribution will depend on when you retire, your current and future tax brackets, the type of retirement accounts you own, how much you have saved, and how much income you will need during retirement. You will need to carefully consider each of these distribution methods to make the smartest choice. Remember, the name of the game is to maximize your retirement nest egg and to avoid paying unnecessary taxes and penalties. At retirement, your distribution options are:

- Taking a lump-sum cash distribution
- Rolling the money into an IRA
- Leaving the money in your former company's retirement plan
- Rolling the money into a traditional IRA, then converting it to a Roth IRA
- Receiving an annuity payout
- Using a combination strategy: Net Unrealized Appreciation (NUA) and an IRA Rollover

Option 1: Cash It

 Cash distributions account for 18 percent of retirement plan distributions.[9]

Quick cash has its appeal. If you choose a lump-sum cash distribution of your 401(k) funds, your employer will simply send you a check for the vested balance in your plan (minus tax withholding). Think of what you could do with all that money. You could purchase a new house, a luxury car, a boat, or an exotic vacation. Doesn't sound too bad, does it?

For most retirees, taking a cash distribution is usually a grave mistake. Although having cash in hand may be an appropriate option in some limited circumstances, such as emergencies, choosing this option is usually shortsighted because it opens you up to penalties and severe tax consequences. Right off the bat, your employer is required by law to withhold 20 percent of the amount distributed to you as a prepayment of taxes. The government anticipates that you will owe this amount as a result of the distribution. You could get some of this refunded if you're in a tax bracket less than 20 percent. If, however, you're in a higher bracket, Uncle Sam will require you to pay additional taxes when you file a return.

Consider a lump-sum cash distribution only when:
• You are faced with a financial emergency and have absolutely no other source of money.
• You have ownership of highly appreciated company stock (We'll discuss this in Chapter 25).

(Note: The 20 percent withholding does not apply to company stock distributed to you in shares. In this case, the company will send you a stock certificate, often referred to as an "in-kind" distribution. All other cash and securities you own in your plan upon distribution are subject to the 20 percent tax withholding.)

In addition, the entire withdrawal is considered ordinary income for the year in which you take the distribution. When you add the distribution amount to your earned income for the year, you may find yourself thrust into a much higher federal income tax bracket (see Figure 1). If your state imposes local taxes, you will be required to pay those, too.

Figure 1

2004 Federal Personal Income Tax Rates

Tax Rate	Single filers	Married filing jointly	Married filing separately	Head of household
10%	Up to $7,150	Up to $14,300	Up to $7,150	Up to $10,200
15%	$7,151-$29,050	$14,301-$58,100	$7,151-$29,050	$10,201-$38,900
25%	$ 29,051 $70,350	$58,101-$117,250	$29,051-$58,625	$38,901-$100,500
28%	$70,351-$146,750	$117,251-$178,650	$58,626-$89,325	$100,501-$162,700-
33%	$146,751 $319,100	$178,651-$319,100	$89,326-$159,550	$162,701-$319,100
35%	$319,101 or more	$319,101 or more	$159,551 or more	$319,101 or more

And if you are not yet age 59 ½, you will be subject to an additional 10 percent penalty for taking a premature distribution.

When you add up penalties and taxes, depending on your bracket, you could lose almost one-half of your retirement savings by taking a cash distribution — and surprisingly that's not even the worst aspect of this distribution method. You'll feel sick years later when you realize how large your retirement plan could have grown with years of compound interest and tax-deferral.

Still not convinced that taking a cash distribution is a bad mistake? Let's peer into the world of Clark Whittaker. Clark, 57, has a 401(k) balance of $500,000. He is tempted to retire early and take a cash distribution to pay off his mortgage, buy a new car, and take a trip to Hawaii. Since a cash distribution is treated as regular income, this withdrawal would vault Clark into the highest tax bracket. He'd have to pay $150,000 in federal taxes (nominal tax rate 30 percent) and $25,000 in state income taxes. In addition, because he's not yet 59 ½, he'd take a $50,000 hit for the 10-percent early withdrawal penalty. Instantly, he'd turn 45 percent, or $225,000, of his hard-earned retirement savings over to the federal and state governments, leaving him only $275,000 (see Figure 2).

Taxes would be bad enough, but it would get worse for Clark when we consider his nest egg's future growth that would be lost if he cashed out. If the $225,000 he'd have to "donate" to the government remained invested and grew tax-deferred at 8 percent, it would be worth $485,758 in 10 years and over $1 million in 20 years. The leftover $275,000 he would use to pay off his home, buy the new car, and take a trip would grow to $593,704 and almost $1.3 million, respectively, over the same periods (see Figure 3). That's a lot of money Clark would have

Figure 2

Cash Distribution

$500,000 cash distribution

Taxes and Penalties
$150,000 30% federal taxes
$ 25,000 5% state and local taxes
+ $ 50,000 10% penalty

= $225,000 total taxes and penalties

$275,000 amount left over

had to meet his retirement needs over the next 30 years. In fact, choosing a cash distribution would make it impossible for him to reach his retirement goals. Even if he were over 59 ½ and beyond any early withdrawal penalties, he would still be better off to withdraw from his retirement accounts over time. That way he would be able to control his tax burden and keep the power of tax-deferral working to his advantage as long as possible. Clark, like most people, <u>should not</u> take a cash distribution.

Remember, one of the reasons you made pre-tax contributions to your retirement account was to obtain much-needed tax advantages. In most cases, by making these contributions, you avoided paying taxes while earning income in a high tax bracket in hopes of being in a low tax bracket when you take withdrawals during retirement. If you can control when you pay taxes, it makes sense to pay them at a time when your tax bracket is the lowest. Would anyone in their right mind defer paying taxes now so they can pay even higher taxes in the future? If you

Figure 3

Loss of Future Growth

Money used to pay taxes	Money Spent
8% growth rate	8% growth rate
$225, 000	$275,000

20 years

$1,048,715	$1,281.763

$2,330,478

Total

take a lump-sum cash distribution and wind up in a high tax bracket, you would do just that. As long as your funds remain in a retirement plan, the money grows tax-deferred. This privileged status ends as soon as the money is withdrawn from the plan. You should preserve this tax shelter as long as possible.

Are There Any Good Reasons to Take a Cash Distribution?

Some people take cash distributions if they lose their jobs, choose to buy or start a business, want to get rid of unwanted debt, or want to pay off their homes. In each of these cases, dipping into retirement

Figure 4

Sample: Distribution of Benefits Election

Name of Plan: ABC Corp. 401(k)
Plan Participant: John Smith
Social Security Number: 522-22-2221

I select the following distribution option:

X I elect a **LUMP SUM DISTRIBUTION of $400,000. I am entitled to a
distribution of $500,000, but understand that this is reduced by
$100,000 because it is subject to the 20% mandatory withholding
rules. I read the Special Tax Notice Regarding Plan Payments, and
understand the tax consequences of this election.**

> **COMPANY STOCK**
> _____ **Please issue a stock certificate for all company stock in my
> plan.**
> **X** **Please liquidate all shares of company stock held in my plan.**

_____ I elect a **DIRECT ROLLOVER of** _____ **% of my benefit (insert the
percentage you wish to be rolled) into an Individual Retirement
Account (IRA) or another qualified retirement plan. If you select his
option you must also complete the Direct Rollover Instruction form.**

> **COMPANY STOCK**
> _____ **Please transfer all company stock in-kind to my IRA.**
> _____ **Please liquidate all shares of company stock held in my plan.**

Signed:

_____   **Date** _____
John Smith

funds is still a bad idea. It would usually be better to obtain a loan, home equity or otherwise, rather than tap into retirement funds for a purpose other than retirement. This also holds true even for emergencies.

If you absolutely must take a cash distribution, there are ways to control and, in some cases, minimize some taxes:

If you rollover 100 percent of your vested plan balance to an IRA, no taxes or penalties will be withheld upon this transfer. Once your money is deposited into the IRA, you can take multiple distributions over a period of years to spread out your tax burden. In addition, when you pull money from an IRA, the financial institution that holds your money is not required to withhold 20 percent as your employer would. When you pull money out, you can request that taxes be withheld or not be withheld from your distribution. Keep in mind that if no taxes are withheld you will still have to pay all of the taxes you owe on the IRA distribution when you file your 1040 at year's end. Once in an IRA, you can also opt to use 72T distribution rules to avoid paying early withdrawal penalties (see Chapter 5).

If you must take a cash distribution simply obtain distribution paperwork from your employer (Figure 4).

 67 percent of all retirement plan distributions are rolled over to IRAs.[10]

Option 2: Roll It

Two out of every three people eligible to take a withdrawal from a company-sponsored plan roll their money into IRAs. In most cases, rolling your money to an IRA makes the most sense.

IRAs are tax-deferred retirement programs designed by the federal government to encourage retirement savings. An IRA is a type of account; it is not an investment. Think of an IRA as a personal storage unit. It's a place where you store your money, tax-deferred, while investing it in virtually any legitimate investment you choose. In many IRAs, you can buy stocks, bonds, mutual funds, annuities, certificates of deposit, and money market mutual funds. The rate of return your IRA produces is determined by the investments you select.

Types of IRAs

You can open an IRA at a bank or a self-directed IRA through a brokerage firm or a mutual fund company. Self-directed IRAs, which allow virtually unlimited investment options and flexibility, are distinctly different from bank IRAs, which generally pay a low, fixed rate of return. There are better places to invest long-term retirement money than in bank IRAs. The rates for most bank IRAs are comparable to the rates for one- to five-year certificates of deposit (CDs). If you invest in a bank IRA, you are essentially limiting yourself to one investment option: a fixed-interest-rate account.

It's true that a bank IRA offers FDIC insurance, which protects your principal up to $100,000. However, it doesn't protect you from one of the most serious retirement risks: inflation. Investing long-term retirement money in short-term, low-interest accounts can be a costly mistake. If you keep your funds from growing, it may be difficult to reach your retirement goals. By contrast, a self-directed IRA held at a brokerage firm or a mutual fund company offers almost endless investment choices and more opportunities to increase the value of your savings.

Opening a New IRA Account

Although there is a limit on the amount of new money you can contribute annually to an IRA, these limits do not apply to rollovers or transfers. Any amount can be rolled over from a qualified retirement plan or from another IRA. If you leave your company, you can have the entire balance of your retirement plan rolled into an IRA. Your money will continue to grow tax-deferred without incurring any taxes or penalties.

Once you open an IRA account, you can add to that account each year you have earned income. However, there are limits on the amount you can add. The annual contribution limit in 2004 was $3,000 per person or $3,500 for those over age 50. Recent tax law changes have upped this contribution amount (see Figure 5). To contribute to an IRA, you must have earned income or have a spouse who has earned income. If you participate in a company-sponsored retirement plan, your IRA contribution may or may not be deductible, depending on your income level.

Figure 5

IRAs/Roth IRAs

Year	Contribution Limit (Under age 50)	Contribution Limit (Over age 50)
2001	$2,000	$2,000
2002	$3,000	$3,500
2003	$3,000	$3,500
2004	$3,000	$3,500
2005	$4,000	$4,500
2006	$4,000	$5,000
2007	$4,000	$5,000
2008	$5,000	$6,000

The Advantages of a Self-Directed IRA

Rolling your money into a self-directed IRA opens up a panorama of investment choices, giving you better ability to diversify your holdings to reduce risk. In a self-directed IRA, you can choose from about 17,000 mutual funds, thousands of stocks and bonds, hundreds of fixed or variable annuity contracts, and more. This lets you uncover better investments than those available in a bank IRA or in your former company's retirement plan. With additional investment options, you can also further diversify your portfolio and build a successful investment strategy. Recent corporate failures have highlighted the risk of not diversifying and leaving your retirement savings in your company's stock. Moving money to a self-directed IRA and creating a diversified investment portfolio is the best way to protect against such risk.

The flexibility of a self-directed IRA allows you to control how much money you want to withdraw from your IRA and how frequently you make withdrawals. You can take a distribution from your IRA at any time you choose, in any amount, and for any purpose. The same early withdrawal penalty applies to distributions taken before age 59 ½, unless the distribution qualifies for an exception to this penalty. Withdrawal flexibility will prove essential if you decide to take early withdrawals (before age 59 ½) from your IRA under the penalty exception of Section 72T of the IRS Code (see Chapter 5).

If you own company stock in your plan, you can roll it into your IRA without having to sell it. This is called an "in-kind" transfer. Your company will issue a stock certificate for the number of shares you own and send it directly to the institution handling your IRA, presuming the institution can hold individual securities. Once in the IRA you can sell the stock anytime.

The ability to sell company stock when you wish is an important element of IRA flexibility. Many companies place restrictions on selling company stock in an employer-sponsored retirement plans. For example, if you sell company stock while it's being held inside your company's plan, you will usually receive the closing price of the stock on that trading day, not the price at the time you requested the stock be sold. This could result in costly losses to you if the stock drops dramatically between the time you call and the end of the trading day.

In a self-directed IRA, you can use limit orders to ensure that a stock is sold before it goes into free-fall and seriously erodes your retirement savings. This mechanism is invaluable in protecting your hard-earned nest egg. For example, you may want to protect your stock from loss by entering a stop-loss order and having your stock sold automatically if it falls below a price you specify. In addition, you may want to enter a limit order to have your stock automatically sold when it appreciates to a certain target price. Specifying a price to sell usually cannot be done in a company-sponsored retirement plan.

If you are ever unhappy with your IRA provider, simply transfer your account to another firm. You can do this as often as you like, as long as you have the money transferred directly from one institution to another without it ever touching your hands along the way. You are limited to one transfer per year if you physically receive the IRA money and then redeposit it in a new IRA at another institution. This is called a 60-day rollover. As the name suggests, you have 60 days to deposit the money into another IRA before you will be taxed and penalized (if applicable).

IRAs also give you the flexibility to make changes to your investments immediately, if you're not happy with their progress. Also, it is very easy to set up a withdrawal plan from your IRA. Most people at retirement establish a system of regular withdrawals from their IRAs to provide the necessary additional income desired during retirement. You can also hire a financial advisor to help you develop and maintain an investment strategy. If you have IRAs at other institutions, you can consolidate them together for ease of management.

401(k) to IRA: Rollover Methods
There are two ways to take a distribution from your employer's plan and roll the money into an IRA account. Method 1 is cumbersome, and Method 2 is easy.

Method 1: Lump-Sum Cash Distribution and 60-day Rollover
To initiate this method, you must request that your plan balance be sent directly to you just as if you were taking a lump-sum cash distribution.

Upon receiving the money, you have 60 days to deposit it into an IRA to avoid penalties. Be advised, however, that there is a major hitch to this method. Distribution rules mandate that your employer withhold 20 percent of all cash distributions — the prepayment of income taxes that may be owed if the money doesn't get rolled into an IRA. Since the IRS has no idea whether your retirement plan money is going to be rolled over or spent, the withholding is applied to every cash distribution.

This presents a huge problem. How can you roll the full distribution amount to an IRA if 20 percent is taken off the top and sent to the IRS before you even receive the distribution? You know the IRS is not going to be able to refund that money to you within 60 days. Let's do the math: Say you decide to take a $100,000 cash distribution from your company's 401(k) and opt to roll it over into an IRA within 60 days. Your company will send you a check for $80,000 and withhold $20,000. You then have 60 days to deposit the full $100,000 into an IRA to avoid taxes and penalties. This means you will have to withdraw $20,000 from your savings account or elsewhere to make up the difference. (When you file your income taxes at year-end, you will get back the $20,000 initially withheld.)

As you can see, the whole process is fairly complicated and an inefficient way to move money from your company's retirement plan to an IRA. Using a direct rollover will enable you to reach the same result with fewer headaches.

Method 2:   Direct Rollover

To avoid the problems that come with taking direct receipt of your retirement money, instruct your employer to transfer the entire vested balance of your plan to a previously established IRA. This way, you will not receive a check made payable to you for the balance of your plan, and the tax-withholding problem never arises. Because the check is made payable to your IRA institution, the IRS knows the money was transferred directly to an IRA account — no taxes are withheld in the process.

Some plans will mail the rollover check to your IRA provider, and others will mail the check to you. In either case, it will be made payable to your IRA provider for and in behalf of you. In cases where the check is mailed to you, don't be alarmed. Simply forward it to your IRA provider to deposit in your account.

At year's end, you will receive a 1099R form from your former employer showing that a distribution was made. You will also receive a statement from your IRA provider showing the money was deposited into your IRA. As long as these transfer balances match, there will be no tax consequences or penalties.

Steps for Initiating an IRA Rollover

The direct rollover process is very simple. First, open an IRA account at the financial institution of your choice. After completing the necessary paperwork, you will be assigned an IRA account number. You will need your IRA account number and the IRA provider's address to complete the rollover.

Retirement plan administrators usually process distributions in one of two ways. Some will provide you with retirement distribution forms (see the sample forms in Figures 6 and 7). If this is the case, complete these forms and return them to your employer. The second method processes the rollover via the telephone. When phone distributions are available, simply call your 401(k) provider (usually a mutual fund company or brokerage firm) and request your money be rolled into an IRA account. Distributions processed by phone usually speed up the process. In either case, you will likely be asked for the following:

1. Your Social Security number (and Personal Identification Number (PIN), if processing the transaction over the phone).

2. Your IRA account number and the address of your IRA provider.

3. Whether or not you would like to sell your company stock or transfer it to your IRA in-kind. (If you transfer stock to your IRA, you will have more control of the price at which it is eventually sold, but you will probably have to pay some commission fees to do so. If you request that your employer sell the stock for you, you will usually receive the closing price on the day of your request and you won't pay any trade commissions. Before making a final decision about your company stock, read Chapter 25 on Net Unrealized Appreciation. You may be able to obtain favorable tax treatment upon selling your stock if you own highly appreciated shares.)

4. Whether or not you would like taxes withheld; indicate that you do not.

5. If you have received and read the Special Tax Notice explaining the tax considerations associated with each retirement plan distribution option. If you haven't read this notice, your rollover request will not be processed.

Allow two to four weeks for the distribution to be sent to your IRA.

When you request an IRA rollover, the investments in your employer's plan will be liquidated and a check for the balance will be sent to your IRA provider. New investments will need to be purchased in the IRA. The process for developing a successful investment strategy was discussed in Chapters 9-18.

Other Rollover Considerations

Have you borrowed any money from your retirement plan? If you have an outstanding loan balance at the time you retire, you should repay it before taking a distribution. Plan loans must typically be repaid within 30 to 60 days from the time you leave the company. If the loan is not repaid and you leave money in your former employer's plan, or choose to roll over money to an IRA without repaying it, the loan amount will be treated as a distribution and be subject to taxes and penalties.

If you have stock in your company's retirement plan, you can choose to have the shares sent directly to you and roll the balance of the plan into an IRA. This combination distribution method is used in the Net Unrealized Appreciation strategy and may allow you to qualify for favorable tax treatment.

You may have some after-tax contributions in your retirement plan. If so, this money can also be rolled into your IRA; however, be sure to keep track of the amount of the after-tax rollover. This is easily done when you report your after-tax rollover on IRS form 8606. If you don't track it, you could wind up paying taxes on this money twice: when contributed and when withdrawn. When you begin taking withdrawals from your IRA, you won't have to pay taxes on money contributed on an after-tax basis. Unfortunately, you can't withdraw all the after-tax money out of the IRA first and then begin pulling out the taxable money. If your IRA contains after-tax contributions, withdrawals are made on a pro-rata basis. Part of your withdrawal is considered taxable and part is not taxable.

There are other considerations you should keep in mind. If you are over age 55, once your money transfers into an IRA, you are no longer eligible to take a penalty-free, lump-sum distribution (see Chapter 5). In addition, depending on your IRA provider, you may be required to pay an IRA custodial fee and commissions to purchase investments in your IRA. While invested in your company's retirement plan, your employer pays these fees.

Figure 6

Sample: Distribution of Benefits Election

Name of Plan: ABC Corp. 401(k)
Plan Participant: John Smith
Social Security Number: 522-22-2221

I select the following distribution option:

_____ **I elect a LUMP SUM DISTRIBUTION of $400,000. I am entitled to a distribution of $500,000, but understand that his is reduced by $100,000 because it is subject to the 20% mandatory withholding rules. I read the Special Tax Notice Regarding Plan Payments, and understand the tax consequences of this election.**

　　　　COMPANY STOCK
　　_____ **Please issue a stock certificate for all company stock in my plan.**
　　_____ **Please liquidate all shares of company stock held in my plan.**

__X__ **I elect a DIRECT ROLLOVER of __100__ % of my benefit (insert the Account (IRA) percentage you wish to be rolled) into an Individual Retirement or another qualified retirement plan. If you select his option you must also complete the Direct Rollover Instruction form.**

　　　　COMPANY STOCK
　　__X__ **Please transfer all company stock in-kind to my IRA.**
　　_____ **Please liquidate all shares of company stock held in my plan.**

Signed:

_____   _____
John Smith　　　　　　　　　　　　 **Date**

Figure 7

Sample: Direct Rollover Instructions

Name of Plan: ABC Corp. 401(k)
Plan Participant: John Smith
Social Security Number: 522-22-2221

FOR A DIRECT ROLLOVER TO AN IRA:

Name of IRA Trustee: _____

IRA Account Number: _____

IRA Trustee Address: _____

FOR DIRECT ROLLOVER TO COMPANY SPONSORED QUALIFIED PLAN:

Name of New Company Plan: _____

Plan Account Number: _____

Plan Address: _____

_____

Signed:

_____   _____
John Smith   **Date**

Option 3: Leave It

Deferring distribution and leaving your money in your former company's retirement plan is the simplest thing to do because you don't have to do anything. There are no forms to fill out and no additional investment decisions to make. Because you are not taking a distribution, there are no taxes or penalties to pay, and your money will continue to grow tax-deferred. In addition, there are no fees or commissions. Although the mutual funds you own in your 401(k) charge annual management fees, you don't actually pay anything out of pocket. Many employers cover account and transaction-related costs and will continue to do so if you defer your distribution.

Another advantage of leaving your 401(k) money in place is the federal creditor protection you receive. Money in 401(k) plans is shielded against bankruptcy, malpractice, divorce, and lawsuits. If you run a high risk of being sued, you may want to keep your money put.

Consider deferring distribution if your former employer's plan:
- Offers numerous investment choices.
- Offers investment choices that are above average.
- Offers flexibility of investment changes.
- Allows participants to sell company stock.

The Downside

Leaving money in your former employer's plan does have its downside. Most company-sponsored retirement plans have limitations, primarily concerning the number and quality of the investment choices offered. This inhibits your ability to properly diversify. The average retirement plan only offers 12 investment choices.[11] Although a dozen investment options could easily provide an acceptable level of diversification, many retirement plans lack important components of a well-balanced portfolio, such as a combination of both growth and value stocks, mid-cap and small-cap stocks, and international positions.

In addition to diversification limitations, it is unlikely that each of the 12 investments offered is among the best available, compared with the thousands accessible outside the plan. If your plan offers only one large-company growth stock fund, for example, and it's not among the best funds in its category, you'll be stuck with it if you want exposure to large-company growth stocks. In an IRA you could choose from over 1,000 large-company growth stock funds and hand-pick the best one.

Leaving your money in place also costs you some control and flexibility. Once you're off the company payroll, you can no longer make contributions, and you cannot obtain a loan from the plan. Some plans may limit how often you can make changes to your investments. Also, you may be unable to set up a systematic withdrawal program, like you could from an IRA, to supplement your other retirement income.

In some plans, leaving your money in the plan may not even be an option. Not all employers allow former employees to keep money invested in the retirement plan and may mandate that you take a distribution from the plan by a certain date. This is almost always the case for accounts with balances of $5,000 or less.

If the limitations presented by leaving your money in your former employer's plan concern you, your choice is clear. You'll want to look at other choices. If the limitations are insignificant and the plan offers plenty of good investment choices, consider deferring distribution and leaving your money in place.

Consider converting your IRA to a Roth IRA if:
- You are in a low tax bracket now and anticipate being in a higher bracket during retirement.
- You would like to withdraw some retirement funds before age 59½ without penalty (applies to principal only).
- You would like to be "tax diversified" at retirement.
- Your adjusted gross income is less than $100,000.

Option 4: Roth It

A Roth IRA is very similar to a traditional IRA when it comes to annual contribution limits, investment choices, and flexibility. It differs, however, when it comes to the way taxes are applied.

Money contributed to a Roth IRA is done so on an after-tax basis. Traditional IRAs and company-sponsored plans consist of pre-tax contributions. Money invested in Roth IRAs grows *tax-free*, not *tax-deferred* like traditional IRAs. This means that you can withdraw money from your Roth IRA, tax-free, upon reaching age 59 ½. For many Americans, it makes sense to take advantage of these tax differences.

In order to deposit your 401(k) retirement plan money into a Roth IRA, you must initially transfer it to a traditional IRA and then convert the IRA to a Roth. There is no cap on the amount you can convert. This conversion option is only available to those who have modified adjusted gross incomes under $100,000. The amount of the IRA conversion, while taxable as ordinary income, is not included in this figure.

Does tax-free growth coupled with tax-free withdrawals sound too good to be true? You think there has to be a catch?

The Catch

In a sense, there is a catch. You will be required to pay federal and state income taxes on any amount converted from a traditional IRA to a Roth IRA (see tax brackets in Figure 1). The entire amount converted will be added to your taxable income in the year of the conversion; you pay taxes now to avoid paying taxes later.

You can control the way you make this transfer. Because taxes are due in the year of conversion, you may want to convert money from your traditional IRA to a Roth IRA a little at a time to avoid having your tax bracket ratcheted higher. You can convert any amount from an IRA to a Roth IRA and do so as often as you choose; the 10 percent early withdrawal penalty does not apply when making a conversion from an IRA to a Roth.

Pay Now or Later

Should you convert your IRA to a Roth? To find the answer, you need only ask yourself one question: Do I want to pay my taxes now or later? Determining whether to convert or not depends on your current tax bracket and your future bracket, and when you begin withdrawing the funds. For example, if you are in the highest tax bracket now, 35 percent, and you anticipate being in a lower bracket, say 15 percent, during retirement, converting to a Roth IRA wouldn't make much sense — you would pay high taxes now to avoid paying lower taxes later.

On the other hand, if you are in a 15 percent tax bracket now and anticipate being in a higher bracket during retirement, then it makes perfect sense to convert your IRA to a Roth.

This was the case with Gary Kruger a 60-year old executive

who retired in 2002 from a large bank. His plan was to withdraw money he'd accumulated in his non-retirement bank and brokerage accounts during the early years of retirement and then tap into his IRA later. In 2003, Gary had no earned income, which dropped him from the 33 percent tax bracket to the 15 percent bracket. In several years, his non-retirement accounts will be drained, and he will be forced to withdraw large sums from his IRA to meet his living expenses. The money he will pull from his IRA will be taxable, and his tax bracket will get bumped up to 25 percent. Anticipating these tax-bracket changes, Gary began converting portions of his IRA to his Roth IRA in 2003. He decided to pay taxes on some of his IRA money while in a lower tax bracket so he can avoid paying taxes later when his tax bracket goes back up.

If your tax bracket doesn't change between now and retirement, both options will yield the same result. See Figures 8, 9, and 10 to compare traditional IRAs to Roth IRAs in different tax situations.

Become Tax Diversified

If you are in a tax bracket that is neither very high nor very low, there is a middle ground you can pursue. Convert some of your IRA to a Roth IRA. This will make you "tax diversified." Some of your money will be invested in before-tax accounts, while your Roth IRA money will have already been taxed. If tax rates are higher at some point during retirement, you can take money out of your Roth IRA and not pay any taxes. If tax rates are lower, you can take money from your traditional IRA. This diversified approach makes sense for people who are in the midrange tax brackets.

Another benefit of the Roth IRA is liquidity. Unlike a traditional IRA, you can withdraw your principal without penalty or taxes prior to age 59 ½. However, to avoid a premature withdrawal penalty, withdrawals cannot take place for five years after the Roth conversion. For those retiring prior to age 59 ½, the ability to tap some retirement funds without penalty may be very helpful.

Roth IRA Conversion Process

The process for rolling your money to an IRA and then converting to a Roth is identical to that for rolling your company retirement plan over

Figure 10

Figure 9

Figure 8

to an IRA except for one additional step. Once your retirement plan money has been rolled over into a traditional IRA, your financial institution will provide you with an IRA/Roth Conversion Form, on which you indicate the amount of your IRA you would like converted to a Roth. At year-end, you will receive a 1099R form from your IRA provider indicating the taxable conversion amount.

Option 5: Annuitize It

 Only 12 percent of plan distributions are taken as annuity payments.

When you choose to take annuity payments, your vested account balance is used to buy an immediate annuity. Annuity payments will be made to you for your entire lifetime and possibly your spouse's as well, depending upon the payout option you choose. With annuity payments, you do not have to worry about the management of the balance in your plan or the stock market's ups and downs. Although the annuity payout is generally lower than what could be produced by an investment portfolio moderately invested, the freedom of not having to manage the money or worry about market downturns makes this option a nice fit for some.

 Consider annuity payments if:
• You don't want to be involved in the management of your own portfolio.
• You want to guarantee your income for life.

The various annuity payout options are usually identical as those offered to people receiving company pensions. Examples of these annuity options are outlined in detail in Chapter 7.

The downside of annuity payments, in addition to a possible lower payout rate, is the inability to reverse your decision. Once the decision is made to annuitize, it is irrevocable. You are guaranteed a lifetime income; however, you can never again tap into your total retirement plan balance.

Option 6: Stock It

Consider this strategy if you're in a high tax bracket, own company stock in your 401(k), and would rather pay taxes at capital gains rates instead of income tax rates.

Investors in high tax brackets who own low-tax-basis shares of company stock in their 401(k)s can save thousands in taxes by using a little-known strategy called Net Unrealized Appreciation (NUA). Bruce Richardson, the retiree mentioned at the first of this chapter, who without thinking rolled his 401(k) money to an IRA could have saved a lot of money using this strategy.

To initiate the NUA strategy, all Bruce would have had to do is request that his $600,000 of company stock be transferred into a non-retirement account and that the remaining $25,000 balance of his 401(k) be rolled to an IRA. Once in the non-retirement account, Bruce could sell the company stock at some point and pay *capital gains* taxes (15%) on the gains instead of income taxes (33%) on the entire balance. Unfortunately, because he rolled his money to an IRA, his withdrawals will be taxed at income tax rates. The NUA strategy would have allowed Bruce to pay fewer taxes on his retirement nest egg. In addition, had he initiated the NUA strategy and never sold the company stock, no taxes would be due during his lifetime. Due to the complexity of this strategy, Chapter 25 has been dedicated entirely to outlining how it works. If you own company stock in your 401(k) plan, you may be able to save thousands of dollars using the NUA strategy.

Making a Final Distribution Decision

Which distribution option should you choose? It's not a decision to take lightly because of the impact it will have on your retirement years. Before choosing, look at your options side by side, comparing the long-term effects of each. By making educated decisions about your money during job changes and at retirement, you can ensure that one of your largest and most critical assets is managed properly.

TWENTY-FIVE

A Tax Loophole

✓ RETIREMENT DECISION #20 (continued): *Which retirement plan distribution option should I choose?*

At retirement, Grace Vincent had accumulated more than $450,000 in her 401(k). Of that amount, $300,000 was invested in highly appreciated company stock. She wondered whether she should roll it all to a retirement account or if there was a better strategy.

To fully maximize her nest egg, Grace decided to use a little-known distribution tax strategy referred to as Net Unrealized Appreciation (NUA). Using NUA, she'll be able to lower the taxes she'll be required to pay on withdrawals from her investment portfolio during retirement. To make this strategy work, she simply rolled the money invested in mutual funds in her 401(k) to an IRA. She then transferred the company stock into a non-retirement brokerage account. With money in both accounts, Grace has a choice where to withdraw the money she needs to meet retirement expenses. If she pulls money from the IRA, she'll have to pay income taxes at a rate of 28 percent. If she sells stock and pulls money from the brokerage account, she'll only have to pay capital gains taxes of 15 percent on her stock's appreciation.

Let's see, would you rather pay taxes at 28 percent or 15 percent? Grace opted for the tax savings and is pulling money from her brokerage account to meet her living expenses.

Upon withdrawal, the money you've invested in mutual funds in a 401(k) and other types of employer-sponsored retirement plans must be liquidated. Most people choose to roll this money into IRAs. As we saw in Chapter 24, rolling money into an IRA is often the best distribution method for plan money invested in mutual funds. It may not, however, be your best choice for the portion of your plan that is invested in company stock.

According to research, 401(k) participants invest about one-third of their retirement savings in their company's stock.[1] In fact, in some corporations, company stock represents more than half of the total plan balance. You'll find this overconcentration in plans where employers provide matching contributions in their own stock. If you own company stock in your employer-sponsored retirement plan, you may be able to save thousands of dollars upon distribution by using this rarely-considered IRS tax strategy: Net Unrealized Appreciation.

This strategy works best in situations where an investor is in a high tax bracket, has low-cost-basis stock in his or her plan, and desires to hold on to the stock for many years after distribution.[2] It also works extremely well in combination with the IRA rollover distribution method covered in Chapter 24.

It's inevitable that the money in your retirement plan is going to get taxed at some point. The NUA strategy allows you some control over how it is taxed. If you sell your company stock while in the 401(k) plan or after rolling it into an IRA, you will be required to pay income taxes on the entire balance when you withdraw the proceeds, whether that occurs immediately or during retirement. The NUA strategy allows

Figure 1

2004 Federal Personal Income Tax Rates

Tax Rate	Single filers	Married filing jointly	Married filing separately	Head of household
10%	Up to $7,150	Up to $14,300	Up to $7,150	Up to $10,200
15%	$7,151–$29,050	$14,301–$58,100	$7,151–$29,050	$10,201–$38,900
25%	$29,051 $70,350	$58,101–$117,250	$29,051–$58.625	$38,901–$100,500
28%	$70,351–$146,750	$117,251–$178,650	$58.626–$89,325	$100,501–$162,700–
33%	$146,751 $319,100	$178,651–$319,100	$89,326–$159.550	$162,701–$319,100
35%	$319,101 or more	$319,101 or more	$159.551 or more	$319,101 or more

your company stock gains to be taxed at capital gains tax rates, which, depending on your tax bracket, are generally lower than income tax rates.

Compare your income tax rate with the capital gains rates in Figures 1 and 2. You will probably see a significant difference.

Figure 2

Capital Gains Rate

Long-Term Capital Gains (holding period longer than one year)	15%
Long-Term Capital Gains (holding period rate for those in 15% tax bracket)	10%
Short-Term Capital Gains (holding period less than one year)	Income Tax Rates

What is Net Unrealized Appreciation? It is the value of company stock upon distribution from the plan minus the value of the stock when it was given to you (the cost basis). For example, let's say your employer contributed $10,000 of company stock to your plan (this is the cost basis), and it is now worth $60,000 — you have NUA of $50,000. When you retire from your company, you must decide what to do with the company stock held in your retirement plan. You have four options, as listed below. Three of these options were covered in Chapter 24.

1. Sell the stock in the plan and take a cash distribution. Income taxes are due immediately as well as applicable penalties.
2. Sell the stock and rollover the cash balance into an IRA. Income taxes are due when you eventually take a withdrawal from your IRA.
3. Don't sell the stock, but roll it over "in-kind" into an IRA. Again, you must pay income taxes when you eventually sell and take a withdrawal.
4. Don't sell the stock, take a stock distribution in-kind and deposit the shares into a non-retirement account. Capital gains taxes are due when you eventually sell shares.

The last option is the Net Unrealized Appreciation strategy. A quick comparison of each of these options shows the value of the NUA strategy. Option one triggers immediate income taxation upon distribution. In options two and three, income taxes must be paid when withdrawals are taken in retirement. But the fourth option, the NUA strategy, allows you to pay capital gains taxes upon selling your company stock, rather than pay income taxes. Using the NUA strategy defers taxation on the appreciation of the stock until it is eventually sold, at which point capital gains taxes are imposed only upon the appreciation.

Let's take a closer look at this strategy.

How the NUA Strategy Works

To initiate this strategy, you must request a lump-sum distribution and have the "qualifying" company stock in your plan sent directly to you in-kind. Qualifying shares are those contributed to your plan by your employer and those non-deductible shares purchased by you (to the extent that they are both part of a lump-sum distribution from your plan).[3] Deductible shares purchased by you do not qualify for this favorable tax treatment.[4] A lump-sum distribution is defined as a payment of your entire plan balance occurring in one taxable year that takes place after a "qualifying event," such as separation from service (including retirement), attaining age 59 ½, or death.

After you make the request, your stock shares will be sent to you in certificate form. These shares can then be deposited into a taxable brokerage account (a non-retirement account). Money that is not invested in your company's stock can be rolled into an IRA. Mutual fund shares, for example, will be liquidated and distributed to you in cash; the cash portion of the distribution can subsequently be rolled into an IRA.

Some plans will allow you to split your plan distribution. If this is the case, your eligible stock shares will be sent to you in-kind while the remaining balance of your account can be directly rolled to an IRA.

Sound complicated? It is. Therefore, I recommend that you talk to your financial advisor or a tax advisor before you take a distribution of your employer's stock.

The distribution of the stock is subject to immediate taxation because you are moving money from a retirement account to a non-retirement account. This may set off some alarms in your mind, but don't worry, you're going to save money in the long run.

Upon taking a stock distribution, you will be required to pay taxes (at income tax rates) on only the cost basis of the stock — the average value of the shares at the time they were initially purchased in the plan — NOT the stock's total current value. Your employer will not withhold any tax upon distribution of stock shares. The 20 percent mandatory withholding tax we discussed in Chapter 24 applies only to cash distributions. If you are not yet age 55, you will also be required to pay a 10 percent premature withdrawal penalty. Again, though, this penalty is imposed only on the cost basis, not the entire value of the stock distribution. Having to pay taxes immediately is a sticky point for many people who are simply unwilling or unable to pay taxes now, even if it will save them money in the long run. However, if your cost basis is very low, the tax and penalty will not be a heavy burden.

You are not required to pay any tax on the appreciation of the stock (its Net Unrealized Appreciation) until you sell it. At that time, any appreciation is subject only to capital gains taxes, not income tax. This means you have a built-in 15 percent capital gains ceiling, a far-cry cheaper than the maximum income tax bracket of 35 percent.

Who Should Consider the NUA Strategy?

Those with low-cost basis stock and who are in the highest tax brackets will gain the greatest benefit from the NUA strategy. As a general rule, the current value of the stock should be at least double, and probably three or four times the cost basis, for the strategy to make sense.[5]

NUA vs. IRA: Which Strategy Is Best When You Want to Sell Stock Immediately and Spend the Proceeds?

If you have low-basis stock, are in a high tax bracket (usually over 28 percent), and would like to sell your stock upon distribution and spend the proceeds, it's generally advantageous to use the NUA strategy.

Let's look at an example: Robert Stewart accumulated 5,000 shares of company stock in his 401(k) plan. The average purchase price was $5 per share for a total of $25,000 (his cost basis). When he retires in the near future, he is planning to sell the stock and use the proceeds to buy a retirement home in Palm Springs. He is trying to decide between a stock distribution to a taxable account (NUA strategy) or a rollover to his IRA. Which should he choose?

If he requests a stock distribution and deposits the shares into a taxable, non-retirement account, he will owe income tax on the cost basis ($25,000). In Robert's 28 percent tax bracket, that amounts to $7,000. Robert is over age 59 ½, so there are no early withdrawal penalties applied to his distribution. He plans to sell his stock shares at $60 per share. Multiplying that price by his 5,000 shares will give Robert $300,000. His NUA is $55 per share, or $275,000. (This is calculated by subtracting the $25,000 cost basis from the total value of the stock.)

When he sells those shares, he will owe capital gains tax (15 percent) on the $275,000 of appreciation, for a total of $41,250 in taxes. This $41,250 is due in the year he sells the stock. If he never sells the stock, he will never have to pay the tax. Assuming he does sell, however, his total tax bill will equal $48,250 ($7,000 of income tax on the cost basis, plus $41,250 in capital gains taxes when the stock is sold). After taxes, Robert is left with *$251,750* to buy the property. Remember this number.

Now let's say Robert chose to roll his stock shares directly into an IRA account, realized the same appreciation, sold the shares at the same time, and then took a distribution from his IRA to buy the property. In this case, he would owe $84,000 in federal income taxes (in his 28 percent bracket) and possibly some additional state income taxes, leaving him with just $216,000. Even worse, if he took the entire $300,000 out of his IRA all in one year, he would find himself in the highest income tax bracket (35 percent) and would be left with only $195,000 after taxes.

Robert could maintain his tax bracket at 28 percent if he chooses simply to take distributions over a period of years rather than all at once. This won't help him, however, if he needs a large sum of money now to buy a property in Palm Springs. In this scenario, the Net Unrealized Appreciation strategy actually saved Robert $35,750 (if he stayed in a 28 percent tax bracket) or $56,800, if the distribution had launched him into the highest bracket.

Saving this amount of money makes the effort to transfer the shares into a separate taxable account worthwhile. The higher the tax bracket and the greater the Net Unrealized Appreciation, the more valuable the NUA tax break becomes. See Figure 3 for a summary of this example.

Figure 3

Sell stock immediately and spend proceeds

Low-Basis Stock	NUA	IRA Rollover
Total value of shares at time of distribution	$300,000	$300,000
Cost basis of shares	$25,000	N/A
Net unrealized appreciation of shares at time of distribution	$275,000	N/A
Income tax on cost basis of shares paid at time of distribution (28%)	$7,000	N/A
Capital gains tax on stock when sold (15%)	$41,250	N/A
Income tax on IRA distribution (28%)	N/A	$84,000
Total Tax	$48,250	$84,000
Advantage to NUA	**$35,750**	

Assumptions: No dividends; capital gains rate 15%, income tax rate 28%; employee is over age 59 1/2, so there are no early withdrawal penalties upon the distribution of the company stock.

Who Should NOT Consider the NUA Strategy?

If you are planning to sell your stock immediately upon distribution to reinvest and diversify the proceeds into other investments, the tax advantages are lessened. Also, the NUA strategy will not yield as many benefits if you own high-basis stock in your plan or are currently in a low tax bracket.

When you sell stock immediately to reinvest into a diversified portfolio, you will have to pay income taxes on the cost basis of the stock and capital gains taxes on the appreciation. The money left over can be reinvested; however, in a taxable account, some of your portfolio growth will be lost to taxes each year. If your objective is to diversify your stock position, it is generally wiser to sell the stock in a retirement account and let the proceeds continue to grow tax-deferred.

Let's look at another example. William Atkinson is age 59 and about to retire. His primary objective is to sell his 5,000 shares of company stock ($5 per share cost basis) and reinvest the proceeds into a more diversified portfolio. He doesn't plan on spending any of this money for 20 years. Which strategy should he choose?

Following the NUA strategy, he would transfer 5,000 shares of low-basis stock into a taxable brokerage account. If he sells the stock at $60 per share ($300,000) and pays the $48,250 in taxes (income and capital gains), he would have $251,750 after taxes to reinvest in a diversified portfolio. William is considering what his portfolio will be worth if he averages a 10 percent growth rate. Now that his money is in a taxable account, some of that growth (interest, dividends, and capital gains) is subject to taxes each year. Assuming that 15 percent of his return goes to pay the taxes, he will average just 8.5 percent growth after taxes have been paid.

Because William's objective is to diversify and invest for the long term, it would make far more sense for him to rollover his money to an IRA. This will allow his growth to take place in a tax-deferred account (see Figure 4). Most people do not withdraw money from their IRAs all

Figure 4

Sell immediately and diversify into other investments

Low-Basis Stock	NUA	IRA Rollover
Total value of shares at time of distribution	$300,000	$300,000
Cost basis of shares	$25,000	N/A
Net unrealized appreciation of shares at time of distribution	$275,000	N/A
Income tax on cost basis of shares (paid immediately 28%	$7,000	N/A
Capital gains tax on stock (paid immediately 15%)	$41,250	N/A
Balance of portfolio in 20-years (after tax)	$1,286,957	N/A
Balance of IRA in 20 years (before tax)	N/A	$2,018,250
Income tax on portfolio upon withdrawal (28%)	N/A	$565,110
Ending balance after tax	$1,286,957	$1,453,140
Advantage to IRA		$255,378

Assumptions: Capital gains rate is 15%, pre-tax growth rate for diversified portfolio is 10%, after tax-rate is 8.5%; employee is over age 59 1/2, so there are no early withdrawl penalties upon the distribution of the company stock. Tax rate applied to IRA distribution is 28%. The rate would be higher if the investor took a distribution all in one year rather than spreading it out over several years.

at once. If, for instance, money is withdrawn over a 20-year period during retirement, the tax rate may be reduced even further. This makes the IRA rollover strategy even more advantageous.

If you own high-cost-basis stock, it is usually better to keep the stock in a retirement account. In this case, if you did use the NUA strategy, you would pay income tax on most of the value of the stock due to its high cost basis. Capital gains tax would only be applied to a small portion of the stock's value (the amount above the cost basis).

In addition, the NUA strategy may not be as effective, if you are not yet age 55. In this case you will be required to pay a 10 percent early withdrawal penalty on the original cost basis of the stock. Again, this is money that won't be compounding toward your retirement. The good news is that no penalties are owed on your stock appreciation.

NUA and "Stepped-up" Cost Basis for Heirs

If you roll your stock into an IRA, you not only face paying income taxes whenever you take a withdrawal, but income taxes must also be paid upon your death.

When you pass away, your spouse can transfer your IRA balance to his or her IRA and avoid taxation. However, upon your spouse's death, your heirs must pay ordinary income tax on the entire balance of the IRA.

Let's go back to the case of Robert Stewart. Assume that when he and his wife pass away the stock is worth $100 per share and has a total value of $500,000. Their heirs would be required to pay income taxes on the entire $500,000 if it was held in an IRA. This would inevitably place Robert in the highest tax bracket (35 percent) when computing the final income tax owed. Before his heirs received anything, the government would take $175,000 (assuming it was taxed at the highest marginal bracket).

If, however, he had used the NUA strategy and transferred his 5,000 shares of company stock into a non-retirement account, his heirs would enjoy some big tax advantages. They would be required to pay capital gains tax on the Net Unrealized Appreciation of the shares while they were in the employer-sponsored retirement plan. This is referred to as "income in respect of the decedent." In Robert's case, he had $275,000 of Net Unrealized Appreciation at the time he took an in-kind distribution from the plan. However, any appreciation that occurred after the stock was distributed from the plan will receive a "stepped-up basis" and will be tax-free after death.

If Robert dies when his stock is selling at $100 per share ($500,000), the $100 price would become the new cost basis for the heirs. The appreciation from $60 (value of stock at the time of distribution from the plan) to $100 (the value of the stock upon death) is tax-free. In Robert's case, this amounts to $200,000. If the heirs subsequently decide to sell the stock, they will pay capital gains tax on the difference between $100 and the price at the time they sell. If, for example, they sold the shares for $105, they would pay capital gains tax only on the appreciation since Robert's death, and only $5 per share would be taxed.

No Mandatory Distributions

If you own an IRA, you must begin taking mandatory distributions at age 70 ½ whether you need the money or not. Mandatory distribution is synonymous with mandatory taxation. If you opt for the NUA strategy and deposit your company stock in a taxable account, you are not required to take any distributions at any age. Having funds in different types of accounts (both retirement and non-retirement) can help you stretch your nest egg and provide more money to your heirs.

What Is the Process for Initiating the NUA Strategy?

Your first step should be determining the cost basis of your employer's stock. This will help you determine its increase in price (the NUA) since being purchased in your retirement plan and whether or not it makes sense to pursue this strategy.

Next, determine if your company stock shares are eligible for the NUA strategy. It may take several phone calls or letters to acquire this information. You'll need to contact your benefits department or the company that administers your employer's retirement plan. Because this information is sometimes difficult to obtain, you should start requesting it at least six months before you expect to retire or separate from service. Due to the technicalities involved, it may be advantageous to hire a tax professional. IRS Tax Code Section 402(e)(4) may also be helpful.

You will need to complete the distribution paperwork. If you are going to take advantage of the NUA strategy, you must request a lump-sum distribution and have the stock shares sent directly to you. If your employer allows split distributions, you can roll the remaining balance of your plan directly into an IRA. If it does not allow for split distributions, you will receive your stock shares and a check for the balance of your plan (non-employer stock). Of course, your company must withhold 20 percent from the money distributed that was not invested in stock. You will have 60 days, upon receiving the check, to roll it into an IRA to avoid taxes and penalties. (See 60-day rollover section in Chapter 24.) At year-end after distributing the stock, your employer will provide you with a copy of Form 1099R and will report the transaction to the IRS.

Figure 5

IRA Rollover	In-Kind Distribution (NUA)
No taxes at time of rollover	Cost basis taxed at income tax rate upon distribution. Potentially lower overall taxes.
Tax-Deferred Growth	Partial tax-deferment
When stock is sold and distributed from the IRA, ordinary income taxes must be paid (maximum tax rate 35%).	When stock is sold in taxable account capital gains taxes are paid on appreciation only (maximum tax rate 15% for long term gains).
Non-spouse heirs must pay income tax upon death of IRA owner.	Heirs will receive a step up in cost basis upon inheriting shares. All gains between holder's retirement and death are tax-free. Capital gains taxes are due on appreciation of shares while in plan (income in respect of decedent).

Before deciding what to do with your company stock, obtain a retirement plan distribution analysis, so you can compare each of your six distributions options side by side. Depending on your goals and objectives, you may be able to save a lot of money in taxes by using the NUA strategy.

 NUA Stock Calculator: www.troweprice.com (go to individual investors, investment planning and tools, retirment planning tools, company stock tool)

A Parting Thought

The biggest reward you'll receive from addressing all twenty of the financial decisions addressed in this book isn't necessarily making more money, although the strategies we discussed will definitely help you improve your investment performance. The biggest reward for all your planning and effort is peace of mind. Once you've built and implemented a well structured financial plan you can relax. Routine check ups will keep you on track. In between check ups, go visit your kids and grand kids, travel the world, enjoy your hobbies and develop new ones, do some charity work, or do whatever it is that you've been waiting until now to do. Whatever you do, if you have a solid plan in place, you shouldn't have to worry about your money.

Everyday is Saturday. It's time to enjoy life. Good luck and remember the best is yet to come!

▒ END NOTES ▒

Chapter 1 Retiring Now!

1. Americans Savings Education Council, "The 1999 Retirement Confidence Survey (RCS) Summary of Findings," http://www.asec.org/rcssummary.pdf
2. American Savings Education Council and Employee Benefit Research Institute, "The 2003 Retirement Confidence Survey Summary of Findings," 2. http://www.ebri.org/rcs/2003/03rcssof.pdf
3. http://www.medicarewatch.org/2001basic/reform-proposals-1.html
4. http://www2.homefair.com/calc/citypick.html
5. Sharon E. Epperson , "Death and the Maven," *Time*, 18 (December 1995), 61.
6. U.S. Department of Labor, Past Annual Inflation (CPI) Rates.
7. "The 2003 Retirement Confidence Survey Summary of Findings," 4.
8. "The 2003 Retirement Confidence Survey Summary of Findings, 6.
9. Lynn O'Shaughnessy, *Retirement Bible* (New York: Hungry Minds, Inc., 2001), 11.
10. "The 2003 Retirement Confidence Survey Summary of Findings," 4.

Chapter 2 Double Your Money

1. Zig Ziglar, *See You at the Top*, 149
2. Office of Investor Education and Assistance, Securities and Exchange Commission, "The Facts On Savings and Investing" (April 1999), 18.
3. Jack Sirard, "Confused? Written Financial Plan Helps," *The Sacramento Bee* (March 14, 2000), D1.
4. Farrell Dolan, CFP and Van Harlow, CFA, Fidelity Investments, Viewpoint, "Retirement Issues Research Report" (November 2003), 5.

Chapter 3 Fire Your Broker!

1. American Express, *Chief Executive Officer David Hubers on February 2, 2000*4.
2. Dede Pehl, "Personal financial planning and ISO: breaking new ground in standards-setting," ISO Bulletin, June 2002, P. 8.
3. Christopher Farrell, "Mutual-Fund Investors' Enemy: Themselves,"

Business Week Online, www.businessweek.com, (March 1, 2001).

4. DALBAR Inc., DALBAR Issues 2001 Update to "Quantitative Analysis of Investor Behavior" Report, "More Proof that Market Timing Doesn't Work for the Majority of Investors," www.dalbarinc.com/content/showpage.asp?page=2001062100, (June 21, 2001).

5. *Financial Planning* magazine April 2004, Eric Garland, pg 25

Chapter 4 More Life than Money

1. Scott Burns, "Dangerous Advice from Peter Lynch, "www.scottburns.com, (October 1, 1995).

2. Scott Burns, "The Trinity Study," http://www.scottburns.com/wwtrinity.htm, (May 17, 2002).

3. The Retire Early Home Page, "What's the "Safe" Withdrawal Rate in Retirement?," http://www.geocities.com/WallStreet/8257/safewith.html, (May 16, 2002).

4- The MetLife Retirement Income Test, findings from the 2003 national survey of American pre-retirees

Chapter 5 Tapping Your IRA Early

1. The 2003 Retirement Confidence Survey, Summary of Findings, pg 4
2. IRC, Section 72 (T).
3. Ibid.
4. Oppenheimer Funds, IRA Section 72(t) Distributions, (July 30, 1997), 10-11.
5. College for Financial Planning, Certified Financial Planner Professional Education Program, Retirement Planning Book #7, (Denver, College For Financial Planning, 1998), 19.

Chapter 6 Tax Refunds Every Year for Life

1. Much of the information from this chapter was obtained from the Social Security Administration's website: www.ssa.gov
2. The 2003 Retirement Confidence Survey, Summary of Findings, pg 6

Chapter 7 Maxing Your Pension

1. A. Pension Benefit Guaranty Corporation www.pbgc.gov, 2004

2. This calculation assumes the portfolio is depleted in the thirtieth year.
3. See note 1 above.
4. Standard and Poors 500 Index.
5. Lehman Brothers Govt/Corp. Index.
6. Hypothetical Illustration, $500,000 hypothetical investment made from 12/31/1975 to 12/31/00. Assumes all interest and dividends are reinvested and $35,000 withdrawn from the portfolio annually.

<u>Chapter 8</u> Avoiding the 10 Most Common Investor Mistakes

1. Vanguard 500 Index January 2, 1984 to December 31, 2003. Morningstar Principia. All distributions reinvested.
2. Jeff Schlegel, "Time to Reappraise Market Timing," Financial Advisor Magazine, August 2004, 55.
3. Terrance Odean and Brad Barber, "You Are What You Trade," Bloomberg Personal Finance, May 2000, 1.
4. Mark Hulbert, "The Blinding Power of Data," New York Times, www.nytimes.com, 8 April 2001.
5. Brian O'Reilly, "Why Johnny Can't Invest," Fortune Magazine, www.business2.0.com, 9 November 1998, 1.
6. Dan Wheeler, "Disciples of Discipline," Investment Advisor Magazine, May 2004, 48
7. Matthew Miller, "Your Own Worst Enemy," Forbes.com, 12/22/03.
8. SEI Investments. The average return of top ten mutual funds in 1999 was 67.2% while the Wilshire 5000 returned 23.82%. In 2000 the average return of those same ten funds was a dismal –24.97% while the Wilshire 5000 returned 10.89%.
9. Morningstar Principia for mutual funds, (12/31/02). The Nicholas-Applegate Global Tech I fund closed on 2/14/03. Assets were merged into the Nicholas-Applegate Global Sel I fund.
10. Ameritrade
11. Morningstar Principia for mutual funds, (12/31/01), 376 Technology Funds Measured.
12. Stocks: 40% Large-Cap, 16% Mid-Cap, 8% Small-Cap and 16% International stocks with equal exposure to both growth and value in each market segment. Bonds: 8% Long-term governments, 9% Long-term Corporate Bonds and 3% International Bonds.

13. Michael Pretzer , "Men Behaving Badly ," Investment Advisor, www.djfpc.com, (October 1999).
14. Ibid.
15. Morningstar Principia for mutual funds, (12/31/03).
16. Sharon E. Epperson , "Death and the Maven," Time Magazine, 18 December 1995), 61.

<u>Chapter 9</u> The Most Important Investment Decision You'll Make
1. Frank Armstrong, CFP, Excerpt from *Investment Strategies for the 21st Century*, Chapter Six: "The Asset Allocation Decision," found at http://www.fundsinteractive.com on Sept. 16, 2002.

<u>Chapter 10</u> Investment Consistency
1. Dow Jones Midcap Value Index
2. Wilshire Target Small Company Value Index
3. Salomon Brothers Non-$ World Government Bond Index
4. Lehman Brothers Long-Term Government Bond Index
5. Morningstar Principia Pro for Mutual Funds, (December 31, 2003).
6. Williams Companies (WMB)

<u>Chapter 11</u>: Know Your Team
1a. "The Facts on Savings and Investing," Securities and Exchange Commission, Office of Investor Education and Assistance, April 1999
1. Ibbotson Associates, (2004).
2. "The Facts on Savings and Investing," Securities and Exchange Commission, Office of Investor Education and Assistance, April 1999
3. Morningstar Principia Pro, December 31, 2003
4. S&P/Barra Growth Index.
5. S&P/Barra Value Index.
6. S&P/Barra Growth Index & S&P/Barra Value Index.
7. Standard and Poors 500
8. Lehman Brothers Long Credit
9. FACT: Only 38% of investors understand that when interest rates go up bond prices usually go down.
10. EBRI/ICI Participant-Directed Retirement Plan Data Collection Project, "401(k) Plan Asset Allocation, Account Balances, and Loan Activity in 2000," EBRI Issue Brief no. 239, (November 2001).

11. Morningstar Principia Pro, December 31, 2003

Chapter 12 The Choice
No footnotes

Chapter 13 Divorce Your Stock
1. EBRI Special Report, "Company Stock in 401(k) Plans: Results of a Survey of ISCEBS Members", Information compiled at year-end 2000, 2.

Chapter 14 Ready! Set! Buy!
1. Morningstar, 184 large-company value mutual funds measured for the 15-year period ending Dec. 31, 2004.
2. Morningstar, 587 U.S. Stock funds measured for the 15-year year period ending Dec. 31, 2003.
3. Morningstar Principia Pro for Mutual Funds (Dec. 31, 2001).
4. Investment Company Institute, *Mutual Fund Factbook 2001 Edition*, excerpts taken from http://www.ici.org, 44.
5. Office of Investor Education and Assistance, Securities and Exchange Commission, "The Facts on Savings and Investing," p. 11 (April 1999).
6. Separate Account Solutions, http://www.separate.com, "About Separate Account Solutions" (June 20, 2002).
7. The Cerulli Report, "Asset Management: The State of Separate Account Consultant Programs," from http://www.cerulli.com, (June 20, 2002).
8. Morningstar (Dec. 31, 2003).
9. Morningstar (Dec. 31, 2003).
10. John C. Bogle, Founder of the Vanguard Group, to the United States Senate Government Affairs Subcommittee (Nov. 3, 2003).

Chapter 15 "No-Load" Means Lower Costs
1. National Association of Securities Dealers (NASD), NASD Launches Major Public Disclosure, Investor Education Initiative, Press Release (February 19, 1997).
2- Expense Ratio of the average Class B domestic stock fund according to Morningstar, 6/30/03.

3. John C. Bogle to the United States Senate Statement Governmental Affairs Subcommittee on Financial Management, the Budget, and International Security, November 3, 2003

4- Expense Ratio of the average No-load domestic stock fund according to Morningstar, 6/30/03.

5- AIG SunAmerica Anchor Polaris I/II, annual insurance expense equals 1.52%, average annual fund management expenses equal 0.92%, Morningstar, 9/30/03.

6- Vanguard Variable Annuity, annual insurance expense equals .37%, average annual fund management expenses equal .35%, Morningstar, 9/30/03.

7- Fee Planners Network (no-load UL vs. load UL offered from the same insurance company)

8- www.ulivi.com

9- Consumer Reports, "Who needs whole life," July 98, Vol. 63, Issue 7, p42.

10 - Compiled by LIMRA and published in the Transactions of the Society of Actuaries, 1988-89-90 Reports
- Andrew M. Wray III and William B. Howard Jr., "Fee Insurance Benefits Clients and Planners," Journal of Financial Planning, October 1992, Vol. 5, Issue 4, Page 150.
- www.peachtreeplanning.com, "Financial Insights-Life Insurance Simplified," Peachtree Planning Corporation 2002.
- Note: LIMRA would not disclose the current industry statistics on policy cancellations.

11- Class B share mutual funds usually convert to a class A shares in year 7 or 8 and qualify for a lower expense ratio at that time.

Chapter 16 Safer Ways to Own Stocks

1. As measured by the S&P 500. Morningstar Principia for mutual funds, (6/30/04).

2. Morningstar Principia for mutual funds, (6/30/04).

3. Morningstar Principia for mutual funds, (6/30/04).

Chapter 17 A Mission Statement for Your Money

No footnotes

Chapter 18 Routine Check Ups
1. Morningstar Principia for mutual funds, (12/31/04).
2. Morningstar Principia for mutual funds, (12/31/04).

Chapter 19 Heart Surgery Isn't Cheap
1. www.insure.com, "The HIPAA law: Your Rights to Health Insurance Portability," (September 16, 2002).
2. www.insure.com, "Know Your COBRA Rights," (September 16, 2002).
3. www.insure.com, "Know Your COBRA Rights," (September 16, 2002).
4. www.medicare.gov, "Does Medicare Pay For Prescription Drugs?" FAQ, (September 16, 2002).
5. www.medicare.gov, "What is a Medigap Policy?" FAQ, (September 16, 2002).
6. Robert Kuttner, "The American Health Care System—Health Insurance Coverage," New England Journal of Medicine, Vol. 340, No. 2., 14 January 1999. Note: "The proportion of Americans without insurance increased from 14.2 percent in 1995, to 15.3 percent in 1996, and to 16.1 percent in 1997, when 43.4 million people were uninsured."

Chapter 20 Toileting and Retirement
1. National Association of Insurance Commissioners (NAIC), "A Shopper's Guide to Long-Term Care Insurance," 2003, 39
2. Ibid. Original Source: Stillman and Lubitz, "Medical Care" 40 (10): 965-967 (2002).
3. HIAA "Guide to Long-Term Healthcare." 12/28/99:
4. Money Tree Silver Financial Planner Software, Long-term care analysis section.
5. Ibid.
6. National Association of Insurance Commissioners (NAIC), "A Shopper's Guide to Long-Term Care Insurance," 2003, 39
7. Long-Term Care Quote[SM], "A Consumer's Guide to Long-Term Care Insurance," 2
8. Public Attitudes on Long Term Care: "The EBRI Poll": A National Public Opinion Survey Conducted by The Gallup Organization, Inc.,

Released August 1993, 15.

9.   National Association of Insurance Commissioners (NAIC), "A Shopper's Guide to Long-Term Care Insurance," 2003, 7.

10. New England Journal of Medicine, 1991; 324(9), 595.

11. Stillman and Lubitz, "Medical Care" 40 (10):965-967 (2002).

12. National Association of Insurance Commissioners (NAIC), "A Shopper's Guide to Long-Term Care Insurance," 2003, 4

13. James Palma, "Long-Term Care Insurance Revisited," National Center on Women and Aging, http://heller.brandeis.edu/national/ltcr499.htm, (April 1999).

14. National Association of Insurance Commissioners (NAIC), "A Shopper's Guide to Long-Term Care Insurance," 2003, 20.

15. David Braze, "The Spectre of Long Term Care," www.Fool.com, (January 31, 2000).

16. Money Tree Silver Financial Planning Software, 2004, Long-Term analysis section.

17. Ellen Hoffman, "Long Term Care Policies That Will Last," Business Week, http://www.businessweek.com, 20 November 2000.

18. National Association of Insurance Commissioners (NAIC), "A Shopper's Guide to Long-Term Care Insurance," 2003, 20.

19. www.ltcq.net premium price quote, quotes from, The State Life Insurance Co., Metropolitan Life Insurance Co., Prudential Insurance Co. of America. 5/26/04

20. National Association of Insurance Commissioners LTC standards (NAIC), the Health Insurance Association of America (HIAA), and the Association for Aged and Retired Persons (AARP)

Chapter 21 Please! No More Life Insurance Premiums
No footnotes

Chapter 22 To Pay or Not to Pay?

1.   Forget the Deduction: Why You Should Pay Off Your Mortgage Before You Retire, Wall Street Journal, Jonathan Clements, 10/6/04 (cited: Federal Reserve Survey of Consumer Finances)

Chapter 23 You Can't Take It With You
No footnotes

Chapter 24 Cash it, Roll it, Leave it, Roth it, Annuitize it, Stock it!

1. IRA Rollover Trends, Financial Research Corporation, 2003.
2. The 2003 Retirement Confidence Survey, Summary of Findings, pg 8
3. 401(k) Plan Asset Allocation, Account Balances, and Loan Activity in 2003, Perspective, Investment Company Institute, pg 12, volume 10, no. 2, August 2004
4. The Cerulli Report, www.cerulli.com/report.rollover.htm, The Rollover IRA Market: Retirement Markets in Transition, (June 20, 2002).
5. 401(k) Plan Asset Allocation, Account Balances, and Loan Activity in 2003, Perspective, Investment Company Institute, volume 10, no. 2, August 2004
6. IRA Rollover Trends, Financial Research Corporation, 2003
7. IRA Rollover Trends, Financial Research Corporation, 2003
8. "Targeting High-Balance Rollovers, 2001," Pension Benefits, July 2000, 6.
9. The Cerulli Report, www.cerulli.com/report.rollover.htm, The Rollover IRA Market: Retirement Markets in Transition, (June 20, 2002).
10. The Cerulli Report, www.cerulli.com/report.rollover.htm, The Rollover IRA Market: Retirement Markets in Transition, (June 20, 2002).
11. Lynn O'Shaunessy, www.money.msn.com, "What's Wrong with Your 401(k)—and How to Fix It," http://money.msn.com/articles/retire/basics/9092.asp?special=msn, (April 1, 2002), 4.

Chapter 25 A Tax Loop Hole

1. Jack L. VanDerhei, "Company Stock in 401(k) Plans: Results of a Survey of ISCEBS Members," Employee Benefit Research Institute (EBRI) Special Report (January 31, 2002).
2. Vern Hayden, "Looking for a Great 401(k) Tax Break? Try Your Employer's Stock," TheStreet.com, (June 28, 2000).
3. IRC § 402 (e) (4) (A) and (B)
4. IRC § 402 (e) (4) (D)
5. Dan Kadlec, www.time.com